THE EUROCURRENCY MARKETS, DOMESTIC FINANCIAL POLICY AND INTERNATIONAL INSTABILITY

The Eurocurrency Markets, Domestic Financial Policy and International Instability

Heather D. Gibson

Lecturer in Economics
Keynes College
University of Kent at Canterbury

St. Martin's Press   New York

First published in the United States of America in 1989

Printed in Hong Kong

ISBN 0–312–02826–1

Library of Congress Cataloging-in-Publication Data
Gibson, Heather D., 1961–
The eurocurrency markets, domestic financial policy, and
international instability/Heather D. Gibson.
p.   cm.
Bibliography: p.
Includes index.
ISBN 0–312–02826–1
1. Euro-dollar market.   2. Monetary policy—Great Britain.
3. Economic stabilization.   I. Title.
HG3897.G53   1989
332.4'5—dc19   88–7949
                                                    CIP

To my mother and father

Contents

x   *Contents*

List of Tables

List of Figures

Acknowledgements

I am deeply indebted to Peter Oppenheimer who has supervised the whole of this research. His many helpful comments and suggestions have guided my research and have been invaluable throughout.

There are a number of people who have made useful comments on various chapters. In particular, I would like to thank Christopher Allsopp, Tony Thirlwall and Andrew Glyn. However, I remain solely responsible for any errors that remain.

A number of bankers in the City of London provided me with useful insights into the more practical aspects of the subject and I thank them for having taken the time to talk with me.

This book is the result of research for the degree of DPhil. I acknowledge with thanks the financial support of the ESRC during my first three years in Oxford. For financial support during the last year I am indebted to The Walter Scott Research Foundation. In addition I am grateful to all those at Walter Scott and Partners who provided help in arranging the interviews with banks in London.

I would also like to thank my friends, Euclid Tsakalotos, Gelina Harlaftis and Vassilis Karasmanis who all contributed to making my time in Oxford most enjoyable. In particular, Euclid Tsakalotos has provided constant encouragement and support in all aspects of my life.

Finally, my greatest debt is to my family who have given me constant encouragement, love and assistance throughout the whole of my studies.

HEATHER D. GIBSON

Introduction

This book looks at the process of the internationalisation of capital markets and its implications for domestic financial policy (monetary policy and banking supervision and regulation). We focus in particular on the Eurocurrency markets,[1] which have played a key role in the trend towards internationalisation. The book makes two main contributions. Firstly, it examines the effect of the Euromarkets on the domestic monetary policy of a small country, through a case study of the effect of the abolition of UK capital controls. Secondly, it investigates the impact of the internationalisation of credit markets on the structure of the banking industry and especially the relationship between competition, market failures and stability.

The issue of interdependence and integration is one of the central themes of this book. Chapter 2 outlines what we mean by monetary independence and its relationship with financial integration. It also discusses why the ability to have an independent monetary policy might be desirable.

Chapter 3 provides a theoretical background to the empirical work in chapter 4. In the former, we focus further on the theoretical reasons for the existence of the Euromarkets. We show that the movement of capital 'offshore' can be explained in terms of an attempt by banks to avoid regulatory mechanisms imposed at national government level. In the light of this we analyse the effect of the Euromarkets on arbitrage and monetary interdependence.

Chapter 4 investigates the relationship between US and UK monetary conditions. It looks at the implications of the removal of capital controls in the UK in October 1979 and the conduct of monetary policy in the increasingly financially integrated environment of 1974–84.

The 1970s were characterised by an increasing liberalisation of capital controls throughout the developed world. Chapter 5 investigates the impact of the increasingly liberal environment on the banking industry. It discusses the connection between increased competition and stability and provides a theoretical background to the work of chapter 6, suggesting an informal model of international banking based on recognition of the market failures which exist.

This informal model is tested in chapter 6 by examining the international banking environment of the 1970s and 1980s and, in

1

particular, the role of the banks in the international debt crisis.

Chapter 7 concludes by highlighting the policy implications of increased financial integration. Firstly, we summarise our conclusions of chapter 4 on the effect of increased integration on small open economies such as the UK: increasingly monetary policy has to be viewed within an international context. Secondly, we look at the implications of our findings on the structure of the banking industry for supervision of banking. We conclude by pointing out the inadequacies of the present attitude to the international debt crisis and by suggesting the need for much greater co-ordination of domestic financial policies at the international level.

1 The Eurocurrency Markets: History and Structure

The purpose of this chapter is firstly to provide an analytical sketch of the history of the Eurocurrency markets and secondly to examine the competitive structure of international banking markets. Rather than proceed in a strictly chronological fashion, I propose to look at some factors that appear to have been relevant in the development of the markets and to introduce some of the themes which will be analysed in later chapters. Section 1.1 examines the size of the markets and their currency composition. Section 1.2 looks at the factors responsible for the growth of the Eurodollar market, by far the largest section of the Eurocurrency markets. The key factors include the return to convertibility, the US balance of payments, monetary policy and capital controls in the US, the breakdown of Bretton Woods and the subsequent floating of exchange rates, the international debt crisis, and finally the interbank mechanism and other financial innovations. Section 1.3 deals with aspects specific to the non-dollar Euromarkets, in particular the Eurosterling and Euro-Deutschmark (hereafter EuroDM) markets.

Section 1.4 examines the competitive structure of the Eurocurrency markets, by considering the development of London and New York as major international banking centres and by analysing the innovative environment which has been characteristic of the Euro-markets since their inception.

1.1 THE GROWTH AND IMPORTANCE OF THE EUROMARKETS

The Bank for International Settlements (hereafter BIS) 20 years ago defined a Eurodollar as; 'a dollar that has been acquired by a bank outside the United States and used directly or after conversion into another currency for lending to a non-bank customer, perhaps after one or more redeposits from one bank to another'.[1] They pointed out that 'a precise statistical picture of the Eurocurrency market is not

3

feasible'[2] and that any measure of the size of the market must be approximate because of some grey areas that exist.[3] Nonetheless, it can still be shown that the Eurocurrency market has grown rapidly. Any reasonable interpretation of the statistics allows such a conclusion to be drawn.

The initial emergence of the markets was seen in the late 1950s for reasons we shall discuss later.[4] Statistics relating to their total size were not collected by the BIS until 1963, but by examining total liabilities and claims on non-residents of the overseas and foreign banks in London, its initial geographical centre, one can derive some indication of its growth between 1957 and the last quarter of 1963; the BIS estimated non-resident deposits to have increased over this period by about $4000 million.[5]

Throughout the 1960s, the markets grew at a great pace. Not only did they grow in size; they also spread geographically, moving to other centres in Europe and Asia. London nevertheless maintained its central role (see section 1.4). Tables 1.1a and 1.1b give some indication of the growth.

Between 1963 and 1981, total short-term foreign currency positions of reporting banks *vis-à-vis* non-residents grew by $928 billion,[6] of which $675 billion was denominated in dollars.[7] This is an average of 27.66 per cent per annum – for the 1960s averaging 34.18 per cent per annum as against 26.07 per cent in the 1970s. This rate of growth was much higher than the growth of national banking.[8]

A feature of the markets from their inception is the prominence of the US dollar. As can be seen from table 1.2, the dollar has consistently accounted for over 70 per cent of the total markets. In the later 1960s, the dollar proportion was as high as 80 per cent.

Over the whole period, the Deutsch mark (hereafter DM) has grown in importance, initially in the 1960s at the expense of sterling, but since 1971, at the expense of the dollar. The reason for the growth of the EuroDM market has been the increasing attractiveness of the DM as a currency to hold both for private agents and as reserves with the central banks. Sterling's importance decreased over the 1960s, steadying at around 1–2 per cent in the 1970s. Since 1978–9, it has enjoyed some revival, reflecting the demand from OPEC countries. This may be attributed at least in part to the removal of UK exchange controls (see chapter 4.5).[9]

The figures used on p. 5 have been gross estimates of the markets' size, in the sense that 'they include interbank deposits between countries; however, they do not include interbank deposits within

Table 1.1a Overall Growth of the Euromarkets – Foreign Currency Assets of Reporting Banks *vis-à-vis* Non-residents, 1963–83 (in millions of US$)

Year	European dollars	European other currencies	Japan & Canada dollars	Japan & Canada other currencies	Total
1963	7670	2820	1660	230	12380
1964	9200	3040	2120	400	14850
1965	11770	3560	2620	380	18330
1966	16070	4180	5760	460	26470
1967	19890	4960	6850	410	32110
1968	30430	7270	8220	460	46380
1969	47630	10540	11640	500	70310
1970	60370	17880	14300	620	93170
1971	71500	29630	12900	910	113940
1972[a]	98000	33840	16940	1150	149930
1973	132110	55510	25940	2300	214710
1974	156230	58940	29850	2930	247950
1975	190180	67550	29600	2620	289950
1976[b]	224020	81300	33420	2970	341170
1977	268430	116410	32410	3450	420700
1978	339520	162450	42950	4660	549580
1979	427980	211960	53340	5760	699040
1980	518730	232510	75800	7750	834790
1981	593530	246520	89500	10910	940460
1982	1023600		129700		1153300
1983	1027200		150900		1178100

a – excludes the BIS deposits from 1973 onwards
b – includes Austria, Denmark and Ireland from 1977
c – now includes external lending by banks in their domestic currency – dollar and other currency total
See also note 7 for a more comprehensive explanation of the figures here.
Source: BIS Annual Reports

Table 1.1b   Percentage Growth Rates of Total Foreign Currency Assets *vis-à-vis* Non-residents, 1963–83

Year	%	Year	%
1963	–	1974	15.50
1964	19.95	1975	16.90
1965	23.40	1976	17.80
1966	44.40	1977	23.10
1967	21.30	1978	30.60
1968	44.40	1979	27.20
1969	51.60	1980	19.40
1970	32.50	1981	12.20
1971	22.30	1982	22.60
1972	31.60	1983	2.70
1973	43.20		

Source: Calculated from table 1.1a

each country'.[10] It is customary in national banking statistics to net out interbank positions. Following this principle, we can net out the various interbank positions since they 'double-count the flow of credit from original non-bank depositors in the market to final non-bank borrowers'.[11]

The principle of double-counting can be illustrated by the following example: assume that a flow of funds is occurring from a bank or non-bank in country A to a bank or non-bank in country D, and that the flow passes through banks in countries B and C, which are both in the reporting area. In this example, the flow will be double-counted because of the interbank transaction between countries B and C. This should be netted out of both the liabilities and assets of the Eurocurrency markets.

However, not all interbank transactions represent double-counting and the BIS 'net' measure therefore includes some interbank transactions. Firstly, an interbank transaction between a bank within the reporting area and a bank outside the reporting area is included. The logic behind this, as Johnston (1983) points out, 'is that the BIS concept attempts to show the intermediary role of the Euromarket in international banking or credit flows rather than only the volume of Eurocurrency flows directly between non-bank suppliers and borrowers of Eurocurrency funds'.[12] The crucial distinction, therefore, is whether a bank is situated geographically inside or outside the reporting area. To the extent that banks outside the area redeposit in

Table 1.2 Currency Breakdown of the Assets of Banks in the European
Area – Foreign Currency Assets *vis-à-vis*
Non-residents, – percentages

Year	$	£	SFr	DM	Yen
1964	75	8	6	9	–
1965	77	6	5	9	–
1966	80	4	5	7	–
1967	81	4	4	8	–
1968	81	2	5	10	–
1969	81	1	5	11	–
1970	77	1	5	13	–
1971	71	2	8	16	–
1972	76	2	6	16	–
1973	72	2	8	17	–
1974	74	1	7	16	–
1975	72	1	6	16	–
1976	75	1	6	16	–
1977	72	1	6	18	–
1978	71	2	6	20	1
1979	70	2	6	20	1
1980	73	2	7	17	1
1981	74	2	7	15	2

Source: Calculated from BIS Annual Report Data

the Eurocurrency markets, this double-counting is not identified by
the BIS.

Secondly, two types of interbank transactions *within* the reporting
area are included. The first type is described in the following
example.[13] A reporting area bank (say in Germany) may obtain
domestic currency which it switches into a foreign currency and then
deposits in the Eurocurrency markets in another reporting area bank
(say in London). Although this is an interbank transaction, it is
included because the original source of the funds is outside the
Eurocurrency market. Similarly, if a German bank borrows dollars
from a London bank and then switches into DM and on-lends in the
German domestic market, this represents an end-use. The volume of
such switched positions are estimated by the BIS and included in
their 'net' concept.[14]

The second type of interbank transaction within the reporting area
which is included in the BIS 'net' figure occurs when a reporting bank
borrows or lends its domestic currency to a reporting bank in another
country on behalf of a domestic customer.

Table 1.3   Percentage Interbank Liabilities in Total Cross-border
Liabilities

Year	Quarter	Broader	a	Narrower	b
1973	Q1	71			–
	Q2	70			–
	Q3	71			73
	Q4	71			75
1974	Q1	71			75
	Q2	71			74
	Q3	70			72
	Q4	68			71
1975	Q1	69			69
	Q2	69			70
	Q3(1)	70:	63		71
	Q4		63		71
1976	Q1		63		71
	Q2		64		71
	Q3		63		70
	Q4		62		70
1977	Q1		63		70
	Q2		63		70
	Q3		63		69
	Q4(1)		63:	64	71
1978	Q1		63		71
	Q2		63		71
	Q3		63		71
	Q4		65		73
1979	Q1		64		71
	Q2		65		71
	Q3		65		70
	Q4		65		71
1980	Q1		66		71
	Q2		65		72
	Q3		65		71
	Q4		67		73

(1)   Breaks in the series
a   Broader definition of the Euromarkets
b   Narrower definition of the Euromarkets
Source: Ellis (1981).

Ellis (1981), in a study of the interbank market, compiled the data
found in table 1.3 using the BIS principle outlined above. The overall
percentage of such interbank balance sheet positions in the Eurocurrency system has remained constant between 1973 and 1980. Such
constancy, as Ellis notes, is not necessarily an expected result.
Attempts to explain it proved ineffective. One theory is that the

Table 1.4   The Volume of International Bank Lending Conducted in the
Eurocurrency Market, 1973–83
end-year figures, billions of US dollars

Year	European Assets[a]	Total Assets[b]	%[c]
1973	187.6	291.6	64.4
1974	215.2	362.1	59.4
1975	258.1	442.3	58.4
1976	305.3	548.0	55.7
1977	384.9	689.8	55.8
1978	502.0	893.2	56.2
1979	639.7	1,111.0	57.6
1980	751.2	1,321.9	56.8
1981	846.6	1,549.5	54.6
1982	866.8	1,689.0	51.3
1983	879.6	1,753.9	50.1

[a] – External assets in foreign currencies of banks in the 12 European reporting countries (that is, Austria, Belgium, Luxembourg, Denmark, France, Germany, Ireland, Italy, Netherlands, Sweden, Switzerland and the UK).
[b] – Total external assets of BIS reporting banks.
[c] – Eurocurrency assets as a percentage of total assets.
Source: BIS (1984) *International Banking Statistics*, 1973–83

interbank market is a residual source of funds for any one bank when its non-banking sources are inadequate; but a regression of fluctuations in interbank deposits on other deposits provided no evidence to support such a theory. An alternative hypothesis that the interbank market's growth is positively related to the strength of the dollar was similarly rejected.

For an analysis of the *growth* of the Eurocurrency market, the use of gross figures is sufficient because of the above-mentioned stability in the ratio of interbank to total items. With respect, however, to the importance of the market in terms of its *liquidity creating* effects, the actual proportion of interbank transactions may be important. Whether interbank transactions have important liquidity creating effects depends on the extent to which there is maturity transformation of deposits.[15] Johnston (1983) concludes that because of the 'nearly perfectly maturity matched position of the London banks *vis-à-vis* other banks in the London interbank market, . . . interbank trading can indeed be netted out when attempting to measure the direct liquidity effects of the Eurocurrency markets'.[16]

Table 1.4 shows the importance of the narrowly defined Eurocurrency markets in international banking from 1973 to 1983. It also points to the more recent trend in the growth of offshore banking facilities by showing the changing importance of the Euromarkets in international banking. In these offshore centres, tax regulations, for example, are often more favourable than in the 12 European countries represented here. The share of the Eurocurrency markets in international banking has declined significantly since the end of 1973 – when US controls on capital outflows were removed – but still accounted in 1983 for one half.

We concentrate on the Euromarkets in this book, because data for these markets is readily available. However, the theoretical background to the empirical work applies generally to the international credit markets.

1.2 CAUSAL FACTORS IN THE DEVELOPMENT OF THE EURODOLLAR MARKET

1.2.1 The Return to Convertibility and Associated Events

The summer of 1957 witnessed a key initial boost to the market with the sterling crisis. The Bank of England reimposed restrictions on the granting of external sterling credits: in particular, they prohibited the sterling financing of non-UK trade. It had been usual for banks in London and indeed other European centres to provide their customers with dollar deposits, but up until 1957, they had been reinvested in the US.[17] When restrictions were re-introduced to limit UK banks' ability to use sterling for external purposes (for example trade credit), they resorted to using dollars for their external operations.

Progressively during the 1950s there had been a change in the US balance of payments, with the large persistent surplus of 1945–50 being replaced by a deficit by 1957.[18] This deficit resulted in increased foreign holdings of dollars. 'By mid–1958, a European market in dollar deposits and loans had become established'.[19]

The return to convertibility in Europe at the end of 1958, with its associated relaxation of exchange controls, gave further impetus to the market. It permitted an increase in the supply of privately held dollars which could now be swapped into local currency. Foreign exchange markets became more active, encouraging arbitrage between the various Eurocurrencies and national markets, and potentially increasing the extent of financial integration and interdependence.

1.2.2 The US Balance of Payments

As noted in section 1.2.1, a basic deficit on the US balance of payments emerged in the late 1950s. The net outflow on the long term capital account had been running at between $2 and $2.5 billion per year between 1959 and 1963, and increased thereafter because of US companies' direct investment overseas.[20] There has been much debate concerning the role, if any, played by the deficit in the growth of the Eurodollar market. Friedman (1969) argued that the deficit was neither a necessary nor sufficient condition for the market's growth. It was not necessary, because one could point to the case of West Germany, and the existence of a market in EuroDM despite the German balance of payments surplus. It was not sufficient because, although a deficit provided dollar holdings for foreigners, it could not be presumed that they would be held in the form of Eurodollar deposits. This depended on the expected return on such deposits relative to other investments.

Klopstock (1970) suggested that the deficit had been an important source of funds for the growth of the market. He implied that the source was central banks rather than private individuals: when individuals went to exchange domestic currency into dollars, to make deposits with Eurobanks, that is, banks dealing in Eurocurrencies, they drew on central bank holdings of dollars, which were the result of the US deficit. In addition, central banks placing monetary reserves in the Eurodollar market were also employing dollars accumulated as a consequence of the deficit.

The BIS (1964) argued that the deficit was useful in the market's initial period of growth, but that once the market had become established, dollars were directly attracted to it from US residents. This added to the US deficit.[21]

1.2.3 Monetary Policy and Capital Controls in the US

In an attempt to deal with the worsening balance of payments, the US authorities introduced the Interest Equalisation Tax in 1963 to discourage foreign bond issues in New York, and this was followed by the Voluntary Foreign Credit Restraint programme and the Foreign Direct Investment regulations (1965). Limitations were placed on loans to foreigners and investment in other foreign assets. The programme applied only to businesses located in the US, so resulting in a shift of operations to foreign branches of US firms and in particular to the Eurodollar market.[22] The role of the external deficit in this instance was an indirect one, in contrast to the direct role it played in the initial development of the market.

Under the Voluntary Foreign Credit Restraint (VFCR) programme, credits to non-residents by US banks' offices in the US were limited during 1965 to 105 per cent of their December 1964 level. These restraints continued in a similar fashion throughout the rest of the '1960s. The limits led overseas borrowers to turn to the Eurodollar market, which in turn helped to keep Eurodollar interest rates at a relatively high level. Johnston (1983) quotes evidence from Brimmer and Dahl (1975) on the resulting growth of overseas branches of US banks. In 1964, the number of US banks with branches overseas was 11: this had increased to 79 in 1970. Over the same period, the assets of overseas branches increased from $6.9 billion to $52.6 billion and the number of overseas branches from 181 to 536. The effect of US and indeed other regulations on capital flows was to shift emphasis of international banking away from national banking systems to the Eurobanks.

The second effect of US monetary policy was through Regulation Q.[23] This prohibited the payment of interest on demand deposits, as well as authorising the Federal Reserve to set a maximum interest rate payable on savings and time deposits in US banks.

Between 1966 and 1969, the Federal Reserve relied to a great extent on the operation of Regulation Q to enforce tight monetary policy. Normally, the ceiling set by the Federal Reserve was inoperable because market interest rates were lower than the ceiling rate. In contrast, in times of tight monetary policy, interest rates rose and would have risen above the ceiling were it not for its existence. The mechanism through which this operated can be described as follows. The level of interest rates in the money market was raised through slowing down the growth of the money supply. However, while money market interest rates rose, the interest rates payable on time deposits were held down by the ceiling. Investors moved their time deposits from the banking system, causing the banks to experience a shortage of funds. The banks then looked to the Eurodollar market for funds, and in 1966, when money was tight, borrowing from European branches of US banks by their head offices rose by $2.5 billion. Moreover, banks began to regard the market as a substitute source of dollars even when Regulation Q was not effective as in 1967. Funds raised through this method were then used to continue lending to customers in the US.

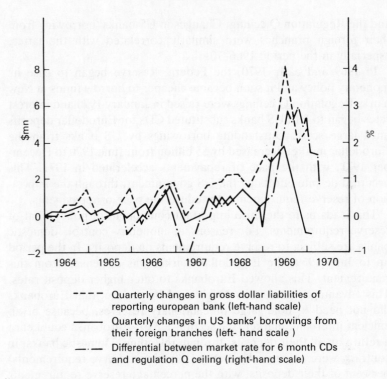

Figure 1.1   Effect of Regulation Q

Source: BIS 40th Annual Report, June 1970, p. 148

Regulation Q, as the BIS recognised,[24] stimulated the growth of the Eurodollar market in two ways. Firstly, it reinforced the market's ability to offer higher interest rates on deposits – even deposits at call. Two other reasons why they could offer higher interest rates were: *i)* Eurobanks operated on lower margins (see section 1.2.6); and *ii)* the effect of domestic reserve requirements (see later in this section).

Secondly, the growth of the market was stimulated because of the demand for dollars from commercial banks in the US in order to circumvent domestic credit restraint policies.

Figure 1.1 illustrates the effect of Regulation Q identified above for the period 1964–70. Changes in the gross liabilities of the Eurodollar market were highly correlated with the differential between the market rate for six months' Certificates of Deposits (hereafter CDs)[25] and the Regulation Q ceiling. Changes in US banks' borrowing from their foreign branches were similarly correlated with the latter, especially in the period 1966–70.

In 1969 and early 1970, the Federal Reserve began to ease its monetary policy and it soon became cheaper to borrow funds in New York. Regulation Q ceilings were raised in January 1970 and interest rates began to fall. US banks substituted CDs for Eurodollar deposits on a large scale. Outstanding borrowings by US banks from the Eurodollar market decreased by $5 billion from June 1970 to December 1971, with the pace of repayments accelerated in 1971. This occurred despite efforts by the US government, through the imposition of reserve requirements, to reduce the pace of repayments.

This leads us to the third important component of policy, that of reserve requirements. For reasons of monetary control, domestic banks are subject to reserve requirements on deposits. In the period up to June 1969, the Eurodollar market was dispensed from this requirement. This allowed Eurobanks to offer higher deposit rates. This advantage was further heightened by the fact that Eurobanks did not need to hold large precautionary reserves, because of an efficient interbank market (see section 1.2.6); Eurobanks could earn a return on all their deposits, through relending. Domestic banks, in contrast, were able to relend only (100 minus reserve requirements) per cent of their deposits, with the percentage reserve requirements earning no interest. In June 1969, the US government imposed what was effectively a 10 per cent marginal reserve requirement on Eurodollar borrowings. This was an attempt to reduce the rate of repayments by ensuring that if the US banks did repay, and subsequently reborrowed from the market, the cost of such borrowing would have substantially increased.[26] The reserve requirement was applicable on the amount by which US bank borrowings from foreign branches exceeded their level of 28 May 1969. On 30 November 1970, the Federal Reserve increased the marginal reserve requirement to 20 per cent. The measures proved to be ineffective since US interest rates continued to fall, causing the cost of maintaining Eurodollar borrowings to become too expensive.

In January 1974, the US removed the capital controls it had introduced in the 1960s. As we saw above, the imposition of the controls stimulated the Eurodollar market. Paradoxically, their removal also enhanced the market in the same respects. After the removal of the controls, US banks could freely arbitrage between the

US domestic market and the Eurodollar market. This led to a greater integration of the national and Eurocurrency segments of the dollar market. Johnston (1983) argues that the removal of capital market controls in West Germany in 1974 and in the UK in 1979 had a similar effect in integrating the EuroDM and the Eurosterling markets with their respective national markets.[27] The effect of US monetary policy in the late 1970s and early 1980s will be examined in chapter 4. It will be interesting to see whether US policy at that time exercised as much influence as it did under Regulation Q and the other policies examined so far.

1.2.4 The Breakdown of Bretton Woods and the Floating of Exchange Rates

A major economic event of 1971 was the breakdown of the Bretton Woods system of fixed exchange rates. The official link between the dollar and gold was broken and the exchange rate parities realigned under the Smithsonian Agreement (December 1971). When it became clear that there might be further realignment with a devaluing of the US dollar, there was a demand to borrow dollars to buy stronger European currencies. After the UK decision to float (June 1972), Germany and Switzerland imposed capital controls and more restrictive monetary policy to reduce inflation. An intensified dollar outflow resulted and the dollar was devalued a second time in February 1973. In the following month when the flight from the dollar continued, European countries decided to move to floating exchange rates.

Bell (1973) points out that the inflows into Europe in 1970 and 1971, led to increases in European central banks' holdings of dollars. The Bundesbank was affected to a greater extent than other central banks, and this was reinforced after February 1971 by speculative pressure against the dollar and in favour of the DM and to a lesser extent the Swiss-Franc (SFr). Given that the dollar inflows from the underlying US balance of payments deficit were perhaps only a quarter of the total dollar flow in Western Europe and Japan over the year to August 1971,[28] the Eurodollar market may have greatly magnified the problem of the dollar. Bell concludes that the existence of the Eurodollar market probably caused realignment and the subsequent breakdown to occur sooner than it would have done in the absence of a Eurodollar market.

1.2.5 Recycling and the International Debt Crisis

Shortly after the breakdown of the Bretton Woods system, the quadrupling of oil prices created both a demand and a supply stimulus to the Euromarket. The IMF's oil fund facility was inadequate to meet the resulting demand for balance of payments deficit financing especially by the non-oil developing countries. Moreover, with the breakdown of the pegged rate international monetary system there was little hope for an international political initiative on the problem of balance of payments adjustment. The partial placement of OPEC surpluses, amounting in 1974 to some $58 billion with the Eurodollar market providing an obvious and politically convenient channel for capital to be moved from surplus to deficit countries.[29] In December 1973, the external liabilities, in domestic and foreign currency of banks in countries reporting to BIS *vis-à-vis* OPEC countries were $16.0 billion. By December 1974, this had increased to $43.5 billion. The Eurodollar market was attractive because it offered slightly higher deposit rates on funds placed short term, allowing good returns to be made, whilst the OPEC countries decided what long term investments they wished to undertake. Along with this, there were political advantages for OPEC to be able to invest dollars in Europe rather than in the US.

The Eurobanks became inextricably linked with the recycling role in the face of continued balance of payments disequilibrium in the international monetary system. The implications of this intermediary function for the stability of the international system and the supervision of banking are investigated in chapters 5 to 7.

1.2.6 The Interbank Market and Financial Innovations

Both domestic and international financial markets have two major components: firstly, the interbank mechanism, and secondly, the channelling of funds from initial depositors to ultimate borrowers. However, in the Euromarkets the former plays a far more important role. With respect to the latter, the markets introduced important innovations.

In the Euromarkets the interbank market accounts for around 70 per cent of the banks' aggregate liabilities. In the case of, for example, the US domestic markets, the Federal Funds interbank market accounts for only 12.5 per cent of the aggregate liabilities of US banks.[30] The existence of such a large interbank market allows banks to match the inflow and outflow of funds from deposits and loans by lending excess funds or borrowing to meet lending commitments. This reduces the need to maintain a stock of liquid assets which would act as a safety margin. Ellis (1981) finds that there is much variety in the reliance on interbank funds between different banks. The larger, better known banks tend to have a smaller percentage of their foreign currency liabilities in the interbank market, for example for American banks over the period 1978–81, the percentage varied between 42 per cent and 54 per cent. This is in contrast with consortium banks whose reliance on the interbank market over the same period was about 80 per cent. Another feature is that these better known banks were not borrowers. Ellis concludes that 'the very large interbank segment of the Euromarket performs a necessary and valuable role in linking non-bank depositors and lenders in different parts of the world'.[31] The general efficiency of the interbank mechanism in allowing banks access to funds at very short notice, as well as allowing them to place funds in the market for short periods to earn some interest, helps to reduce the transactions and information costs in the Eurocurrency markets, allowing them to operate on smaller margins. However, Ellis (1981) also recognises that the interbank mechanism has led to increased interdependence, increasing the speed at which crises might spread through the system. We consider this point in more detail in chapter 5.

Two innovations, which are associated with end-uses of funds (that is, lending to non-banks) and which have facilitated the expansion of the Eurocurrency markets, are roll-over credits and the syndicated loan system.

The introduction of roll-over credits reduces the risk of interest rates moving against a bank when it tends to borrow short and lend long. It enables banks to offer higher interest rates on short term deposits whilst at the same time being able to commit these funds long term, through reducing the risk of making losses if deposit rates should rise again. On the borrower's side of the market, such roll-over credits imply that interest rates at the time of borrowing are less important, because if they should fall over the course of the loan, the borrower will reap the benefits. Naturally, he will also pay the cost if interest rates rise, the implications of which have become increasingly recognised since 1982. We discuss this in more detail in chapter 7.3. The presence of the former benefit, however, kept borrowing buoyant in the early 1970s though the fact that real interest rates were low also helped.

The second innovation is that of syndication of loans. 'A syndicated credit is a loan in which a group of financial institutions makes funds available on common conditions to a borrower'.[32] It allows credits of large sizes (over $1 billion in some cases) to be put together, a factor that was especially important in the financing of national balance of payments deficits.

From the lender's point of view, it reduces the risks of international bank lending,[33] through diversification of loans to political entities. It also provides more protection against selective defaults: unwillingness of a nation to repay its debts will be met with pressure from several countries, whose banks are involved. Negotiations were also made feasible, because at the same time there are few enough creditors involved. On the other hand, a possible danger of the process, which has become increasingly recognised, is that in the event of a default, the repercussions will be spread over a wide part of the Eurocurrency system. This has raised questions regarding the stability of the international banking system, which we return to in chapters 5 and 6.

1.3   NON-DOLLAR EUROCURRENCY MARKETS

Within the Eurocurrency system, there are EuroDM, Eurosterling, EuroSwiss-Francs, EuroFrench-Francs, EuroGuilder, EuroLira and more recently EuroYen markets.

I wish to comment briefly on two of these:

i)   The EuroDM market because it is the second most important Eurocurrency market after the dollar;

ii)   the Eurosterling market, because it has implications for interdependence between the US and the UK, which I will be examining in chapter 4.

A basic question when dealing with these two markets, and indeed all non-dollar Eurocurrency markets, is the extent to which they are phenomena independent of the Eurodollar market, or whether they represent an offshoot of the latter. Evidence concerning the determination of interest rates in these non-dollar Euromarkets suggests that they are an offshoot of the Eurodollar market. The hypothesis that non-dollar Eurocurrency interest rates are determined by the Eurodollar rate minus the forward premium on the appropriate currency *vis-à-vis* the dollar has much support.[34] Chapter 3 offers a theoretical analysis of this hypothesis and its implications. I propose to examine this hypothesis for the Eurosterling – Eurodollar relation in chapter 4.

Domestic monetary policy in West Germany and in the UK has had an impact on the covered interest differential between the domestic and Eurocurrency sections of each market.

In the case of West Germany, Johnston (1983) investigates the effect of the controls imposed by the West German government to reduce capital inflows in 1973–4 and again in 1978. The policy was implemented by varying the reserve requirements on domestic and foreign-owned DM liabilities of the West German banks. Reserve requirements between January 1973 and 1974 ranged from 11.75 per cent to 13.95 per cent on DM domestic liabilities. On liabilities of German banks to foreigners reserve requirements were 35 per cent. Added to this was a marginal reserve requirement of 60 per cent on the growth of West German banks' time liabilities to non-residents. This combined marginal reserve requirement of 95 per cent effectively discouraged any borrowing by German banks from the EuroDM market during the period.

Furthermore, West German companies under the Bardepot Law (July 1972 – February 1974) had to maintain a minimum reserve requirement that varied during the period between 20 per cent and 50 per cent against foreign loans. This made it unprofitable for West German companies to borrow externally. Together these measures insulated the economy from capital inflows, and allowed a differential between domestic and EuroDM interest rates to be maintained.

In the case of the UK, the capital controls that existed before 1979 were on outflows. In chapter 4, I examine the hypothesis that this allowed large differentials between domestic and Eurosterling rates to be maintained.

In short, although the EuroDM and Eurosterling markets are to a considerable extent offshoots of the Eurodollar phenomenon, domestic policy measures have affected the degree to which interdependence has been altered through the growth of the Euromarkets in both West Germany and the UK.

1.4 COMPETITION IN INTERNATIONAL BANKING MARKETS

It is widely acknowledged[35] that the Eurocurrency markets are highly competitive. However, an analysis of the level of competition within the banking industry does not fit easily into any of the standard theories of market structure and competition. Competition can be defined as rivalry between producers. In this sense, it is clear that the perfectly competitive equilibrium represents no competition. Producers are not seeking to compete actively with one another, and the behaviour of one producer will have no effect on other producers. At the other extreme, the textbook case of pure monopoly is not a competitive situation, since one producer controls total production within that industry.

In reality these two extremes are rarely witnessed and most industries can be classified as competitive, albeit to varying degress. In this section I offer two pieces of evidence which suggest that international banking markets are highly competitive. (The implications of the high degree of competitiveness characteristic of these markets are examined more fully in chapters 5 and 6.) Firstly, the past three decades have seen an increasing international integration of financial markets and an increase in the number of banks competing with each other for international business.

Secondly, there has been a proliferation of product innovations within international banking, especially during the 1980s. Innovation lies largely outside the perfectly competitive paradigm.[36] Innovation is risky yet under perfect competition, firms gain no advantage by innovating since there is no prospect of monopoly profits. Thus, it is argued that there is a need for some assurance of monopoly profit to compensate for the risk. Empirical evidence on the degree of competition required to produce an optimal level of innovation is mixed[37] and moreover it is not clear that it is entirely applicable to the banking industry. Most studies examine the relationship between research and development (R and D) expenditure and firm size in manufacturing industry. Financial intermediaries, however, do not have R and D expenditure and innovations are not a costly process as in manufacturing. Innovation within international banking can be seen as a process whereby banks seek to attract customers by offering services which are tailor-made for their needs. In this sense, it is evidence of competition between banks who are seeking to improve their market share and increase profits.

During the late 1960s and 1970s, international banking expanded very rapidly (see section 1.1). This expansion occurred over a wide geographical area including not only the UK, US and continental Europe (the more traditional international banking centres), but also offshore centres (for example, Hong Kong, Singapore, the Bahamas) became popular as a means of avoiding the banking regulations common to most European countries and the US.

London is the world's largest international banking centre. Whilst

Table 1.5   London and New York – Foreign Banks Represented

Date	London direct[1]	indirect[2]	total	growth	New York direct[1]	growth
1967	114	n.a.	114	–	n.a.	–
1968	135	n.a.	135	15.50	n.a.	–
1969	138	n.a.	138	2.17	n.a.	–
1970	163	n.a.	163	15.30	75	–
1971	176	25	201	18.90	81	7.40
1972	215	28	243	17.30	85	4.70
1973	232	35	267	8.99	98	13.30
1974	264	72	336	20.50	114	14.00
1975	263	72	335	−2.89	127	10.20
1976	265	78	343	2.33	144	11.80
1977	300	55	355	3.38	177	18.60
1978	313	69	382	7.06	208	14.90
1979	330	59	389	1.80	244	14.80
1980	353	50	403	3.47	253	3.60
1981	353	65	418	3.59	255	0.70
1982	379	70	449	6.9	285	10.50
1983	391	69	460	2.39	294	3.10
1984	403	67	470	2.12	c307	4.20
1985	399	64	463	−1.52	c320	4.10
1986	400	47	447	−3.58	356	10.10

Notes: 1 – representation through a branch, representative office or, sub-
         sidiary
         2 – representation through a stake in a joint venture or a consortium
Source: Compiled from data in Blanden (1983, 1984a, b, 1985, 1986).

this role is of long-standing importance, the numbers of banks represented there increased steeply in the 1960s and 1970s. This is shown
in table 1.5,[38] which records the number of foreign banks in London
for each year since 1967.

Initially, during the early 1960s, US banks came to London to tap
the Euromarkets for funds which they would pass back to the US (on
some specific episodes, see chapter 1.2.3). Soon, American banks
were building up a presence in London to avoid the VFCR restrictions imposed in 1964.[39] In the 1970s, their numbers increased further
as they began to participate in lending in the Euromarkets. Initially,
this subparticipation was largely through consortium banks[40] because
they offered banks the ability to develop a specialist knowledge in the
area of syndicated lending, whilst at the same time pooling risk with
other large banks. Once this specialist knowledge was secured, the

banks tended to pull out of these consortia as they established their own international departments and set up branches in London (if they were not already represented there in that form).[41]

One factor encouraging US banks to come to London, which has been emphasised in various studies[42] was the liberal regulatory environment which foreign banks in London enjoyed. Throughout the period before exchange control abolition, foreign currency business *vis-à-vis* non-residents was excluded from regulatory control by the Bank of England (see Chapter 4.5). London retained its role as an international banking centre by conducting business in non-sterling currencies.

Moreover, even with respect to sterling business, foreign banks were initially in a more favourable position. Whereas the UK clearing banks were from 1965 to 1971 subject to an 8 per cent cash reserve ratio, a 28 per cent liquid assets ratio, interest rate ceilings on deposit and loan base rates (through the cartel arrangement) and quantitative and qualitative limits in their sterling portfolios, foreign banks only had ceilings on the amount of sterling loans which could be advanced to British residents. After 1971, regulations applicable to domestic and foreign banks became more uniform.[43] However, the Bank of England successfully maintained a rigid distinction between sterling and foreign currency business, the latter being unregulated and indeed positively encouraged thus allowing London to become the major centre for Eurocurrency business.

During the 1970s many banks from other countries established a presence in London. By 1983, 73 different countries from all parts of the world were represented (see table 1.6).[44] Figure 1.2 shows us that although US banks were increasing their representation in London in absolute numbers over most of the period, their percentage share of foreign currency liabilities decreased from just under 40 per cent in 1974 to just over 20 per cent in 1983. This highlights the growth in importance of banks from other countries and especially the Japanese. (Table 1.6 shows that Japanese banks have the second highest representation in terms of the number of banks and this number increased from 33 to 43 between 1983 and 1986.)

The growth of Japanese banking abroad has been heavily influenced by regulation by the Japanese Ministry of Finance. In 1974, the Ministry banned all medium and long-term overseas loans by Japanese banks or their foreign branches. As a result, Japanese banks could operate in markets such as the Eurocurrency market

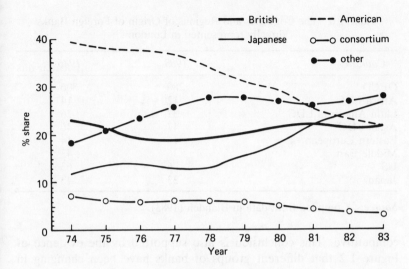

Figure 1.2 Percentage share of liabilities

only via overseas subsidiaries and expansion was curtailed because those subsidiaries did not have access to lender-of-last-resort facilities from the Bank of Japan.

As Japan became a large surplus country and therefore a large holder of foreign exchange, pressure to resume overseas lending increased. After only three years, in June 1977, the Ministry of Finance announced the removal of the controls on medium and long term lending. Japanese banks' foreign currency liabilities in London promptly showed a steep increase (Figure 1.2).

Since 1984, there has been a levelling off in the growth of foreign bank numbers in London. The main reason is that almost all the major banks in the world are now represented there. By 1984, only one bank from the top 100 banks in the world was not represented.[45] The uncertain atmosphere of international banking in the wake of the world debt crisis also affected growth. Some of the US regional banks who had become very involved in the Euromarkets in the late 1970s began withdrawing from international banking especially because of pressure from the Federal Reserve to increase capital ratios (Ipsen (1983)).

The large increase in the number of foreign banks in London in the 1970s suggests that the international banking market is highly

Table 1.6   The Countries and Regions of Origin of Foreign Banks
directly represented in London

Countries	1983	1986
OECD	280	306
Africa LDC	12	14
Latin American LDC	32	26
Asian LDC	47	46
Eastern European	15	14
Middle East	36	43
US	76	63
Japan	33	43

Source: Compiled from data in Blanden (1983).

competitive. This conclusion is also supported by the evidence of
Figure 1.2 that different groups of banks have been changing in
relative importance over the period 1974–83.

Increasing numbers of foreign banks have also come to New York
(see table 1.5). Foreign banking in the US dates back to the middle of
the last century as the US became industrialised. New York became
the focus of international banking activity with the main growth
periods pre-1970 being in the 1920s (the international bond
markets[46]) and the 1950s (when foreign banks found it necessary to
have a representation in the US to serve the needs of their corporate
clients).[47] The main growth period in the 1970s was after 1974 (somewhat different to London, see table 1.5), following the removal of
capital controls (1974) which allowed banks in the US to take an
active role in the recycling process.

International banking in the US has to be distinguished from that
in the UK and many other centres. A considerable number of foreign
banks are established in the US to gain access to the US domestic
market. International banking therefore has two aspects: firstly,
foreign banks engaging in international business; and secondly,
foreign banks wishing to participate in US markets. The presence of a
greater number of regulations in the US compared to the UK restricted the extent to which the first type of international banking
occurred, and helps to account for London's role as a Eurodollar
centre. Before 1978 foreign banks in the US had more favourable
conditions relative to domestic US banks. They were regulated only
at state level and were not subject to Federal Reserve reserve
requirements, deposit interest rate ceilings or restrictions on inter-

state banking. The 1978 International Banking Act introduced Federal Regulatory Laws for foreign banks which gave them the same regulatory status as domestic banks. The desire to strengthen New York's position as an international banking centre led to the creation of International Banking Facilities (IBFs) in December 1981. The result was a significant increase in the numbers of foreign banks in New York (table 1.5). IBFs allow banks (either US or foreign) to conduct their international business free from interest rate restrictions, reserve requirements and FDIC insurance. This represented an attempt by the US to repatriate some Eurodollar business from London.

This pattern of the multinationalisation of banking has been repeated in many other countries.[48] The pattern which has emerged over the last 20 years in international banking is one of deregulation (indeed competition in deregulation, see chapter 7) and encouragement by the supervisory authorities. As the numbers of banks involved in international banking grew, and as these banks established themselves in most of the major banking centres of the world, so competition between them was stepped up.

Further evidence on competition within international banking is given by the increasingly innovative environment of international banking. During the late 1960s and 1970s, the main innovations in international financial markets occurred in the Eurocredit markets. As we saw in chapter 1.2.6, these innovations were important in the markets' development.

Since 1982 uncertainty produced by the international debt crisis has severely squeezed the primary syndicated Eurocredit market. The increase in attractiveness of the bond markets can be seen as a result of the debt crisis and of the rise in real interest rates in the 1980s. Because the banks were heavily involved with countries which were experiencing debt servicing problems, they were reluctant to increase their balance sheet exposure further once the debt crisis broke. They preferred, therefore, to operate through the bond markets, acting more as merchant banks rather than deposit banks. Alongside these difficulties, a proliferation of innovations in these markets has been encouraged and a blurring of traditional distinctions between credit and bond markets has occurred.

The first major innovations of the 1980s occurred in the syndicated Eurocredit market itself – the tentative emergence of a secondary market especially in sovereign debt.[49] The debt is either sold or swapped. This enables banks to rearrange their balance sheets at a time when much of the debt on their balance sheets is static (due to rescheduling and the squeezing of the primary market), limiting room for manoeuvre.

A further incentive to rearrange balance sheets in this way has been the desire to increase income from fees. The more rigorous application of country limits (see section 6.3.5) has meant that the only method of boosting income from fees when the balance sheet is already 'full' with regard to a particular country is either to sell off the older debt prior to its maturity or to swap the debt of one country for that of another allowing new lending.[50] Banks take a partial write-off of existing debt (since it is sold or swapped at a discount), something which has only been possible because of the build-up of reserves and capital over the last four years. Portions of debt can be sold off either until maturity or for only a specified period of the loan, before reverting to the original lender. The bank which takes on the loan benefits from greater international diversification of its portfolio because in many cases subparticipations are sold to smaller banks such as the US regionals.

There is some dispute as to the legal issues involved with these subparticipations. The borrower may refuse to permit the original loan to be subparticipated, if the assets are to be sold to a bank of lower quality. Many of the prime borrowers have clauses in their loan agreements which exclude silent subparticipations thus preventing banks from making any sales without first consulting the borrower who may refuse especially if the loan is sold to a bank considered by the borrower to be inferior. The borrower may also not like the possibility of his debt trading at a discount in a secondary market when he is attempting to raise new money on good terms. In the case of other borrowers (that is, usually non-prime borrowers) they rarely know about the subparticipation.

The main regulatory concern regarding subparticipations is the fact that as long as the borrower's contract remains with the primary bank, it may still have to bear the risk if the borrower cannot repay. To that extent, therefore,[51] the vendor has only cosmetically reduced its country exposure. The increased space in its country limit has resulted, in reality, from an increase in the country limit and not a reduction in exposure.

As a result of these difficulties, a new instrument was introduced in 1984 – a Transferable Loan Instrument or Certificate (TLI or TLC). Under such an arrangement, the subparticipation allows for the transfer of all obligations to the new lending bank. The borrower retains the advantages of Eurocredits compared to Eurobonds; that is, the choice of an interest rate period (usually one, three or six-month) throughout the life of the loan and a staggered drawdown. The lenders have the advantages of greater liquidity (under normal market conditions).

Despite such innovations, the Eurocredit market has been declining in importance in international borrowing since the early 1980s. The Eurobond market, where there have also been many innovations, has been increasing in importance. The first of these is the Floating Rate Note (FRN), which was the application of the roll-over principle to the international bond markets. It provided an alternative to fixed rate bonds. It was originally conceived in the late 1970s to be limited to best quality borrowers who had access to the bond markets. Little competition was therefore envisaged with the Eurocredit market. By the end of 1983, however, it was a genuine rival to the Eurocredit market because, firstly, banks felt that it provided some measure of liquidity which they sought after the debt crisis of 1982. Secondly, the FRN market was accessible even to some of the better risk LDCs. In practice, FRNs may prove to be less liquid under conditions of crisis, when investors, mainly the banks themselves, seek to unload them within a short period of time. FRNs can be cheaper for the borrower (because they are more liquid, in theory) although they have the disadvantage that there is not usually any flexibility to change the interest rate periods throughout the life of the bond. FRNs allow the subparticipation of non-bank investors, but banks are the main takers of the notes, especially for borrowers without a triple A rating (that is, who are not prime risks).

A second innovation within the capital market is the Revolving Underwriting Facility (RUF). This emerged in 1981 and by the end of 1983 there were $7 billion RUFs outstanding. The issuer borrows medium term funds at a rate which is usually below that which it would pay in the loan or FRN markets. The borrowing involves a bank (or group of banks) which underwrites the sale of three-month or six-month Euronotes or EuroCDs. If the paper cannot be placed, the banks have to take them. The problem with this market – and a reason why many international banks refuse to participate in it – is that the underwriting banks generally assume that they will never have to take the notes. However, if at some time spreads in the market as a whole rise, then all the RUFs are likely to require to be taken up by the underwriting bank(s) *at the same time* as investors sell the RUFs to move into notes with higher spreads. Moreover, these notes were not initially covered by the supervisory authorities. Latterly, these off-balance sheet items have been included in capital requirements. A further risk is the risk that the agent bank may not try hard enough to place the notes with non-bank investors over the ten years or so of the life of the facility. The notes require repeated marketing because of their six-month maturity. This is a risk that is faced by both the underwriters (they are more likely to have to take the notes) and the borrower (the note may trade at a discount). The risk can be removed if the agent bank is a major underwriter.

As with the FRNs, Euronotes are taken up mainly by banks. Only an estimated 20–30 per cent have gone to non-banks (*The Banker*, February 1984). Thus in terms of exposure to different countries, banks now have outstandings above those shown on the balance sheet, yet one can argue that the risks associated with these innovations are the same as with syndicated lending. The new instruments appear liquid, but the market is highly dependent on confidence. They are liquid, therefore, under normal conditions and allow some manipulation of the balance sheet of individual banks. But the system does not gain decisively in stability as a result; a crisis would strip most of these assets of their liquidity and banks would find themselves having to honour their underwriting commitments.

This brief review of the new developments in the market supports our earlier conclusions regarding the highly competitive nature of the international markets. The case, however, is not completely conclusive. In particular, there is the question of collusion between banks.

Whilst the number of banks in the international banking market may have increased, this would be indicative of increased competition only if collusion were absent. In the conventional sense of a cartel, collusion is not a factor. However, the herd instinct is to some extent a form of collusion. With respect to the innovations, the banking industry differs from other industries in that banks would prefer their innovations to be used by others. If many banks are involved when a crisis strikes, then the innovating bank is not alone and a co-ordinated resolution of the crisis with the authorities is more likely. To this extent, the herd instinct removes some of the risk inherent in innovations.

1.5 CONCLUSION

This chapter has outlined some of the factors involved in the development of the Eurodollar market and, in a very preliminary way, the EuroDM and Eurosterling markets.

We may conclude that in the 1960s and 1970s, the Eurodollar market was affected to a great extent by US monetary policy. In chapter 4, I shall examine whether this influence has continued in the later 1970s and early 1980s, and if so, what form it has taken.

We have shown that controls on capital movements were influential in the development of both the Eurodollar market and the EuroDM market. We examine in chapter 4 whether UK capital controls affected the development of the Eurosterling market.

Factors such as the recycling role played by the markets, the effects of the interbank market and innovations, in combination with the highly competitive structure of international banking markets, raise interesting questions about the stability of the markets. These questions are pursued in chapters 5 and 6.

Part I
Interdependence, Arbitrage and the Removal of UK Capital Controls

Over the last 25 years capital markets have become increasingly international and interdependent. In this first section of the book we examine closely the processes through which this internationalisation occurred. In chapter 2 we establish the importance of the interest rate parity condition as a measure of financial integration. We then incorporate the impact of the growth of an offshore banking industry (as typified by the Euromarkets) on the interest rate parity condition and arbitrage mechanism into the Mundel–Fleming framework. This allows us to draw some conclusions regarding the impact of the Euromarkets on interdependence (chapter 3).

This analysis is examined in relation to the Eurodollar and Eurosterling markets in chapter 4. Firstly, we investigate the importance of capital controls in the UK prior to 1979 as a policy allowing greater monetary independence. Secondly, we show that the removal of these controls resulted in greater interdependence.

2 Interdependence and Monetary Policy

2.1 INTRODUCTION

In examining various aspects of interdependence it is useful to distinguish two concepts – sovereignty and autonomy (Cooper (1968)).[1] Sovereignty is defined as authority, firstly to form and announce economic policy decisions and, secondly, to renounce such decisions previously made. The entitlement to announce decisions is distinct from the ability of the government to carry them out. The latter may be called autonomy, and is one of the recurrent themes in this thesis. It is the ability to pursue objectives which may or may not conflict with objectives of other countries.

Certain questions arise in relation to *monetary* independence in particular. Firstly, what exactly do we mean by monetary independence and interdependence? The question is closely linked with the definition of financial market integration and its measurement. Different measures assume different definitions and it is important to determine which definition lies behind any analysis. Secondly, why should a country want to have independence of monetary policy? This chapter seeks to analyse some of the issues relating to these questions.

2.2 INDEPENDENCE AND FINANCIAL INTEGRATION

Interdependence involves both costs and benefits. The traditionally emphasised benefit is a more economical use of resources – the familiar argument for gains from trade. The cost is that decisions then have to be taken within a set of additional constraints – that is, there is some loss of national autonomy.

Over the past few decades, policy makers have become increasingly aware that the decisions for which they are responsible cannot be analysed in isolation from those of other political units. In the case of small countries, there has been some loss of control over policy variables. In the case of large countries, there has been a growing

33

realisation that their policies may have repercussions upon the world economic climate.

Interdependence occurs because of economic integration. There can be integration of goods markets, labour markets and so forth. We concentrate in this chapter on financial integration and its relation to monetary interdependence. The literature contains various definitions of integration and interdependence.[2] Firstly, there is the sensitivity of international capital flows to both covered and uncovered interest rate differentials. When interest rates change in a country, in response to monetary policy, capital will begin to flow between that country and other countries. The greater the sensitivity of these capital flows to interest rate changes, and the greater the magnitude of the flows, the less the scope for independence with respect to monetary policy.

This view may be contrasted with that of Logue *et al* (1976), who argue that in an integrated system, interest rates are always uniform and capital flows independent of interest rates. As information becomes available in financial markets, prices adjust without the need for any actual monetary flows. Markets are assumed to be efficient in the finance theory sense of the word. Prices at time *t* reflect all available information at time *t*. If new information becomes available, then prices adjust instantaneously to incorporate the implications of that information (Logue *et al* (1976) p. 95). Kenen (1976) examines this assertion. He argues that the statement is ambiguous in that it implies that even if opportunities for capital flows were highly restricted (for example due to capital controls), price adjustment would still occur and do so instantaneously. Kenen accordingly suggests a modification to the statement in the sense that there is likely to be some anticipation of capital flows which may 'obviate the need for actual transfer of claims between two markets'.[3] Whether transfers actually take place depends on the characteristics of the disturbance causing expectations to change.

For example, he compares two cases. In the first case, an exogenous disturbance affects the quality of assets, and affects all wealth holders alike. Price changes can then occur without the need for any capital movements. Bid and offer prices are changed in the same way by all wealth holders and therefore capital flows will be precluded. Secondly, by contrast, where the disturbance has different implications for different wealth holders, or where the stock quantities demanded or supplied are affected, movements of capital must occur. The price of the asset may change before such movements take place,

depending on whether the change was anticipated or not, but ultimately there is a need for portfolios to be adjusted and justify the
change in prices. Kenen concludes that the efficient markets hypothesis approach is a legitimate way of introducing expectations into our
analysis, but that there is a need to examine more closely the causes
of such a change in expectations before we can determine the likelihood of capital flows. The efficient markets hypothesis, however,
casts doubt on the efficacy of capital controls as Kenen points out.[4]
This will be examined for the case of the UK in chapter 4.

Whatever the verdict on Logue *et al*'s definition, the view that
integration can be adequately defined by the interest sensitivity of
capital flows is not immune to criticism. Logue *et al* argue that there is
no analysis within this approach of the effect of flows on domestic
and foreign economies experiencing them. Most authors, however,
combine the capital flow approach with the ultimate stock effects of
such flows. As interest rates are affected by the capital flows, so shifts
in portfolios will occur, eventually converging to a new stock equilibrium, where investors are satisfied with the amount they hold of
each asset. Logue *et al* view this combination as a separate definition
of integration. Much of the literature, however, would indicate that
the two approaches go very much together. McKinnon and Oates
(1966), for example, build a model modifying the analysis of Mundell
(1963) and Fleming (1962) to take account of stock considerations.
This approach allows us to look not only at the adjustment process
but also at the new equilibrium that is likely to prevail.

There are several ways of specifying the relationship between
interest rates in different countries:
i) The covered interest parity approach makes use of the interest
parity relation which states that in equilibrium the differential between interest rates on assets of the same degree of risk denominated
in different currencies will be approximately equal to the forward
discount/premium.[5] The interest rate parity condition is defined
formally as:

$$(1 + if)F/S = (1 + id)$$

where:
if = the foreign interest rate
id = the domestic interest rate
F = the forward exchange rate in domestic currency per unit of
foreign currency

S = the spot exchange rate in domestic currency per unit of foreign currency

This condition can be reduced to the following if second order terms are neglected:

$$rd = rf - fp$$

where:

fp = the forward premium on the domestic currency *vis-à-vis* the foreign currency.

The interest rate parity condition is a necessary condition for complete integration. In itself, however, it tests only the efficiency of arbitrage between two financial centres. Other considerations need to be taken into account if we are to reach firm conclusions about the degree of interdependence (sterilisation and insulation mechanisms, see below).

ii) The level of interest rates in various countries: in this case, the argument is that integration is greater when there is less divergence[6] among nominal interest rates of different countries. Whereas the interest parity approach looks only at covered interest rates, this approach looks at uncovered interest rates. Its shortcomings are that firstly it does not recognise that actual interest rates may differ because of risk considerations. Secondly, nominal interest rates may differ because of differences in inflation rates between the two countries concerned.

iii) The covariability of interest rates approach deals with the risk problem. Recognising that differences in the level of risk or other factors cause differing interest rates between countries, it looks at the correlation between movements in interest rates on assets of similar risk (for example, US Treasury Bills and UK Treasury bills would be considered as assets of similar risk). Financial integration under this definition may still be present even if interest rate levels are very different. Kenen (1976) argues that covariation is implied by integration but need not itself imply integration, because it could occur as a result of common influences on both markets for example a common history of inflation. To eliminate these effects, it would be desirable to carry our multiple regressions and determine the partial rather than the simple correlations.

At the same time, financial integration may be complete without uncovered interest rate covariation: since we may still have interest parity holding when covariation has broken down. Some of the adjustment to, say, a foreign interest rate change may be absorbed in the short run by the forward premium. The domestic interest rate may not then move in line with the foreign one despite a high degree of integration. In the long run the forward premium must reflect the expected rate of depreciation (appreciation) of the domestic currency because of a higher (lower) inflation rate relative to the foreign country. Whilst, therefore, interest parity can tell us about financial integration, which is a necessary condition for interdependence, two other factors are important in determining the degree of short-term interdependence. The first is insulation mechanisms, 'which refer to certain features of the system (such as movements in the forward exchange rate in response to changes in interest rates), which automatically insulate either domestic interest rates or money supplies from monetary developments in other countries'.[7] Consider such movement in the forward exchange rate. The consequence is that a change in the covered interest differential is less than the change in interest rates (domestic or foreign).

The covered interest rate differential, c, (derived from the interest parity condition on page 36) is given by:

$$c = rd + fp - rf$$

where:

rd = domestic interest rate
fp = forward premium on domestic currency
rf = foreign interest rate.

When the insulating mechanism is operating, the change in c is less than the change in $(rd - rf)$ and adjustment in the forward premium modifies the impact of a change in rf on rd. A key insulation mechanism is that of flexible exchange rates which may preserve some independence of monetary policy despite financial integration.

Secondly, sterilisation mechanisms[8] are deliberate policy measures introduced to offset any external influence on the domestic money supply when there are fixed exchange rates. The authorities may engage in open market operations, for example, in response to a change in the external component of high powered money, thus neutralising the effect of the change on the domestic money supply. The cost of such action is higher volatility of exchange reserves. It does, however, provide some monetary independence in a financially integrated world. The extent to which such sterilisation can be carried out when the domestic country seeks to maintain a covered interest rate differential against domestic assets is limited in practice by the stock of reserves which the central bank holds. Monetary independence can therefore only be maintained in the short run.

Up till now, we have dealt with interest rates and capital flows as measures of integration and therefore interdependence (to the extent that insulation/sterilisation mechanisms are inoperative). An important question when dealing with financial integration is whether one should consider the relationship between interest rates or money supplies in different countries. Portfolio theory along with the efficient market approach lies at one extreme; proponents of this approach such as Logue *et al* argue that asset prices rather than quantities are important since they are the variables that are affected by changes in information in financial markets. Kenen (1976), however, opts for using the ability to control the money supply in his definition of monetary autonomy. In his view, financial integration and monetary interdependence are to be defined in different ways. He defines integration as the degree to which markets are connected, in the sense that participants are both obliged and able to take notice of events in other markets. Ability to take notice means that there are good information flows, and no barriers (for example, capital controls) preventing investors from reacting to these flows. In this sense, substitutability[9] of assets is not sufficient for financial integration; there is also a need for investors to be able to buy and sell assets when risk-adjusted prices change. Obligation to take notice means that if investors did not take actions, they would not achieve their own objective, for example maximising the return from their portfolio. Kenen points out that if economic information is conveyed to a great extent in prices, then investors will be both able and obliged to take notice and it makes sense to study prices.

Monetary interdependence, on the other hand, is determined according to Kenen by whether the money supplies of the two countries are independent of each other and not their interest rates. However, this view ignores the mechanism through which interest rates and the money supply are related. If financial markets are perfectly integrated then an increase, say, in the money supply in the foreign country results in an increase in the world money supply and associated with this is a decrease in world interest rates. The domestic interest rate also decreases being determined in this case by the world interest rate. In the case of less than perfect financial integration changes in the high powered money supply are associated with interest rate changes through the following mechanism. Llewellyn (1980) sets out a 'mechanical representation of the causal links between an initial policy induced change in the domestic component of high powered money in country A (*Hpa*) and the ultimate induced change in . . . [high powered money] in country B (*HPMb*)'.[10] Assuming either a fixed or a floating exchange rate,

$$dHpa \longrightarrow dHta \longrightarrow dHPMa \longrightarrow dia \longrightarrow d(ia - ib - fp) \longrightarrow dK \longrightarrow dReb \longrightarrow dHPMb$$

where:
$\longrightarrow$ = causal link
d = change in
HPM = high powered money
Hpa = policy domestic component of HPM in country A
Hta = total domestic component of HPM in country A
ia = interest rate in country A
ib = interest rate in country B
fp = forward premium of A's currency in relation to B's (its adjustment is dependent on the exchange rate regime)
K = the capital account balance between A and B ($dK = 0$ if exchange rates are fully flexible, resulting in independence of $HPMa$ and $HPMb$)
Reb = The external component of HPM in country B.

Policy induced changes in the money supply of country A are transmitted to country B through changes in the interest rate of country A and the interest rate differential. The latter changes result in international capital movements which then affect the endogenous external component of *HPM* in country B, depending both on the degree to which the forward exchange rate is flexible (the insulation mechanism) and on the extent to which sterilisation is carried out. If one invokes such a mechanism, Kenen's distinction is not important.

Since 1976, the UK monetary authorities have been adopting publicly announced targets for monetary growth. Deviations from such targets are supposedly corrected through the authorities operating on the general level of interest rates and through direct controls.[11] Interest rates are of importance even when following a policy of controlling the money supply: the ability to determine interest rates independently of other countries is valuable. Indeed some criticisms of the lack of success in controlling the money supply through the level of interest rates, and the need at times for direct controls, can be attributed to problems raised by interdependence and the difficulty of achieving an appropriate interest rate if it is different from that prevailing in other countries.

In chapters 3 and 4, I concentrate on the mechanism by which changes in the foreign money supply or interest rates are transmitted to the domestic country and the effect of the internationalisation of capital markets on that mechanism. I therefore combine an examination of the interest party condition (investigating any deviations from it) with analysis of:

i) The insulating mechanism of the forward exchange rate, which is present during periods of flexible exchange rates;

ii) the sterilisation policies, such as capital controls employed in the past by UK governments in particular;

iii) the exchange rate policy being pursued by the government. Even although the period covered in chapter 4 is the period of floating exchange rates, there were periods where government intervention in the foreign exchange markets was very prevalent.

The examination of the interest parity condition will enable us to determine the extent of financial integration. When combined with *i)* and *ii)*, this will allow an assessment of the degree of monetary interdependence.

2.3 MONETARY INDEPENDENCE

This section begins with some remarks on how monetary policy affects the economy. Secondly we consider the nature of monetary interdependence in either removing altogether the instruments of an independent monetary policy, or else frustrating attempts to achieve particular targets devised by the government. This helps to bring out the reasons why an independent monetary policy is desirable.

Monetary policy is useful in an uncertain world. Monetarists advocate adherence to a constant monetary growth rate. Such a policy relies on the assumptions that the demand for money is relatively stable in the long run, that there is a natural rate of unemployment, and that the market economy is stable. This last assumption is particularly debatable. The existence of inconsistent decisions in an economy because of uncertainty and lack of information can cause disequilibrium within the system, which is then aggravated by accelerator/multiplier responses. Discretionary monetary policy under such circumstances is desirable and control over the methods through which such policy can be channelled is important. Monetary policy has a key role to play through its ability to alter the relative yields of different assets, and through changes in wealth. Through these changes, expenditure decisions in the economy may be affected.

The standard textbook account typified by Goodhart (1975) recognises two categories of expenditure decisions which are affected, through changes in relative yields:

i) Savings/consumption decisions;
ii) Investment decisions.

Changes in financial conditions may lead to changes in decisions regarding the amounts to be consumed now rather than later. We can identify both a substitution and an income effect of a change in interest rates. A fall in yields, for example, will cause a decrease in the number of future consumption goods that can be derived from one unit of present consumption goods. The resulting substitution effect will make for a decrease in the amount saved out of present income (in the case of net savers) and will encourage borrowing against future income (in the case of net borrowers). On the other hand, a decrease in interest rates that is expected to be permanent will also lower future incomes from current savings and reduce the future consumption options for the saver. In order to maintain consumption over future periods at a level consistent with the past, there may be a need to save more out of present income. This is the income effect.

If we assume the life-cycle of model of savings and consumption, where we have a period of employment followed by retirement, then those who are receiving an income from labour services rendered will be on balance net savers. Thus the substitution and income effects work in opposite directions. Depending on the relative strength of these two effects, a fall in interest rates may either decrease or increase an individual's net savings. The key question in determining whether a decrease in interest rates increases consumption is whether the income effect is important. The income effect is not only offset by the substitution effect. It may also be offset by a wealth effect. As interest rates fall, the market value of assets already held by investors will rise and the owners of these assets will feel better off and increase their consumption. If the combined wealth and substitution effects outweigh the income effect, the overall impact of a decrease in interest rates on the savings/consumption relationship is expansionary.

With regard to the investment decision, a decrease in interest rates causes an increase in investment. In a simple monetarist model, where financial assets are close substitutes for real assets, as interest rates on the former fall, the relative yield of the latter rises, giving rise to an incentive for investors to run down surplus financial assets and invest in additional real assets. As demand for real assets rises, so their price is bid up and their production stimulated.

In a simple Keynesian model interest rates alter investment expenditure in more indirect ways. Firstly there is the effect of changes in interest rates on business confidence – Keynes' 'animal spirits' and 'spontaneous optimism'.[12] Higher interest rates pointing to a tighter monetary period will tend to have a dampening effect on confidence and an adverse effect on investment. Lower interest rates may similarly induce greater optimism. Secondly, an increase in the money supply may increase the demand for real assets indirectly as the demand for liquid financial assets rises. The purchase of liquid assets induced by the increase in the money supply raises the price and lowers the yield of these assets. This in turn raises the demand for less liquid assets and so on along the liquidity spectrum until finally the demand for real assets rises. In this mechanism the final effect on real assets is small – the effect of the initial rise in the money supply decreases as assets are substituted along the liquidity spectrum.

Another influence of monetary policy on expenditure decisions may occur through the wealth effect of money itself and of financial assets not backed by real capital assets. For example, a fall in interest rates results in a rise in the present value of the National Debt. This increase in wealth is offset in theory by a rise in the present value of the tax liability of the community. In practice, however, it can be argued that the private sector will not discount the future tax liabilities fully, resulting in a real economic effect. Thus changes in the real value of the public sectors's financial liabilities which are held by private individuals, although not contributing to a change in the net wealth of the whole community, may have real economic effects because the public sector (which cannot go bankrupt) will not react to the altered real value of its net liabilities to offset the change in private sector behaviour. An increase in the money supply, given constant prices, increases the wealth of the private sector and so generates an increase in private consumer's expenditure.

Monetary policy, firstly though changing relative yields and secondly through inducing changes in wealth, is aimed at influencing the level of aggregate demand in the economy. If the existence of efficient arbitrage makes it more difficult to use monetary policy effectively, then policy makers lose one of their policy instruments that influence the level of aggregate demand. This cost associated with increased interdependence must be weighed against any benefit arising from increased financial integration resulting from a more efficient distribution of resources.

Aside from its direct effect on aggregate demand, monetary policy influences the exchange rate. Many authors refer to the problem of maintaining an independent monetary policy under fixed exchange rates.[13] If balance of payments disequilibrium arises, reserves come under increasing pressure leading eventually to the need to alter the level of aggregate demand in the domestic economy. It was argued (for example, Friedman (1953)) that under a floating exchange rate regime, these problems would disappear because the exchange rate could adapt to correct a balance of payments disequilibrium.

In a floating exchange rate regime, there may be a problem of achieving the correct exchange rate. This can be defined as that exchange rate which reflects the competitive position of the country in world markets. In the long run, it can be argued that the correct exchange rate is that rate which, together with the country's inflation rate, results in purchasing power parity. Over the short to medium term, however, achieving the correct exchange rate (that is, one that gives an 'appropriate' current account)[14] may be a problem. The major question is to whether financial integration and specifically the existence of the Eurocurrency markets either makes it less likely that the market mechanism produces the correct exchange rate or makes it more difficult for policy makers to achieve the correct exchange rate; and, once it is achieved, do capital flows make it more difficult to maintain?

Traditional theories of the exchange rate determination paid most attention to the role of the current account.[15] It was recognised, however, particularly with the advent of floating rates, that the capital account was also important and this led to the development of the asset market view of exchange rate determination.[16] Subsequent work has been done on the interactions of the two accounts. The view that seems to be emerging from the analysis is that the exchange rate is determined in the short run by financial asset variables, and in the long run, by the current account and the level of competitiveness although the direction of causation is uncertain.[17]

Since 1973, there has been much variability in exchange rates, which could not conceivably represent the changing competitiveness of the various countries or areas concerned. When capital account factors dominate short run exchange rate movements in such a way that the rate deviates widely from the long run competitive exchange rate, exports and imports may be severely affected. If the exchange rate is too high relative to the long run competitive level, then exports and import competing goods will suffer because they will become too high cost relative to competing goods in world markets.[18]

In a small country such as the UK, where trade plays a major role, depression of export demand can cause unemployment and a reduction in overall aggregate demand through a multiplier effect. This is liable to result from the exchange rate being wrong because of asset market pressures and expectations with the influence of the level of competitiveness of the economy being small in the short run.[19] Monetary policy can help to readjust the exchange rate. The existence of highly efficient international financial markets, such as the Eurocurrency markets, however, makes it more difficult, because they may allow arbitrage to be more efficient through reducing the transaction and information costs, as well as increasing the opportunities for arbitrage, both necessary conditions for integration. These issues will be examined in chapter 3.

Asset market factors assume a greater prominence over current account factors, thus altering the strength of policy required to override this. This is one of the motivations for a dual exchange rate system, either fully fledged or similar to that of the UK before the abolition of exchange controls. Prior to 1979, the UK operated a system of partial segregation. Despite London's prominent position in international finance, there was a fairly strict separation between the domestic and international sectors of the financial markets. The authorities achieved this by ensuring that some capital transactions, namely the bulk of investment overseas by UK residents, took place through a separate market with an exchange rate that reflected the demand for and the supply of foreign securities by UK residents (the 'investment currency' market – see chapter 4 for a fuller discussion).

In a fully-fledged dual exchange rate system, the range of capital transactions channelled through the financial market is widened to include non-resident's capital as well. Provision of a stable exchange rate for transactions purposes will be achieved through intervention in the official market, the exchange rate in the financial market being allowed to vary to clear any excess demand or supply for the domestic currency. If, however, the purpose is also to insulate the economy from the effect of capital flows on the domestic money supply, then intervention in the official market could be accompanied by a reciprocal transaction in the financial market.[20] This prevents changes in the external component of the high powered money supply. Monetary insulation, as well as a stable exchange rate for current account transactions, is thus provided.

In general, policy is introduced by governments to correct some deficiency in the market mechanism. Macro-economic policy is usually used to correct deficiences which result in rationing effects in different sectors of the economy, but more especially the labour market.

The economy may be seen as divided into two broad sectors. In one agents are sluggish to respond to new information, and the eventual response is liable to involve quantity changes. The other sector, interacting with the first, is a highly efficient financial sector that responds to new information quickly and does so through price changes. Before the advent of the Eurocurrency market and of the tendency towards financial deregulation, the financial sector was more tightly controlled by the government which used it to enable their policy targets to be realised. Control took the form of the legal imposition of reserve requirements, interest rate ceilings, credit rationing at times of great demand for bank loans, and other mechanisms, which varied from country to country. With the advent of the Euromarkets, regulation became more difficult because many of the controls that were applicable to domestic banks did not extend to these new markets. Indeed, as we noted in chapter 1, the existence of these domestic controls helped to promote the growth of the Euromarkets.

The financial sector, therefore, became more efficient. This increase in efficiency occurred in international markets and therefore led to greater integration of financial markets and subsequent problems for policies. Its effect on the 'real' economy was strengthened (as financial sector disturbances were transmitted more quickly and strongly to the real sector), whilst the ability of monetary policy to achieve various objectives was weakened. Policy makers were affected from both sides of the problem.

The key impact of monetary interdependence on the leverage of policy is through disintermediation. Disintermediation is the ability to move one's borrowing or lending activities from a regulated market to an unregulated market. The scope for disintermediation increases with interdependence, because it then becomes possible to move one's lending or borrowing activities to an unregulated 'off-shore' market (in this case the Euromarkets). The result is that the monetary aggregates in the countries affected will understate the true amount of credit available to their residents, thus reducing the reliability of monetary aggregates as indicators of domestic monetary conditions.

Moreover, during periods of monetary restraint, the existence of these offshore markets allows some economic agents to circumvent such constraints by moving to the Eurocurrency sector of the domestic currency. Tobin and Brainard (1963) developed the theory of the impact of an unregulated intermediary on monetary policy. Johnston (1983) examines the effect of the existence of the Euromarkets in such a framework. Two financial intermediaries, domestic banks and Eurobanks are examined. The liabilities of the financial intermediaries are close but not perfect substitutes because of the different risks associated with each type of deposit and the different regulatory environment of the two markets (see Johnston (1983) p. 91). In contrast, borrowers consider loans from the market to be perfect substitutes in line with the general principles of portfolio theory (see Johnston (1983) chapter 4.3). There is therefore an identical lending rate in both markets, but a different deposit rate, with that of the Euromarket higher because of the non-existence of reserve requirements. We assume no lending margin for services to simplify the analysis, and hence the only factor causing differential loan and deposit rates is reserve requirements, which affect only the domestic markets.

Assume that the supply of bank reserves is contracted or reserve requirements increased to tighten the domestic monetary policy stance. This action tends to raise the loan rate and lower the deposit rate in the domestic money market relative to those in the Euromarkets. The differential between domestic loan and deposit rates widens due to the increased cost imposed by the reserve requirement increase whereas the differential in the Euromarkets is unaffected. The domestic supply of loans decreases and therefore, given that the demand for loans is unchanged, the domestic loan rate rises in absolute terms.

Equilibrium is re-established through arbitrage movements by investors. Marginal wealth holders will move out of domestic deposits into Eurocurrency deposits because the Eurocurrency interest rate is now higher. Similarly, marginal borrowers move to the Eurocurrency market where loan rates are relatively lower. Equilibrium will be re-established when and where the Eurocurrency loan rate is equal to the domestic loan rate. This loan rate will be higher than the initial loan rate, but lower than that existing in the domestic market immediately after the change in policy. (The domestic loan rate falls slightly because demand for loans decreases as borrowers move to the Eurocurrency markets). This new loan rate in the Euromarket is again equal to the Eurocurrency deposit rate (because of the lack of reserve requirements and because we have assumed no lending margin). A new equilibrium is thereby established with the key difference being that the Eurobanks' balance sheets are larger than prior to the policy change; those of domestic banks are smaller.

What effect does this result have? The impact of the domestic monetary stance has been to move business to the unregulated area of the financial markets and borrowing by domestic residents has not decreased by the amount desired. This weakens the restrictive stance of monetary policy, but provided that policies do not become perverse, the desired level of monetary restriction can be achieved. It is theoretically possible for the change in policy to cause a very large shift of funds to the Euromarket, large enough to increase the combined lending of the two markets and cause a fall in lending rates. The restrictive monetary policy becomes perverse under such circumstances (see Johnston (1983), p. 258).

Disintermediation may also have allocative effects. The nature of the Eurocurrency market is such that only large deposits/loans can be made, which means that the market is a 'wholesale' one. Commercial banks and central banks are the most active in the markets, and the amounts dealt in are rarely less than one million currency units. As a result the non-interbank market is accessible only to large industrial and commercial firms and institutional investors. In a situation of restrictive domestic monetary policy, larger firms will be able to circumvent the policy's effects through going instead to the Eurocurrency markets and borrowing there. Smaller companies, who are unable to borrow in the Euromarkets because they require only small amounts of funds, will still be affected by the restrictive policy, although to the extent that the demand for domestic loans by larger companies has been reduced, conditions might be slightly easier. Despite this, it will be true that the restrictive policy limits small businesses more than larger ones.

We can argue that this phenomenon, the result of financial integration and monetary interdependence, is undesirable in that restrictive monetary policy now has a more uneven effect across the economy. Were financial markets less integrated, this would still occur, but on a smaller scale.

Disintermediation thus causes both a weakening of monetary policy measures, frustrating attempts to achieve a target variable, and distributional effects. For these reasons, it is not desirable from the point of view of the policy maker. One method of forestalling these effects is capital controls. Johnston (1983) shows that they helped in the case of the U. K. in that after their removal in 1979 the disintermediation effects increased. We shall examine the effect of capital controls on interdependence in chapter 4.

2.4 CONCLUSION

We have sought here to establish the criteria by which we determine the extent to which financial integration occurs and how that is related to monetary interdependence. We argued that an extension of the interest parity condition gives some indication of the degree of financial integration. When combined with an analysis of the importance of insulation and sterilisation mechanisms, it is possible to assess the extent to which monetary interdependence exists.

The second part of the chapter argued that independence of monetary policy was useful for influencing the level of aggregate demand and, more importantly, for influencing the exchange rate.

3 The Effect of the Eurocurrency Markets on the Arbitrage Process

3.1 INTRODUCTION

The purpose of this chapter is to examine the effect of the Eurocurrency markets on monetary independence with specific reference to arbitrage and capital flows. Through an analysis of the workings of the market and interest rate determination therein, we shall endeavour to assess the effect of the Eurocurrency market on arbitrage efficiency; the new channels it has introduced and the extent to which it has resulted in greater integration of international capital markets. However, greater efficiency of arbitrage need not entail greater interdependence as we saw in chapter 2. A major issue is whether floating exchange rates, and in particular the forward exchange rate, will adjust to restore interest parity. The pressures on the interest rate of a small country, arising from a change in the interest rate of, for example, a large country such as the US, are thus absorbed.

In the opening section of the chapter, I shall restate the principle Mundell–Fleming results,[1] to be used as a benchmark for discussion of policy aspects in the rest of the chapter. The Mundell–Fleming results emphasise the importance of the exchange rate regime and capital mobility when dealing with issues of interdependence. The impact of the Eurocurrency markets may be related to the Mundell–Fleming model; it makes a key contribution to what the model describes as 'perfect capital mobility'.

3.2 THE MUNDELL–FLEMING PROPOSITIONS

The literature on the effectiveness of various types of financial policy under fixed and flexible exchange rates, initially developed by Mundell (1963) and Fleming (1962), now provides results for all possible combinations of policies and exchange rate regimes. I focus on monetary policy under both fixed and flexible exchange rates, assuming various degrees of capital mobility. Assume:

i)   Two countries, a small domestic one and a relatively large foreign one. The model is of a Keynesian type with underemployment and fixed domestic prices.[2] A change in aggregate demand will influence output and real incomes rather than prices.

ii)   The balance of payments comprises the net current account and the net capital inflow to the country. The only role for the current account (net exports) is as a component of demand for domestic output. Depreciation leading to an increase in net exports (that is, exports minus imports) will raise demand for domestic output; and conversely, for an appreciation.

iii)   The degree of capital mobility may vary. Perfect capital mobility implies that domestic and foreign bonds are perfect substitutes for each other, that is, returns are equalised for the given level of risk that they both possess. Portfolio adjustments occur instantaneously with any change in prices being immediately reflected in a shift in portfolio composition. This contrasts with the adjustment process in the original Mundell–Fleming model, where interest rate adjustment occurs because of capital flows between the two countries. Here, however, we include stock considerations. Imperfect capital mobility, by contrast, implies that the domestic interest rate can differ up to a point from the foreign one with no resulting pressure to change.

iv)   Exchange rate expectations are assumed to be unit elastic. Expectations are considered further in section 3.3.

With these assumptions, we can express goods market equilibrium as follows:

$$Y = f(e, Y^*, r, I, G) \qquad (1)$$

where:

Y = domestic real income
Y^* = foreign real income
e = real exchange rate
r = domestic interest rate
G = government spending (exogenous)
I = investment (exogenous)
* = indicates foreign country variables

Similarly, money market equilibrium requires that;

$$Ms = Md(Y, r) \qquad (2)$$

where:

Ms = the supply of money (exogenous)
Md = the demand for money

And for the balance of payments,
$$b = g(NX, k) \tag{3}$$
where:

NX = net exports

k = net capital account excluding official reserve changes.

The external balance is constrained to be zero when exchange rates are flexible. In the original Mundell–Fleming model, the net capital account is assumed to be a function of the differential in interest rates between the domestic and foreign country.[3] In the portfolio models (see, for example, McKinnon and Oates (1966)) this somewhat unsatisfactory assumption is replaced by one which takes stock considerations into account. Individuals allocate their wealth among certain assets. The demand for domestic bonds increases with the domestic interest rate and falls with the foreign interest rate. If the foreign interest rate increases, that is, a differential opens up in favour of foreign assets, then individuals will desire to hold more of their wealth in foreign bonds. A temporary capital outflow will result, which is a direct consequence of individuals' desires to alter their stock of assets. We assume that with perfect capital mobility, in equilibrium, r must equal r^*; otherwise, r can diverge from r^*.

The model has three equations in three unknowns: under flexible exchange rates, the endogenous variables are Y, r and e with $b = 0$; under fixed exchange rates, the endogenous variables are Y, r and b with e given. From this model, several results can be generated. I shall examine one particular aspect which will serve to highlight international monetary interdependence. What effect does a change in the money supply[4] of a large country such as the US have on a small country such as the UK? If the small country experiences no effect on output and employment, there is complete independence. If, on the other hand, the UK experiences a change in output matching that of the US, there is complete interdependence. Output rather than prices change because of the Keynesian nature of the assumptions.

Assume initially that e is fixed and that there is a decrease in the foreign money supply, Ms^*. This leads to an increase in r^*. Under perfect capital immobility, the resultant divergence of interest rates will cause no domestic capital outflow. Asset holders, by definition, are unable to alter their portfolios. The only effect is to reduce expenditure abroad, causing the demand for imports to fall. The resulting decrease in the demand for home produced goods sold for export causes a deficit on the balance of payments that is financed by official reserve flows. The Mundell–Fleming analysis stops here and does not consider the effects of these flows on the stock of reserves. Given that the domestic country experiencing the deficit does not have an unlimited supply of reserves, it will eventually have to introduce deflationary policies or devaluation to eliminate the deficit.

Under perfect capital mobility, the resultant increase in r^*, following the decrease in the foreign money supply, causes a rise in the interest rate of the domestic country in anticipation of capital outflows should the interest rate differential be maintained. The rise in the domestic interest rate will result in real effects on income. Only when $r = r^*$ will equilibrium be re-established and the world interest rate will be higher than previous to the disturbance. Output in both the home and foreign country will have decreased. The effects of the disturbance are transmitted from one country to another under fixed exchange rates and perfect capital mobility.

This is in contrast with the effects of a monetary policy disturbance under flexible exchange rates. The model now constrains $b = 0$. A decrease in Ms^* causes r^* to diverge from r. Complete insulation results from capital immobility, as the exchange rate depreciates to correct the incipient home country deficit, with income unchanged.[5]

Under perfect capital mobility, the decrease in Ms^* resulting in the increase in r^*, causes expectations of a capital outflow, resulting in an incipient capital account deficit for the home country and corresponding surplus for the foreign one. On current account the decrease in Ms^* reduces aggregate demand in the foreign country, causing its demand for imports to fall. An incipient deficit emerges on the home country's current account and a surplus on the foreign country's. The effect of these incipient deficits on the home country is pressure for depreciation. With Ms given and an increase in r, resulting from the outflow of capital from the home country, money market equilibrium requires income in the home country to increase. This counter-intuitive conclusion is the result of either assuming an exogenous money supply, and more specifically that the money supply is unaffected by flows of capital from one country to another, or because the demand for money function (an increasing function of the price of traded goods, P^*) is highly sensitive to changes in P^*, which has increased because of depreciation.

The foregoing discussion of the Mundell–Fleming model has attempted to sketch the importance of the exchange rate regime and the degree of capital mobility for interdependence. Under flexible exchange rates, the degree of insulation is greater than under fixed, but perfect capital mobility implies some interdependence even with floating rates. With fixed exchange rates, there are always spillover effects, and indeed with perfect capital mobility, there is complete interdependence, with the large country's monetary policy being transmitted fully to the smaller country. Under both exchange rate regimes, therefore, increased capital mobility results in greater interdependence between countries, but this is more marked under fixed exchange rates.

3.3 THE EUROCURRENCY MARKETS

3.3.1 Background

The Mundell–Fleming result does not indicate the extent to which capital mobility exists. Introduction of the prevailing institutional framework will help to fill that gap.

The following sections outline a model of the role of the Euromarkets in international finance. We initially consider the case where there is total international integration and no scope for Eurocurrency markets. The arbitrage possibilities that exist are then discussed. Creating scope for the Euromarkets, we examine the way they exploit existing arbitrage channels and create new ones. One of the crucial points that emerges is that efficient arbitrage does not necessarily imply complete interdependence. Efficient arbitrage is a necessary condition, but the question of forward exchange rate adjustment becomes paramount in determining the consequential extent of interdependence, as we noted in principle in chapter 2.

3.3.2 A Financial System with no Scope for the Euromarkets

We want to build up a stock model of interest rate determination in the Eurocurrency markets. We focus on stock equilibrium rather than flow equilibrium because, as we argued in section 3.2, a stock equilibrium is conceptually more satisfactory. Both theory and empirical evidence suggest that the portfolio stock model is a better representation of reality than the flow model.[6]

Take initially an extreme case where there is no scope for the development of a Eurocurrency market. It is a situation of complete international financial integration, implying an absence of information and transaction costs and of controls such as reserve requirements and interest rate ceilings; banks are free to carry on their business as they please. Assume that we are in a general equilibrium world where the banks are acting in a competitive manner. The volume of deposits and loans is determined by the preferences of borrowers and lenders. The interest rate, being the price variable, operates to equate demand and supply for deposits and loans such that it equals the amount paid to the marginal depositor and the marginal borrower (we assume there are no transactions or intermediation costs). Any change in preferences on the part of borrowers or lenders results in a change in the interest rate to re-equate demand and supply.[7] Equilibrium requires that the marginal cost of loans equal the marginal return paid to depositors.

In such a world, there is no advantage to being a Eurobank. Domestic banks can carry out all international transactions at the competitive rate which is faced in the market by all, adjusting for their levels of risk. Risk-adjusted returns are equalised not only within the countries, but also between countries.

This is achieved by a process of arbitrage. Within the framework above, we can derive a stock model of arbitrage and thereby determine the relation between international and domestic bank lending.

We make the following additional assumptions;

i) Deposits in both market – say the UK and the US – are perfect substitutes for each other: they have the same maturity and marketability.

ii) Funds can move freely between both domestic markets, that is, both banks and residents may hold foreign deposits if they wish.

iii) Banks hold no non-interest-bearing reserves with the central bank. Under these conditions, the supply of funds to and the demand for funds from the international banking market will be dependent on investor preferences. In equilibrium, given the level of risk, there is no difference between the return on domestic assets and on foreign assets. Thus the amount investors are willing to invest in foreign markets will be determined by their portfolio preferences. We can expect the supply of funds to both markets to depend on the return being earned.

We need to study the mechanism by which markets remain in equilibrium. The forward exchange market is one channel through which the markets are related to each other. An important relationship for the integration of capital markets is the interest parity condition, defined in chapter 2.2 as:

$$(1 + if)F/S = (1 + id)$$

Discussion of the forward exchange market traditionally takes place under the assumption that it is the forward rate rather than either of the interest rates that adjusts to maintain parity. In the event of a change in the foreign interest rate, interest parity is restored by changes in the forward premium, allowing the new interest rate differential to be maintained, at least in the short run. Only in a situation of full long run equilibrium, where the interest rate differential has to reflect the inflation differential between the two countries, is adjustment of the domestic interest rate considered. We can see why this long run result holds if we look at forward exchange policy, which is sometimes used as an indirect means of influencing domestic monetary conditions rather than through the more direct method of open market operations.[8] If foreign interest rates rise, then the UK central bank could attempt to narrow the forward discount by selling sterling spot and buying sterling forward, maintaining interest rate parity without changing domestic interest rates. The main problem is that such intervention in the forward market may result in large losses being sustained by the monetary authorities in their attempt to maintain the policy direction. The losses occur because of speculation (see Llewelyn (1980) pp. 140–1). In the long run, therefore, it is difficult to continue to support an interest rate differential which is out of line with the inflation differential: such exchange rate policy is unsustainable. Here, however, we do not assume that the forward premium will necessarily adjust in the short run since such a presumption would preclude short run interdependence, where this is defined as the extent to which one can have differing interest rates (chapter 2).

Two important classes of people are involved in the forward exchange rate mechanism.

i) Arbitrageurs seek to exploit any interest rate differentials that may arise between two financial centres. When investing in a foreign currency, there is always the risk that the exchange rate may move against an investor before his funds mature. In order to remove this risk, he may cover himself in the forward exchange market by selling forward the amount he will receive on the maturity of his investment. Hence the direction of capital flows from one country to another depends on the forward premium/discount as well as on the interest rates. Even if the crude interest rate differential were favouring sterling assets, funds may move from sterling to dollars if the forward discount on sterling with respect to the dollar is great enough. When the forward discount approximately equals the interest rate differential, interest parity is said to hold between the relevant assets.

In this theoretical world, if the interest parity relation is disturbed by some exogenous shock, one or more of the following adjustments will be made:

i)   A change in the domestic interest rate
ii)   a change in the foreign interest rate
iii)   a change in the forward exchange rate
iv)   a change in the spot exchange rate.

For example, take a situation where a differential opens or widens in favour of UK assets. Investors' portfolios are now in disequilibrium. Investors want to conduct a once-for-all change in their portfolios in response to the change in the differential. The spot rate of sterling appreciates as investors move into sterling assets; the forward exchange rate depreciates as they sell sterling forward to cover their investments; the UK interest rate falls as funds are invested in the UK; and the foreign interest rate may rise as funds move out of the foreign centre. The extent to which the foreign interest rate rises depends on the size of the foreign centre. If it is large, like the US, then the movement of funds would be small relative to the total stock of assets and the foreign interest rate will only change a little, if at all. Hence there would need to be more adjustment of the other variables.

If we assume that the interest rates and spot exchange rate are exogenous and given, we derive the result that if a differential opens up, the forward rate will adjust to eliminate the arbitrage opportunities. By allowing the interest differential to be maintained, the adjustment of the forward exchange rate allows a measure of independence for monetary policy. We want now to look at the determination of the forward exchange rate in order to investigate whether there is any theoretical reason why it should bear the burden of adjustment whilst the other variables remain constant.

We derive the arbitrageur's demand and supply schedules for foreign exchange (AA in figure 3.1 below) with the forward discount on the vertical axis. Changes in interest rates are represented by shifts of the schedule: changes in the forward discount are represented by movements along the schedule.

When the forward discount is at E, both the interest parity relation holds and there are no flows of capital. If the discount were to widen (that is, to move below E), this implies that the forward dollar is depreciated against the spot dollar by more than the interest rate differential; arbitrageurs would move into sterling assets, simultaneously purchasing forward dollars. For analogous reasons, when the forward discount narrows, arbitrageurs will purchase forward sterling as the counterpart of a move into dollars.

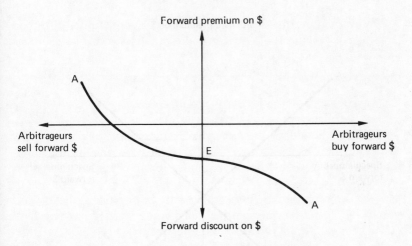

Figure 3.1   Arbitrageurs' Demand Schedule

ii)   Speculators are the second set of actors in the forward exchange market. They buy and sell forward exchange on the basis of their expectation of the future spot exchange rate. If all speculators have uniform expectations, then when the forward rate is equal to the expected future spot rate, no speculative sales/purchases of foreign/ domestic currency are undertaken. If speculators expectations are not uniform then no net speculative transactions will occur when the forward rate is equal to the marginal investor's expected future spot rate. We can derive the schedule, SS in figure 3.2, which is the demand and supply of funds by speculators.

If the expected future spot rate of dollars is above the current forward rate, then speculators will want to buy forward dollars, because they expect to make a profit, buying the dollars for less pounds than they will receive from the forward contract. To the right of the y-axis, the converse will apply. The curve is drawn assuming a given set of expectations. Any change in expectations shifts SS. The curve is drawn such that in equilibrium, no sales or purchases by either arbitrageurs or speculators takes place that is, the equilibrium is at E,[9] where the expected future spot rate is equal to the forward rate.

To the right of the equilibrium point, the forward discount on sterling is increasing. At M, for instance, the forward premium on dollars (ME) is greater than the expected change in the spot rate (OE); hence, speculators move into sterling by selling forward dollars.

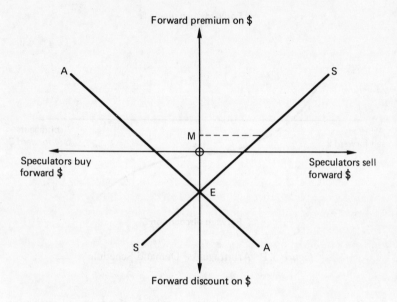

Figure 3.2   Equilibrium in the Forward Exchange Market

In an analogous fashion, to the left of E, speculators will be buying
forward dollars.

The introduction of speculators shows us that the interest parity
condition alone does not determine the forward discount. We now
have two conditions for stock equilibrium, taking the case of the UK
and the US;

$$i\pounds = i\$ - fp$$
$$E(S) = F$$

where:

$E(S)$ = The expected value of the spot rate
F = the forward rate of exchange
$i\pounds$ = domestic UK interest rate
$i\$$ = domestic US interest rate
fp = forward premium on sterling.

We can now examine more fully the effects of a disturbance to the
interest parity condition.

Firstly, in the case where both spot and forward exchange rates are
fixed, it is clear from the above equilibrium conditions that in
response to a change in $i\$$, $i\pounds$ must alter to restore interest parity and
must change by the amount of the initial change in $i\$$.

Secondly, assume that the spot rate is fixed by the authorities, but the forward rate is free to adjust. If a differential opens up in favour of UK assets, arbitrageurs move into sterling, and there is pressure on the pound to appreciate. The authorities have to intervene to sell spot pounds to prevent appreciation and maintain the spot exchange rate. Adjustment to restore equilibrium will therefore fall on one or more of the other three variables. Assuming the foreign authorities are fixing $i\$$, the UK can maintain $i£$ only if the forward rate depreciates. In other words, independence can be achieved only through adjustment of F. As F depreciates (as arbitrageurs sell forward sterling), so the speculators' condition for stock equilibrium is disturbed. Speculators will buy forward pounds if they believe that the government will maintain the spot exchange rate. We will have a flow equilibrium. To return to speculators' stock equilibrium, the forward rate must appreciate. If the government wants to maintain $i£$ fixed, it has to prevent appreciation of F (to maintain interest rate parity). The government must support F through intervention (selling forward sterling), a policy that could prove costly and unsustainable in the long run because of pressure on the domestic money supply.

Thirdly, if we assume flexible exchange rates, both spot and forward rates can adjust allowing the UK to maintain a different interest rate from that in the US in the short run. However, the introduction of speculators shows us that even with flexible exchange rates, there may be times when interest rates bear the majority of the adjustment to a change in $i\$$. This will occur when speculators are very confident that the exchange rate will move in a certain direction. In terms of our four variables, this case can be represented by fixing the forward premium, causing readjustment to equilibrium to come about through a change in $i£$. For example, assume speculators are putting cumulative downward pressure on sterling leading to a widening forward discount. At the same time, interest rates in the US are raised. Restoration of interest rate parity requires either a narrowing of the forward discount on sterling or a raising of $i£$. If speculators expectations do not alter, and the forward discount continues to widen, interest parity and stock equilibrium for arbitrageurs must be restored via a change in UK domestic interest rates.

3.3.3 The Eurocurrency Markets

A model of the financial system leaving no scope for international financial markets like the Eurocurrency markets is in need of some modification to take account of the prevailing institutional environment of banking and finance.

Two important factors distinguish the Eurocurrency markets from domestic financial markets. First, transaction and information costs are smaller in the Euromarket than in national financial markets. There are several reasons for this. One is the wholesale nature of the Euromarkets. Only very large amounts are transacted there. The main operators are commercial banks themselves, central banks, industrial and commercial enterprises and institutional investors. There are only a few individual investors. Deposits are mostly in currency units of one million or more. Transaction costs associated with such amounts not only become insignificant in relative terms but also diminish in absolute terms because of economies of scale.

The second reason why transaction costs are smaller is that the Eurocurrency markets are characterised by a greater degree of competition than is found in national financial markets (see chapter 1.4). In these latter, the structure of the market is usually oligopolistic with the interest rates offered by the leading banks often set by conventions or tied to officially adjusted banks rates. The competitive environment of the Euromarkets results in narrower bid-offer spreads.

A third reason for low transactions costs is found in the financial innovations which have increased the qualitative appeal of the Euromarkets (see also chapter 1.2.6). The introduction of roll-over credits, where the price of credit is altered every three, six or 12 months in line with LIBOR reduces, although it does not eliminate, risks faced by long term borrowers and lenders of paying more or receiving less than the current interest rate when these change over the course of the loan.[10] The syndication approach to medium term lending also reduces the risk faced by individual banks because risk now becomes shared. Lower risk means lower costs associated with a particular loan.

Finally, there is the contribution made by the interbank mechanism. Its function is to 'make it possible for initial suppliers to one group of banks to be matched with final users who deal with different banks.[11] Johnston (1983) recognises at least three ways in which the interbank market reduces costs. First it allows easy liquidity smoothing in the face of deposit withdrawals, thereby lowering transaction costs directly by reducing the volume of unrenumerative precautionary balances that banks need to hold. Secondly, the interbank mechanism facilitates liquidity transfer. A feature of the Euromarkets is that there is a difference across all banks between the degree to which they rely on primary depositors. The well-known US and UK banks tend to attract the largest proportion of their deposits from non-banks sources. In contrast, some of the less well-known banks rely almost totally on the interbank market. There is a gain here from specialisation. Smaller banks can become well informed about the interbank market and need not attempt to compete directly with the larger banks for non-bank deposits, a process that could be very costly (that is because of advertising costs and the cost of offering higher deposit rates to attract non-bank depositors who may perceive smaller banks as a greater risk). Thirdly, there is currency transfer. Traditionally banks have covered themselves against transactions by their clients through the foreign exchange markets. The advent of the Eurocurrency markets brought a new vehicle through which banks could cover themselves, namely by matching the currency composition of assets and liabilities through interbank trading. This provided a competitor for the foreign exchange markets.

All these reasons help to explain why the Euromarkets are able to offer more competitive rates than national markets. The effect on arbitrage of the reduction in transactions costs is that the band within which arbitrage is unprofitable will be smaller than it is among domestic financial markets.

The second major difference between domestic markets and Euromarkets lies in the matter of government regulations. The Euromarkets, as we noted in chapter 1, have commonly been exempt from regulations such as reserve requirements and interest rate ceilings. This enabled them to offer more competitive rates of interest and attract funds.

Johnston (1983) sets out a methodology for empirical research into the interest parity relation, that takes account of the fact that there are, in many instances, differences between the reserve requirements imposed on domestic deposits and on Eurocurrency deposits respectively. The following pages adopt a similar method to that of Johnston. However, whereas he concentrates on interest rate determination alone, the contribution here is to incorporate the effect of a different regulatory environment into our Mundell–Fleming analysis via the arbitrage relation. This allows us to draw some conclusions regarding the effect of the Eurocurrency markets on interdependence. The assumptions are:

i) Deposits in the two domestic markets are perfect substitutes for each other as implied in the Mundell–Fleming framework, that is, they have the same maturity, marketability and risk.

ii)   Domestic banks are required to hold reserves against all deposits in domestic currency. Eurobanks are not obliged to hold reserves and it is assumed that they do not.[12]

iii)   Funds can flow freely between the domestic and Eurocurrency markets. This assumption is important and its violation often explains departures from the model in reality.

iv)   Private non-bank holders of funds are assumed to have strong preferences for deposits in either the domestic markets or the Eurocurrency markets. This is based not on yields but on perceived risk, transactions requirements and portfolio diversification.

v)   For domestic banks, however, there is no difference in the perceived risk of lending in the domestic interbank market or to Eurobanks. This assumption can be justified on the grounds that the banks involved in the two activities are, to a considerable extent, the same. Conceivably, there could be some difference in the perceived risk of the use of funds in each market. This risk factor has become increasingly important in recent years, with the international debt crisis.

The introduction of the Euromarkets adds to the number of arbitrage channels through which policy effects can be transmitted. Along with the channels considered in the previous section of this chapter (3.3.2), two new ones are added. Firstly, there is the opportunity for arbitrage between the Euromarkets and their corresponding national markets (for example, between the Eurodollar market and the US domestic market). This arbitrage differs from our earlier types in that here no exchange risk is involved.

Secondly, there is arbitrage between the markets in the different Eurocurrencies, which does involve exchange risk and therefore the foreign exchange market, but in a very different way from traditional national arbitrage, as we shall see below.

Arbitrage between National and Eurocurrency Markets
This is the first of the new arbitrage channels created by the growth of the Eurocurrency markets. Its extent is determined by the nature of banking controls on domestic deposits and loans, and the different transactions costs in the two markets.

The Eurobank's liabilities are dependent on interest rate differentials between the domestic and Eurocurrency markets, and on domestic monetary regulations. For example, the supply of funds to the Eurosterling market by UK banks will depend on the return offered (that is, the Eurosterling deposit rate), relative to the cost of domestic funds to banks. We might expect the supply also to depend on the domestic interbank rate – the return which UK domestic banks could get on lending the money in the sterling interbank market (*ib*).

The cost of raising funds domestically is not just the domestic deposit rate. Reserve requirements involve a further cost since the reserves that must be held against these deposits have a lower return: in our example, we have assumed the return on reserves is zero, for simplicity. The effective cost per unit is therefore;

$$ie = \frac{id + xd}{1 - Rd}$$

where:
ie = effective cost of funds
id = domestic (in this case sterling) deposit rate
xd = other costs per unit
Rd = domestic reserve requirements.

The term *xd* captures the effect of any other costs incurred because of regulation – such as the Federal Deposit Insurance in the US. Interest rate ceilings under Regulation Q in the US would be represented by a given *id* if they were effective.

Non-banks will similarly be influenced by the interest rate differential – the return on Eurosterling deposits relative to those in the domestic market (*r£* – *i£*, where *r£* is the Eurosterling deposit rate and *i£* the domestic sterling deposit rate). The greater this differential, the greater the supply of non-bank funds to the market. The supply will eventually be limited by the portfolio considerations (*P*) of investors – risk and diversification. Recall that banks are assumed to be indifferent between domestic and Eurobanks: thus their supply will be less affected by *P*.

Taking all these considerations into account, we can write down a function for the supply of funds to the Euromarkets, which is equivalent to the stock of liabilities of Eurobanks:

$$s = f(r£–i£, ie, P, ib)$$

This function applies to the case of arbitrage between national and Eurocurrency markets of the same currency. Exchange rates are not relevant. Were we to consider arbitrage between, say, the UK domestic market and the Eurodollar market, then together with the factors already considered, exchange rates also enter the supply function. The supply of funds would be positively related to the covered Eurodollar rate and the expected appreciation of the dollar.

On the demand side, banks and non-banks are again involved. As for domestic banks' demand for loans from the Euromarket, they will derive funds from this source only when the rate they pay is less than the effective cost of raising funds at home (*ie*). This will depend on the reserve requirements that must be held against both resident and non-resident deposits. As to non-banks, their demand for loans determines the Eurobanks' demand for funds and asset position. The demand for Euroloans is a function of the relative cost of borrowing in the Euromarkets and in domestic market.

$$d = g(r£ - i£, ie)$$

Given the functions determining the assets and liabilities of the Eurocurrency market, we can now identify the effect of efficient arbitrage on the relationship between the interest rates in the two markets.

In the case of the UK and the Eurosterling markets, where exchange rate expectations are not involved, efficient arbitrage should ensure that the Eurocurrency rates stay within a band. The upper limit of this band is the effective cost of raising funds domestically, *ie*. If the Eurosterling rate rose above this, then UK banks would borrow as much as they could domestically and place it in the Eurosterling market. The lower band is the rate at which it becomes profitable for domestic banks to borrow in the Eurosterling market. If the rate fell below that then the demand for funds by banks from the Eurosterling market would be large: depending on the demand for funds they borrow. They will presumably borrow funds only up to the amount they can profitably relend.

This band within which the Eurosterling rate will lie is the result of two aspect of our model:

i)   Reserve requirements or other controls that increase the cost of domestic funds;

ii)   the existence of an efficient arbitrage mechanism between the domestic and Eurocurrency markets (of the same currency).

The Forward Exchange Market

The role played by the forward exchange market when Eurocurrency markets exist is analogous to its familiar role in maintaining interest parity between national markets. Taking the case already mentioned, with the UK domestic and Eurodollar markets, efficient arbitrage implies that the following condition will hold;

$$i£ = r\$ - fp$$

where:

i£   =   UK domestic interest rate

r\$ =   Eurodollar interest rate

fp = the forward premium on sterling per unit of dollar (%).

The forward exchange rate also plays a key role in the other set of arbitrage conditions – those between different Eurocurrencies. However, the process here is different from that envisaged by traditional analysis. Institutionally, all non-dollar Eurocurrency interest rates are determined by the subtraction of the appropriate currency's forward premium on the dollar from the Eurodollar rate. For instance, in the case of the Eurosterling market;

$$r\pounds = r\$ - fp$$

where, $r\pounds$ = the Eurosterling rate.

This essentially stems from the efficient interbank mechanism which is integral to the Eurocurrency system. Arbitrage is assumed to be efficient and therefore to maintain interest parity. The important point about the relationship in this case is that it runs counter to the traditional treatment that makes the interest rate exogenous when dealing with the forward exchange market. When looking at the institutional dynamics, rather than the equilibrium conditions alone, the picture is one of an integrated market where both forward premium and the Eurocurrency rates are jointly determined. An increase in the Eurodollar rate will automatically lead to an adjustment of the Eurosterling rate. Funds probably need not flow to cause this to happen: adjustment occurs in anticipation of such movement. If the forward premium is also allowed to vary, then some adjustment will be borne by it, as it rises in anticipation of excess demand for forward sterling: the forward premium will rise and reduce the rise in the Eurosterling rate.

Interdependence and the Eurocurrency Markets

Now that we have incorporated the Eurocurrency markets, we are in a position to examine the new channels of interdependence that it has introduced. In the absence of Eurocurrency markets, interdependence resulted from capital mobility, fixed exchange rates, and the dominating influence of large countries, reflected in the national interest parity condition. In reality this has never been found to hold continuously.[13] The Eurocurrency markets may enhance interdependence without interest parity relations between national markets being achieved. Assume:

i)   Perfect arbitrage between Eurocurrency markets for the institutional reasons stated above;

ii)   good arbitrage between national and Eurocurrency markets of the same currency;

iii)   poor arbitrage between national markets which will be assumed to be zero for ease of exposition.

Consider now the effect of an increase in the US domestic interest rate. This causes investors to think that they have too little invested in the US and too much in the UK. Those who want to borrow funds turn to the Eurodollar market, increasing the demand for funds from it. There is also a decrease in the supply of funds to the Euromarkets as greater returns can be earned in the US domestic market. Thus there will be an excess demand for funds, putting upward pressure on the Eurodollar rate.

The change in the Eurodollar rate will cause a readjustment of other Eurocurrency rates as well as some adjustment through the forward premium. It is likely that the Eurosterling rate will increase. Arbitrage will then transmit this to the UK domestic market.

In terms of the Mundell–Fleming framework, the results of this 'chain-arbitrage' mechanism indicate that there is potential for greater interdependence through greater capital mobility because of the extra channels through which monetary policy effects can be transmitted. The fact that these markets are outside the control of the domestic government (or at least subject to fewer controls) enhances the finding.

3.4   CONCLUSION

This chapter has looked more clearly at the relationship between interdependence and arbitrage.

We began with a review of the Mundell–Fleming model and the role of the exchange rate regime in offering some independence to policy makers of a small open economy. We concluded that, whilst flexible exchange rates allow greater insulation from foreign policy changes than fixed exchange rates, under perfect capital mobility, interdependence results even with floating exchange rates.

The prevailing institutional framework was subsequently introduced by examining the role of the Euromarkets in the international financial system. We explored further the reasons for the development of the Euromarket phenomenon. The two main ones are, firstly, that information and transactions costs are lower in these markets and, secondly, that government regulation has commonly been absent. Both factors enabled the Euromarkets to offer more competitive interest rates than national financial markets.

An analysis, firstly of traditional arbitrage between national financial centres and, secondly of arbitrage following the introduction of the Eurocurrency markets, allowed us to show precisely what the latter have added to the mechanism. The additions comprise new channels together with a possible 'chain arbitrage' mechanism, as well as a greater volume of private funds available for arbitrage. Potential interdependence has been increased.

4 Some Empirical Analysis of the US and the UK

4.1 INTRODUCTION

There has been much interest in recent years regarding the transmission of US monetary policy to Europe. Chapter 3 drew attention to several possible channels through which monetary policy could be transmitted. Arbitrage between various financial markets was suggested as a key mechanism.

Accordingly, we now examine the following interest rate relations.

i) Arbitrage between the Eurodollar and the Eurosterling markets; does interest parity hold continuously as those involved in the markets suggest?

ii) Arbitrage between the Eurodollar market and the US domestic market, together with the factors that determine the Eurodollar rate. The role of US monetary policy is crucial here.

iii) Arbitrage between the Eurosterling and the UK domestic market, together with the determination of the former rate. The main question here is whether the Eurosterling rate is determined solely with reference to the Eurodollar rate and the forward premium, or whether UK domestic conditions have an influence on it. Arbitrage between these two markets is likely to have been affected by exchange control, and it will be interesting to contrast market behaviour before and after October 1979.[1]

iv) Arbitrage between the UK domestic market and the Eurodollar market, where exchange controls will again be important.

v) The question of forward premium adjustment. Even with efficient arbitrage, the adjustment of the forward premium could still allow an economy some independence of policy. Therefore, we want to determine the role of changes in the forward premium in the insulation of the UK economy from external monetary conditions.

The chapter is divided into five sections. The first reviews existing literature on the efficiency of arbitrage. In the following three sections, points *i*) to *iv*) above are examined using data from the 1970s and early 1980s. Finally, I look at the issue of interdependence and insulation with reference to UK monetary policy from 1974–84 and the influence of the United States.

4.2   EXISTING LITERATURE

There is a large literature on international arbitrage and its efficiency in terms of interest parity. The interest parity condition relates strictly to assets that are homogeneous, that is, perfect or near perfect substitutes, an example being Eurocurrency deposits of different currencies. Arbitrage also occurs, however, between heterogeneous assets: provided there is no limit to the supply of arbitrage funds, profitable opportunities may well be competed away.

When examining the data for profitable opportunities, it is necessary to take into account a number of factors that may legitimately cause deviations from interest parity. Several authors have investigated this. Aliber (1973) notes that with respect to investment in a foreign currency, there are two kinds of risk; firstly, the foreign exchange risk, which is traditionally dealt with through assuming that arbitrageurs cover their investments forward; secondly, political risk. Arbitrageurs, he argues, face greater political risk than speculators who, because they deal exclusively in the forward exchange market, may lose a potential gain, but will never incur a loss through, for example the imposition of capital controls when the contract would simply become void. Political risk is therefore one reason why unexploited arbitrage opportunities may appear to persist in *ex post* data.

Frenkel and Levich (1975), Branson (1969) and others point to another factor – transactions costs, in the form both of broker's fees (in both the foreign exchange market and securities markets) and of the requirement, which banks often impose on their foreign exchange departments, to earn a greater yield on these investments than on domestic ones.[2] Existence of these costs or restrictions implies that there is a band within which arbitrage is unprofitable. Frenkel and Levich (1975)[3] estimated transactions costs at about 0.15 per cent per annum; Branson (1969)[4] found them to be about 0.18 per cent per annum.

Llewellyn (1980) makes a distinction between what he calls global parity and partial parity conditions. Partial parity refers to interest parity between Eurocurrency markets. When we add to this the condition that interest parity holds between homogeneous securities in different countries, which implies that the domestic interbank rate is equalled to the corresponding Eurocurrency rate, then the global condition is also satisfied. This distinction allows us to note that barriers such as exchange controls would not significantly affect partial parity because the uncontrolled Euromarket itself calculates the various Eurocurrency rates with reference to interest parity. Exchange controls may, however, prevent the conditions required for global parity from being satisfied.

Other literature may be classified according to categories i) to iv) above.

i)   We look first at arbitrage between different Eurocurrency markets. Most authors assume that interest parity automatically holds in this case. Non-dollar Eurocurrency rates are calculated through the addition of the Eurodollar rate and the forward premium, so empirical studies should show interest parity holding in these markets.

Marston (1976) examined this contention. He regressed the non-dollar Eurocurrency rate, ix on the Eurodollar rate, ie, and the forward premium, Px;

$$ix = a + b(ie) - c(Px) + u$$

If interest rate parity held then it would be expected that $a = 0$, and the coefficients b and c would each be 1. To allow for any influence of Px on ix, Marston estimated two sets of equations.[5] The first, a normal ordinary least squares (OLS) regression, was estimated for the period 1965 to 1970 using weekly data. In the case of the Eurodollar and Eurosterling markets, the hypothesis that interest parity held continuously could not be rejected. The second approach, an instrumental variables approach,[6] confirmed this result for the period as a whole. Marston concludes that arbitrage seems to determine fully non-dollar Eurocurrency rates.

ii)   Secondly, a number of studies have examined the efficiency of arbitrage between the US domestic and Eurodollar markets, together with the related question of the determination of the Eurodollar rate. In the case of the determination of the Eurodollar rate, Rich (1972) finds that the US bill rate is important in an analysis of monthly data for the period March 1959 to December 1964.

Johnston (1983) and Argy and Hodjera (1973) also find that arbitrage between the Eurodollar and US domestic markets is very near perfect. Their analyses are interesting in that they also looked at the impact of US monetary policy on the Eurodollar market. In modelling the Eurodollar rate, using monthly data from January 1961 to March 1971, Argy and Hodjera highlight the impact of Regulation Q by including the differential between the three month commercial bill rate and Regulation Q interest rate ceiling on time deposits. The ceiling was effective[7] from July 1966 to January 1967 and again from May 1968 until June 1970. In all other months,[8] this variable was set to zero. It is expected that at the times when interest rate ceilings are

binding, additional demand for Eurodollars will be generated, thus
raising interest rates in the market. Empirically, this factor was found
to be important in both periods when Regulation Q was effective; for
every 1 per cent the market rate was above the ceiling rate, the
Eurodollar rate would rise by 0.4 per cent.

Herring and Marston (1977) used the differential between the
interest rate ceiling and the secondary market CD rate to measure
the effect of Regulation Q. Their results suggested that when Regulation Q was not binding, a 1 per cent rise in the US CD rate increased
the Eurodollar rate by 0.7 per cent; by contrast, when Regulation Q
was effective, the Eurodollar rate would rise by as much as 1.2 per
cent. This tended to confirm that tighter monetary conditions in the
US were indeed magnified in the Eurodollar market as demand for
Eurodollars increased.

Johnston (1983) looks at the period up until 1980. He specifies US
monetary policy in terms of changes in reserve requirements on
different classes of deposits in the US. The differential treatment of
Eurodollar and domestic dollar deposits reflects changes in the effect
of domestic conditions on the Eurodollar market. These differentials
are important because they reflect changes in the potential profitabil-
ity of arbitrage between the US domestic and Eurodollar markets. If
we construct a series of US domestic interest rates which take into
account the cost of reserve requirements, then this effective interest
rate should be close to the Eurodollar rate with any differences
reflecting profitable arbitrage opportunities which have been missed.
For the period 1973–78, when US banks were large net suppliers to
the Euromarkets, the effective cost to US banks of raising loanable
funds in the domestic market was compared to the three month
Eurodollar deposit rate. The relationship between 1975 and 1978 was
particularly close. Pre-1975, however, the differential fluctuated
more, for two reasons. Up to the beginning of 1974, bank lending to
foreigners by the US was limited by direct constraints (the VFCR
programme, discussed in chapter 1) allowing the Eurodollar rate to
rise above the effective cost of borrowing funds in the US. In 1974
and 1975, the VFCR programme had been abolished, but the Eurocurrency markets were experiencing a crisis of confidence, centred on
the failure of the Cologne bank Herstatt. The Eurodollar rate tended
to remain above the effective cost of borrowing in the US because
depositors required a risk premium.

Johnston's initial test having indicated that arbitrage between the
two markets is efficient, he conducts an extension of this test on data

from 1979–80.[9] An arbitrage tunnel is constructed within which the Eurodollar rate should fluctuate. The upper limit is the cost to banks of raising funds domestically,[10] and the lower limit is the rate at which it is profitable to borrow in the Eurodollar market and lend domestically.[11] Changes in bank reserve requirements are important because they change the cost of Eurodollar borrowing or lending relative to domestic borrowing or lending (see chapter 3). The statistical evidence of the arbitrage tunnel supports the hypothesis that arbitrage between the two markets is efficient.

iii)   Thirdly, I consider the literature concerning arbitrage between the Eurosterling market and the UK domestic market. Just as US monetary policy and pre-1974 capital controls (VFCR programme) proved to be important factors influencing arbitrage between US domestic and Eurodollar markets, so one might expect that UK exchange controls and monetary policy have played a significant role here. Llewellyn (1980) notes that whereas the differential between the three-month Eurodollar rate and the cost of funds to US banks of funds raised domestically averaged 0.07 per cent (1975–78), the differential in the UK case was 0.48 per cent over the same period, when arbitrage was hindered by controls on outflows. No detailed examination has hitherto been undertaken of the Eurosterling rate, of arbitrage between that rate and the domestic market, and of the effect of exchange controls.[12] This gap is at least partially filled in section 4.5 below.

iv)   With respect to our fourth form of arbitrage – between the Eurodollar and the UK domestic markets – Herring and Marston (1977) found that for the period of the 1960s a 1 per cent rise in the Eurodollar rate would bring about a 0.44 per cent rise in the UK money market rates. This suggests some degree of interdependence between these two markets. Rich (1972) also includes another three variables – the UK Treasury bill rate, exogenous changes in the expected spot exchange rate measured by changes in US official holdings of gold and foreign exchange net of liabilities to official institutions and the US trade balance – which are likewise found to be significant determinants of the Eurodollar rate. He concludes that the significance of the UK Treasury bill rate and of the exchange rate 'supports the view that Eurodollar assets are close substitutes for sterling . . . assets' (Rich (1972) p. 633). He further suggests that the development of the Eurodollar markets has led to a greater degree of financial integration between US and UK interest rates.

v) Finally, there is the question of forward premium adjustment which ultimately given efficient arbitrage determines the degree of monetary interdependence faced by a country.

Rich (1972) and Knight (1977) both found that adjustment of the £/$ forward premium tends to offset some of the change in the US interest rate. This implies that there is some independence of monetary policy in the short run.

Herring and Marston (1977) examine the external relation of the German monetary sector. Their analysis covers the period from 1960 to 1971 and uses quarterly data. They model the DM/$ forward premium as being dependent on the value of exports, the value of imports, the differential between the German interbank rate and the Eurodollar rate and speculative variables. They conclude that although the forward premium adjusts, most of the protection from capital flows for Germany has come from sterilisation policies that were actively pursued by the Bundesbank in the 1960s.

The broad conclusion from these few studies is that movements in the forward premium do allow some degree of monetary independence to non-US countries.

4.3   EURODOLLAR – EUROSTERLING RELATIONSHIP

The purpose of this section is to test the hypothesis that the Eurosterling rate is determined by the Eurodollar rate and the forward discount on sterling *vis-à-vis* the dollar – the alternative hypothesis being that the Eurosterling rate is determined by conditions in the UK money markets.

Figure 4.1[13] shows that there is very little deviation from interest rate parity, especially if we include transaction costs, which create a tunnel within which arbitrage is not profitable. Despite wide fluctuations in the differential and the forward discount, they move almost exactly together. This is consistent with the findings of Marston (1976) and the institutionally held view that arbitrage determines nondollar Eurocurrency interest rates in the way outlined in the initial hypothesis.

Table 4.1 (1967–84) shows the annual mean and standard deviation of the covered interest differential between Eurodollar and Eurosterling interest rates. It might be argued that this is too long a time period for averaging, which could cover up much variation. The

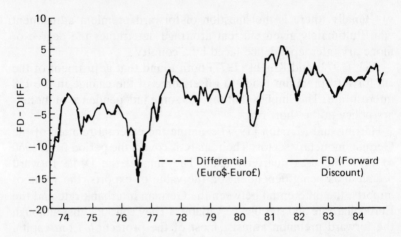

Figure 4.1   Eurodollar-Eurosterling Relationship, 1974–84

majority of the standard deviations, however, are quite small, and therefore the length of period chosen does not seem inappropriate. It is in any case going to be arbitrary.[14]

The results in the table show some deviation from interest parity, but the majority of it can be explained by transaction costs (about 0.18 per cent according to Branson (1969)). If we combine these results with inspection of the figure, we can reasonably conclude that arbitrage has been efficient over the period 1967–84.

Furthermore, Figure 4.7 (see p. 86) indicates the relationship between the Eurosterling and Local Authority loan rate (LA rate, hereafter). The differential between these two rates was far greater than any differential between the (adjusted) Eurodollar and Eurosterling rates. This confirms our hypothesis that the Eurosterling rate is institutionally determined by the Eurodollar rate with little influence exerted by the UK money markets. This result is not surprising for the period prior to the removal of exchange controls in October 1979. Arbitrage between UK money markets and their offshore counterpart was limited by controls on outflows (see section 4.5). We can conclude that the Eurosterling rate has been determined by the Eurodollar rate and the £/$ forward premium.

Notable deviations from this conclusion occurred on two occasions. Firstly, in 1967 (see table 4.1), after the devaluation of sterling the forward discount widened sharply. Before the devaluation the Bank of England had intervened heavily in the market, maintaining the forward discount around 1 per cent. After devaluation, the

Table 4.1   Annual Means and Standard Deviations (SD) of the Covered Interest Differential between Eurodollar and Eurosterling Rates, 1967–84

Year	fp	r$–r£	fp–(r$–r£)	SD (differential)
1967	−0.96	−0.82	−0.14	1.77
1968	−3.36	−3.18	−0.18	0.49
1969	−3.32	−3.44	0.12	1.15
1970	−0.61	−0.40	−0.21	0.26
1971	−0.68	−0.48	−0.20	0.25
1972	−1.93	−1.73	−0.20	0.25
1973	−3.68	−3.61	−0.07	0.25
1974	−5.36	−5.20	−0.16	0.50
1975	−4.78	−4.80	0.02	0.02
1976	−7.87	−8.04	0.17	0.18
1977	−2.76	−2.88	0.12	0.28
1978	−1.65	−1.62	−0.03	0.06
1979	−1.91	−1.96	0.05	0.12
1980	−2.21	−2.04	−0.17	0.47
1981	2.59	2.45	0.14	0.18
1982	1.00	0.77	0.23	0.08
1983	−0.49	−0.61	0.12	0.10
1984	1.42	1.32	0.10	0.13

where:
fp = forward premium on £ *vis-à-vis* $
r£ = Eurosterling 3-month rate
r$ = Eurodollar 3-month rate

government was left with massive commitments to buy sterling at a rate which was well above the new spot rate. Disillusionment about the cost led to a significant withdrawal of support. The forward discount on sterling remained high even after the devaluation because of the lack of immediate success of the devaluation in changing market opinion and because of the withdrawal of support.

Secondly in the fourth quarter of 1973, and the first quarter of 1974, the coal miners' strike and subsequent three-day week and political upheaval resulted in much pressure on the exchange rate and a widening of the forward discount.

4.4   EURODOLLAR – US DOMESTIC ARBITRAGE

In the literature survey above, we noted that Johnston (1983) had shown arbitrage between the Eurodollar and the US domestic markets up to the end of the 1970s to be efficient. This section presents a variant of his analysis to cover the more recent period, 1979–84, and to examine the influence of US monetary policy on the Eurodollar market. An interesting question is whether the influence was as strong as Argy and Hodjera (1973) found it to be from 1966–70 in the presence of Regulation Q.[15]

We argued in chapter 3 that the supply of funds to the Euromarket could be expressed in the equation;

$$s = f(rd - id, ie, P, ib)$$

where:

$rd - id$ = the differential between Eurocurrency deposit rates and domestic deposit rates (influences the non-bank supply of funds);

ie = the effective cost to banks of raising funds on domestic markets (the main influence on the bank supply of funds (Kreicher, 1982));

P = portfolio preference considerations;

ib = the return that domestic banks could obtain by placing funds in the domestic interbank market.

The demand for funds from the Euromarket is given by;

$$D = g(rd - id, ie)$$

which is the relative cost of borrowing in the two markets for banks and non-banks. During the period 1979–84, as table 4.2 shows, US banks were net suppliers of funds to the Euromarkets.[16] We can therefore test the efficiency only of outward arbitrage from the domestic US market to the Eurodollar market.

In theory, there are two possible methods which a bank could employ when engaging in outward arbitrage. The first method, which does not expand the balance sheet of the bank, involves selling CDs (which form part of the bank's assets) in the secondary market. This releases funds for depositing in the Eurodollar market. In this case, if the Eurodollar deposit rate is above the return on holding CDs (the secondary CD rate), the bank should transfer funds to the Eurodollar market.

The second method, unlike the first, may involve an expansion of the bank's balance sheet (Kreicher (1982), Johnston (1983)). The bank raises new funds by issuing CDs. It then deposits these funds in the Eurodollar market. Such a test implies, as expressed in the supply function, a comparison between the Eurodollar deposit rate and the effective cost of raising funds domestically, which is

$$ie = \frac{id + xd}{1 - Rd}$$

Table 4.2   External Dollar Assets and Dollar Liabilities of US Banks, 1979–83 $ millions

	Assets	Liabilities	Net
1979 March	108.6	96.4	12.2
June	115.6	110.2	5.4
September	127.7	122.7	5.0
December	133.9	128.2	5.7
1980 March	131.8	130.6	1.2
June	149.6	128.4	21.2
September	161.5	129.8	31.7
December	172.6	135.5	37.1
1981 March	184.4	130.7	53.7
June	198.1	138.1	60.0
September	211.5	151.8	59.7
December	251.6	174.6	77.0
1982 March	279.1	200.2	78.9
June	318.4	229.8	88.6
September	343.4	237.3	106.1
December	355.7	241.4	114.3
1983 March	375.2	248.0	127.2
June	373.9	248.9	125.0
September	375.5	261.8	113.7
December	388.7	291.6	97.1

Source: BIS (1984), International Banking Statistics, 1973–83

where id is the domestic deposit rate, xd is the cost of federal deposit insurance, and Rd is the reserve requirements placed on US banks.[17] If ie is less than $r\$$, then domestic US banks will find it profitable to borrow domestically and place the funds in the Eurodollar market.

Kreicher (1982) and Johnston (1983) take the secondary CD rate to represent id in the above formula. As Johnston (1983) points out, however, the primary CD rate is the more appropriate rate, since a bank cannot *raise* funds via the secondary CD market. He argues for using the secondary CD rate on the grounds that US banks use it when calculating the cost of funds. There are two possible reasons for this behaviour. Firstly, the banks may use the secondary rate as a proxy for the primary rate. The primary rate is usually around 0.10–0.15 per cent below the secondary rate; the differential can, however, be wider if the primary market is thin (Johnston (1983)). If this is the case then the primary CD rate may not be a good proxy.

A second possible reason why banks use the secondary market rate

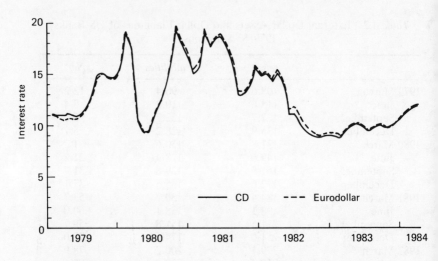

Figure 4.2   Eurodollar-Domestic Dollar Relationship, 1979–84

is that they view it as a form of safeguard, to ensure that arbitrage is always profitable. Given that the primary CD rate is usually below the secondary rate, if arbitrage is profitable when the latter is used to calculate the cost of funds, then it will be profitable *a fortiori* if the former applies.

In Figure 4.2[18] we compare the adjusted secondary CD rate and the Eurodollar deposit rate. Figure 4.3 shows the differential. In spite of very high interest rate variability, especially between late 1979 and end 1981, the relationship is very close.

Given our discussion above, it is also interesting to examine two other series of differentials. Firstly, the differential between the *unadjusted* secondary CD rate and the Eurodollar deposit rate. Do banks undertake arbitrage by selling CDs which they hold in the secondary market and placing the funds in the Eurodollar market? Figure 4.4 suggests that banks do not arbitrage in this manner. The series 'DIFF1' shows a persistent differential in favour of the Eurodollar market. Secondly, we use the adjusted primary CD rate, which imposes a tougher condition for arbitrage to be efficient (as we indicated above). This differential is also shown in figure 4.4 ('DIFF2'). Only after October 1983 does this differential fall within the range where arbitrage is unprofitable (taking into account transactions costs).

In order to determine whether events in the US were the main influence on Eurodollar rates, we need to look at the history of US

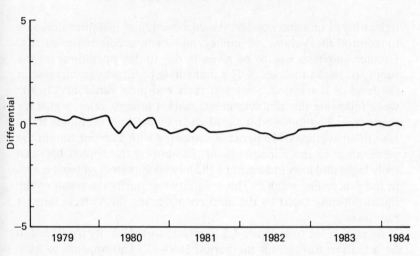

Figure 4.3   Differential between Eurodollar and Adjusted CD, 1979–84

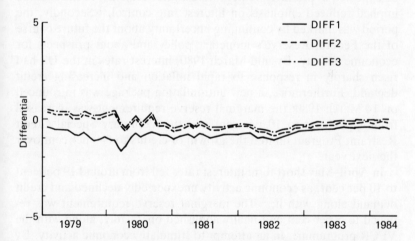

Figure 4.4   Differentials between Eurodollar and Domestic US Market
(DIFF1   =   unadjusted secondary CD rate – Eurodollar rate
DIFF2   =   adjusted primary CD rate – Eurodollar rate
DIFF3   =   adjusted secondary CD rate – Eurodollar rate)

monetary policy from 1979–84. If we find that the observed variability in the CD rate can be explained by factors internal to the US,
then we may conclude that the US domestic monetary policy is a
major determinant of Eurodollar interest rates.

On 6 October 1979, the Federal Reserve announced, along with a tightening of monetary policy, the introduction of measures designed to control the volume of money and bank credit more strictly. Greater emphasis was to be given in day-to-day operations on the supply of banks reserves.[19] The immediate result was an increase in the level of domestic US interest rates and their variability. In the week following the announcement, market interest rates, which for many years had followed the lead given by the Federal Funds Rate, rose to an average of 13 per cent compared with 11.9 per cent in the week prior to the announcement. Moreover, the spread between daily highs and lows increased to 182 basis points from 84 basis points in the preceeding week.[20] This volatility was partly the result of the initial difficulty faced by the markets of finding the 'correct interest rate level'.

As we can see from figure 4.2, interest rate variability continued to be a feature throughout the period 1980–82. This appears to have been the result of two factors. Firstly, Monetary Base Control would be expected to produce greater interest rate variability because of the implied reduced emphasis on interest rate control.[21] Secondly, the period was marked by continuing uncertainty about the future course of the Federal Reserve's monetary policy and about prospects for economic activity. By mid-March 1980, interest rates in the US had risen sharply in response to rapid inflation and increasing credit demand. Furthermore, a new anti-inflation package was introduced on 14 March 1980: the marginal reserve requirement was increased from 8 per cent to 10 per cent and the Voluntary Special Credit Restraint Program limited the growth of credits to 6–9 per cent over the next year.

In April–May short term interest rates fell from around 19 per cent to 10 per cent, as economic activity unexpectedly declined and credit demand along with it.[22] The marginal reserve requirement was reduced to 5 per cent and finally abolished on 24 July, along with the VFCR programme, in an attempt to stimulate economic activity. By the autumn, a recovery in economic activity and an associated increase in the growth of the money supply was evident. M1–B (the narrow measure of the money supply) rose at 10.5 per cent (annual rate) in the second half of 1980 compared to 2.3 per cent in the first half. This was partly a consequence of increased economic activity.[23] The Federal Reserve, in an attempt to control this expansion of money and credit, raised the discount rate twice to 13 per cent during the last quarter of 1980 and imposed a surcharge on frequent borrowers from the discount window. As a result, market interest rates rose substantially within a short period: the CD rate adjusted for reserve requirements and Federal deposit insurance climbed from 13.80 per cent in October 1980 to 19.26 per cent in December. Over the next 12 months, interest rates responded to mixed signals concerning both economic activity and monetary and fiscal policy. The CD rate fell slightly at the beginning of 1981 (see figure 4.2) as the outlook for inflation was thought to be good following slower growth of M1–B, but increased from April onwards in response to the faster growth of M1–B (which overshot its target) and an unwillingness on the part of the Federal Reserve to slacken its monetary stance.[24] Moreover, there was increasing concern that the fiscal deficit would widen as a result of President Reagan's economic programme of tax cuts.

Interest rates remained high until the end of 1981 as the policy of monetary restraint continued. Inflation fell to 8.9 per cent (year-on-year) compared to 12.4 per cent in 1980; GNP fell at a yearly rate of 4.5 per cent in the fourth quarter and unemployment rose. Interest rates declined towards the end of 1981 for only a short period (as figure 4.2 shows). Monetary growth was again higher than the Federal Reserve's objectives at the beginning of 1982 leading to further rises in interest rates in February 1982. The CD rate, which had been as low as 12.9 per cent in November and December 1981, rose to a peak of 15.5 per cent in February 1982. Thereafter rates remained much steadier throughout the rest of 1982, declining in the third quarter as figure 4.2 shows.

This steadier behaviour of rates during 1982 was the result of a more accommodating monetary policy which placed less emphasis on movements in the narrow definition of the money stock (M1–B). Temporary surges in M1–B, which during 1980 and 1981 had been rapidly countered, resulting in sharp rises in interest rates, were now tolerated. The change was made partly in response to the continuing recession (by the end of 1982, real economic activity was slightly below that of 1979).[25] Greater emphasis was placed on broad monetary aggregates, the declared reason being that the narrow definition of the money stock was being distorted by institutional developments which caused funds to flow into accounts technically included in M1–B.[26]

Interest rates continued to be much less volatile through 1983 and 1984 as Monetary Base Control was abandoned:

The committee [the Federal Open Market Committee] in 1983 had to deal with institutional changes that affected the monetary aggregates and their relationships to ultimate economic variables to an uncertain degree. Already during 1982, income velocities had deviated substantially from past patterns. Ongoing financial innovation, deregulation and economic changes suggested that velocity patterns in 1983 were likely to continue to diverge significantly from past experience.[27]

As a result the FOMC sought to achieve its objective by 'setting reserve conditions judgementally rather than allowing them to emerge semi-automatically in response to monetary behaviour'.[28]

Figure 4.2 clearly shows that the Eurodollar rate followed the general movements in US domestic interest rates. Moreover, during 1979 and 1980, this occurred in spite of events in the Eurocurrency markets which may have been expected to put pressures on Eurodollar rates opposite to those operating in the US domestic markets. The second oil price shock brought about a major rise in the supply of deposits to the market. New deposits from oil exporting countries which had been $6 billion in 1978 totalled $38 billion in 1979.[29] While credit demand from deficit countries also rose, the BIS (1980) conclude that supply was probably greater than demand from 1979–81 as indicated by the continuing borrowers' market (see chapter 6.3). Yet the Eurodollar rate rose during 1979, as figure 4.2 shows, in response to the Federal Reserve's introduction of Monetary Base Control.

Whilst the Eurodollar rate seems to have been substantially influenced by the CD rate, the differential between the two was at times quite large (ranging from −0.71 to +0.48). Moreover, there was a sustained negative differential in 1981–2. We divide the whole period into the four subperiods which seem most appropriate based on the behaviour of the differential and calculate the mean and the standard deviation of both interest rates and the differential. Table 4.3 presents the results.

The deviations from interest rate parity (see figure 4.3) which appeared from October 1979 to December 1980 were quite large in absolute terms. Although the overall average of 0.05 per cent was small, the variability of the differential (as reflected in the standard deviation) was high relative to the other periods. The main cause of this variability appears to have been uncertainty of interest rate levels because of US monetary policy. This policy of monetary base control led to high and very variable interest rates in the US, especially

Table 4.3   Mean and Standard Deviation (sd) of the (absolute)
Eurodollar – CD Differential

| Date | r$ | | Adj. CD | | Differential | |
	Mean	Sd	Mean	Sd	Mean	Sd
1979(1)–79(9)	11.05	0.62	11.35	0.62	0.30	0.08
1979(10)–80(12)	14.17	3.06	14.19	3.12	0.05	0.26
1981(1)–82(12)	14.95	2.77	14.56	2.86	−0.39	0.14
1983(1)–84(8)	10.04	0.88	9.93	0.95	−0.12	0.10

Calculated from data in Figure 4.3.

during 1980, as figure 4.2 and table 4.3 both show. Differentials were therefore quite large and volatile.

Between 1981 and 1982 the Eurodollar rate was consistently higher than the adjusted CD rate suggesting that banks were not engaging in outward arbitrage to the extent required to eliminate the differential in favour of the Eurodollar market. Interest rates remained high and were only slightly less volatile. Monetary Base Control was still in operation, although towards the end of the period, the Federal Reserve focused less on the growth of narrower monetary aggregates, as we saw above.

The sustained differential in favour of Eurodollar assets can be explained by two factors. Firstly, Kreicher (1982) points to balance sheet constraints. On the assets side of the balance sheet, growing concern about the capital adequacy of banks in the US led them to reduce the extent to which they were willing expand their balance sheets through arbitrage. This was especially so because arbitrage usually only generates small profit margins thus resulting in a fall in the return on equity.

Secondly, a change in the perceived riskiness of Eurodollar deposits may have occurred during this period because of the debt servicing difficulties of Eastern European countries during 1980–81 and, in 1982, the more widespread international debt crisis. Eurodollar interest rates were higher than US domestic rates, suggesting that the US banks required a risk premium on deposits placed in the Eurodollar market. We emphasised in chapter 2 that the interest rate parity relationship is applicable only to assets of the same risk. During 1981–2, therefore, our analysis of the interest rate parity condition between the Eurodollar market and the US domestic market may not be entirely valid, because US domestic deposits and

Eurodollar deposits were no longer considered by banks to be perfect substitutes for each other.

Since the beginning of 1983, interest rate parity has held, suggesting that the capital adequacy constraint has been relieved (as banks increased their capital-assets ratio) and that the banks no longer require a risk premium on their Eurodollar deposits.

We can conclude that, despite the appearance of larger and more persistent differentials in the period 1979–84, the interaction between the Eurodollar market and US domestic monetary policy has generally been as close as it had been shown to be by others during the 1960s and 1970s.

4.5   EUROSTERLING – DOMESTIC STERLING AND EURODOLLAR – DOMESTIC STERLING RELATIONS

4.5.1   Analysis of Figures

The following figures[30] present first (4.5) the uncovered differential between the three-month Eurodollar deposit rate and the UK Local Authority Temporary Loan (LA) rate together with the premium/discount on forward sterling; secondly (4.6) the LA rate and the Eurosterling rate are plotted together with the differential between them (4.7); finally the covered differential between the Eurodollar rate and domestic sterling is shown in 4.8. Until 1979, large covered interest rate differentials often existed against UK domestic assets. In this subsection I examine the conditions that led to some of the more striking episodes where large differentials appeared.

Figure 4.5 shows that, whilst the LA rate was almost consistently above the Eurodollar rate, there was a persistent covered interest differential against sterling assets (as represented by the LA temporary loans market) up until 1979. The reason for this was two-fold. Firstly, the forward discount on sterling was generally greater than the gap between the Eurosterling and LA rates. Secondly, the differential was only sustainable because of exchange controls which limited outward arbitrage by UK residents.

If exchange controls had not existed, then UK residents would have been expected to move funds into dollars which offered a greater return. The resultant capital outflow and deterioration in the balance of payments would have put upward pressure on interest rates in the UK, causing them to rise even further above Eurodollar

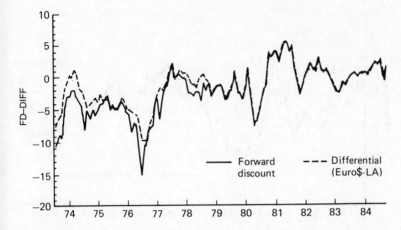

Figure 4.5   Eurodollar – Domestic Sterling Relationship, 1974–84

rates. The selling of sterling spot and its purchase forward would narrow the forward discount absorbing some of the pressure on interest rates. A combination therefore of a rise in interest rates and a decrease in the forward discount would have restored interest rate parity.

It is interesting to investigate the reason why the differential against sterling varied considerably over the period 1974–84. We examine here some of the more striking features of figures 4.5–4.8, by looking at the conditions which gave rise to such configurations of interest rates and forward discount. In doing so, we hope to shed light on the workings of the international arbitrage process.

Significant changes in the differential against sterling in the pre-1979 period appear to have been related to sharp movements in the forward discount on sterling *vis-à-vis* the dollar. Although the forward discount does not enter into the interest rate parity condition for arbitrage between the Eurosterling and LA markets, its influence is nonetheless felt indirectly. The theoretical reason for this apparent role for the forward discount is seen by recalling the method by which the Eurosterling interest rate is determined (section 4.3). The arbitrage condition is given by

$$r\pounds = r\$ + fd$$

If the forward discount (on sterling) widens, then the Eurosterling rate will increase for a given Eurodollar rate. Hence, if the LA rate remains unaltered (a situation possible only because of exchange

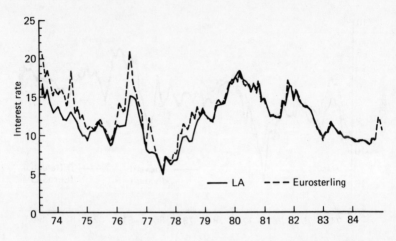

Figure 4.6　Eurosterling – Domestic Sterling Relationship, 1974–84

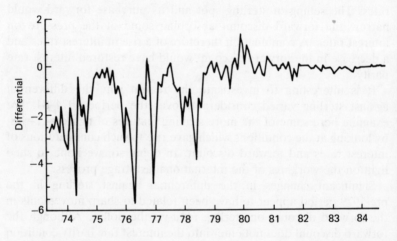

Figure 4.7　Differential between Eurosterling and Domestic Sterling,
　　　　　　　1974–84

controls), then the differential against domestic sterling assets widens. As a result of this, Eurosterling – domestic sterling differentials can usually be explained in terms of the same factors as Eurodollar – domestic sterling covered differentials.

To confirm whether our initial impression of the importance of the forward discount in determining the size of the pre-1979 differential is

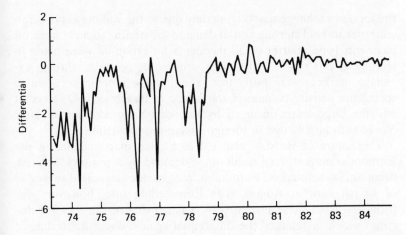

Figure 4.8   Differential between Eurodollar and Domestic Sterling, 1974–84

correct, it is important to analyse the movements in the differential more closely.

At the beginning of 1974, the covered interest differential against sterling was around 4 per cent. The forward discount on sterling *vis-à-vis* the dollar was large because spot sterling was under downward pressure and was expected to fall further. The depreciation of the pound (relative to the dollar) reflected the markets' belief that the US economy would be better able to absorb the oil price rise, as well as the fact that the US balance of payments continued to improve during January 1974. On 21 January, the above factors together with continuing speculation about the imminence of a general election and the continuing three-day week in the UK, culminated in the lowest ever (to that date) £/$ exchange rate of $2.15.[31]

The consequence of the weak pound and the large forward discount was the continuing need for UK interest rates to remain much higher than those in the other major financial centres. Monetary policy during the three months to end-January 1974 was dominated by the need to maintain the UK's interest rate competitiveness, especially in the light of the balance of payments deficit.[32] Such a policy was however consistent with the authorities' desire to control the broadly defined money supply. It was this interest rate policy that ensured that the covered interest differential was maintained around 3–4 per cent.

From February to October 1974, the pound was much steadier on the foreign exchange markets, mainly due to the willingness of Arab countries to hold sterling and to demand for sterling to meet large oil payments (one quarter of all payments for crude oil were made in sterling at this time).[33] Moreover, from June onwards, foreign exchange markets were fairly thin: there was a notable decrease in speculative activity because of the failure of Bankhaus I. D. Herstatt and the large losses incurred by Franklin National Bank of New York, both largely due to foreign exchange speculation.

The failure of Herstatt also led to a crisis of confidence in the Eurodollar market. As a result of the demand by depositors for a risk premium in the market, Eurodollar interest rates increased to a peak of 14 per cent in August. The Eurosterling rate, however, was protected from these increases by a narrowing of the forward discount which maintained the differential against domestic sterling at around 2–3 per cent.

During December 1974, US interest rates were falling faster than those in the UK as the deepening recession had become the main concern of the US authorities.[34] The forward discount on sterling rose to a high level because of this, but also because of the Saudi Arabian decision in mid-December no longer to accept sterling in payment for oil. Sterling came under selling pressure as oil companies sold sterling deposits they had accumulated for the purchase of crude oil. The covered interest differential against sterling increased to over 5 per cent, as a result of the widening forward discount which at 8 per cent was its highest level of 1974. The differential against sterling was allowed to persist only because exchange controls inhibited arbitrage between the domestic sterling and the Eurosterling markets.

The pattern which emerges from the foregoing survey of events in 1974, is that the covered interest rate differential against sterling assets varies with the forward discount and the interest rate policy of the authorities. If there were no capital controls on outflows, a widening of the forward discount would imply a rise in the Eurosterling rate and in the domestic UK rate to maintain interest rate parity with the Eurodollar. In early 1974, despite a large forward discount, the covered differential was only slightly above its yearly average of 3 per cent, because the authorities were maintaining high relative interest rates in an attempt to support the spot pound. Towards the end of the year, however, the sharp downward pressure on sterling and the widening forward discount was not countered by rising interest rates and the covered interest differential against sterling was allowed to increase to 6 per cent, its highest level of 1974.

A month-by-month examination of events before the abolition of exchange controls (see Appendix I, on p. 226)[35] further supports our hypothesis that the forward discount was the major determinant of the size of the covered interest differential against sterling. In periods of a widening forward discount due to downward speculative pressure on the pound (that is, December 1974, most of 1976 and the first half of 1978) the covered interest differential rose. Whereas in the absence of exchange controls, domestic UK interest rates would have been forced to increase, the presence of controls insulated the domestic money markets and enabled UK domestic interest rates to be lower than they would otherwise have been. By contrast, those periods where sterling remained stable (February–October 1974, 1975 and 1977)[36] were characterised by much smaller differentials against sterling.

Moreover, our hypothesis that the differential between the Eurosterling interest rate and the domestic sterling rate was determined by movements in the forward discount prior to 1979 is also supported.

The key factor in the pre-1979 period was the existence of exchange controls. In the absence of exchange controls an exogenous widening of the forward discount would generally necessitate a change in the domestic sterling rate. However, in the presence of exchange controls limiting outflows from the UK, a covered interest differential against sterling *vis-à-vis* the Eurodollar market could be sustained; so the LA rate did not need to change. The higher covered differential could simply be allowed to persist. Up to October 1979, the LA rate was below the Eurosterling rate.

Although exchange controls were only removed in October 1979, the covered interest rate differential against sterling was much smaller from October 1978 than in the past. This can be explained by two factors. Firstly, anticipation by the markets of the removal of capital controls following the partial slackening which occurred in the summer of 1979 (see section 4.5.2). Secondly, the strength of sterling, which stood consistently at over $2 to the pound. The Bank of England argued that this was the result of North Sea oil[37] which ensured that the UK balance of payments was seen as favoured by the 1979 oil price rise. An arguably more important factor was the severe deflationary policy which the new government undertook in its attempt to reduce inflation.

Exchange controls were finally removed completely on 24 October 1979. We can see from figures 4.5 to 4.8 that the interest rate parity conditions held continuously after that period. This important change in policy must be examined in some detail.

4.5.2   UK Exchange Controls – History and Description

Exchange controls of a sort were first introduced in the UK during World War I, when the export of capital was restricted, becoming more comprehensive as the war progressed.[38] In 1924, all restrictions were removed,[39] but in the period up to the return to the gold standard (1925), the Bank of England used the informal method of moral suasion to limit new issues by foreign borrowers.

The Gold Standard (Amendment) Act[40] (21 September 1931) made provision for 'such controls as the Treasury might see fit'.[41] On 22 September, controls were introduced which prohibited 'purchases of foreign exchange or transfer of funds with the object of acquiring such exchange directly or indirectly by British subjects or persons resident in the United Kingdom'.[42]

These were rescinded in March 1932. It was not until World War II that a system of co-ordinated and statutory regulation was introduced (September 1939).

After the war, the Anglo–American financial agreement set the date of 15 July 1947 for the return to convertibility. In preparation, the UK had been liberalising its bilateral payments regime by establishing a system of transferable accounts. Residents of specific countries were authorised to transfer sterling among themselves and into the sterling area for current transactions. In February 1947, this was extended to the dollar area. From then until 15 July, other countries were added.

On 15 July 1947, convertibility was generalised.[43] The time was not right for a return to convertibility; the economy was suffering from the effects of the war and more especially the debts resulting from it. Fuel shortages in February resulted in much lost production and temporary unemployment, together with an increase in the external current account deficit. The UK lost $1 billion of gold and dollar reserves as sterling balances were converted before abandoning convertibility on 20 August 1947. The failure of 1947 seemed to demonstrate the need for controls.

Accordingly, the Exchange Control Act of 1947 was designed to facilitate the conservation of UK foreign currency and gold reserves and assist the balance of payments. The Act essentially enabled the Treasury to control foreign currency and assets held by UK residents; it generally prohibited any transfer of cash or securities abroad without first obtaining permission from the Treasury. It also controlled sterling held by non-residents who required permission to operate a sterling bank account.

Under the regulations laid down in the Act, and subsequent amendments, banks were not allowed to deal in foreign currencies for their own account outside the limits laid down by the Bank of England.[44] There were two kinds of limits.

i) The open limit: this was the difference between the total assets and liabilities in all foreign currencies, both spot and forward together. This limit would not stop a large spot plus being matched by a large forward minus. Hence the further limit;

ii) spot against forward, which controlled the extent to which net spot assets in foreign currencies could be held to cover net forward liabilities. It did not seek to limit the amount of net spot liabilities against net forward assets. In other words, unlike *i)*, it worked only in one direction.

Both limits were designed to ensure that the maximum possible foreign currency was held in the official reserves pool.[45] The actual value of the limits were agreed with the Bank of England by each bank individually, based on the amount of foreign exchange work usually done. Any surplus of foreign exchange over the limits had to be sold for sterling immediately. The aim of the authorities was to prevent speculation against sterling by commercial banks. In pursuing this objective, the authorities also prevented arbitrage up to the amounts required if interest parity were to hold.

The availability of forward cover to UK residents was limited, again to prevent its use for speculation. It could be obtained only for cases where commercial contracts existed and then only with prior permission from an authorised bank. Permission for cover in respect of current account transactions was normally given for up to six months. Permission for cover for capital account payments would be given when only 75 per cent of the foreign currency loan had already been repaid.

All the above limitations related to the dealings that occurred at the official market rate. Another market, the investment currency market, also came into existence in the late 1950s, where a premium was paid when purchasing foreign currency. This market was for the purchase of foreign corporate securities and other assets. The premium was determined by the supply of and the demand for invest-ment currency;[46] it would be recouped at the going rate when the currency was sold.[47] Foreign currency purchased in such a manner could only be held for up to 12 months without investment. After such a time, it had to be sold on the official market, implying no potential recovery of the premium paid. The important point for potential arbitrageurs and speculators was that investments in Government bonds, Treasury bills, CDs and other money market papers with less than six months to maturity were not considered as having been invested. This hampered speculative and arbitrage use of the market.

Exchange controls also exerted an influence on the Eurocurrency markets. Residents of the UK were not allowed to hold foreign currency deposits[48] and hence could not participate in the Eurodollar market in London. There were no restrictions, however, on non-residents dealing in foreign currency in, for example, London banks. This meant that there were no controls governing the growth of the offshore Eurodollar market in London.

UK banks could only deal in Eurosterling to a limited extent,[49] because once a Eurosterling deposit was borrowed by a London bank, it became a resident sterling deposit. The borrower could repay the loan, but could not relend the sterling to non-residents. Therefore, the deposit had to be held in sterling in the UK until maturity. UK residents were not allowed to lend sterling deposits in the Eurosterling market without permission from the Bank of England. This was given only rarely. *Inter alia* this limited the growth of the Eurosterling market by the restriction of the supply of sterling to the market (see section 4.5.3).

Once the UK joined the EEC, it was obliged under the Treaty of Rome to amend the exchange controls structure.[50] It was clear that the exchange control mechanism might have to be dismantled at some future date. In August 1978, the Labour government recog-nised their obligation, but action was postponed until after the general election (May 1979). Some small changes were made in February 1979.[51] In July 1979, the total dismantling of exchange control was declared by the new Conservative government to be the ultimate aim. Overseas direct investment was no longer subject to exchange controls and the requirement to use the investment cur-rency market for the purchase of overseas property was abolished. Several other relaxations were announced before all remaining con-trols were abolished in October 1979.

The advantages of exchange controls were that they gave the authorities some greater control over downward pressure on the exchange rate, lessened the vulnerability of the economy to capital flows and helped to strengthen the UK exchange reserves position. The disadvantage is that over the longer term, freer investment flows are thought by some to be desirable. The 'retention of exchange control has entailed some sacrifice of longer term investment opportunities, a consideration now especially critical given the need to convert the benefits of North Sea oil production into a desirable form'.[52]

In the view of the Bank of England, 'the strengthening of the external position in the last few years . . . [had] altered the balance of the argument'.[53] However, in their account they do not pay adequate attention to the implication of the removal of capital controls for capital flows and interdependence.

In an examination of the causes of the appreciation of sterling (1979–80), the Bank of England[54] point to the impact of North Sea oil. On the visible trade balance the oil balance improved by £1.25 billion in 1979. However, the main effect was arguably felt on the capital account. Relative to other OECD countries, the UK, at the time of the second oil shock, was insulated from the current account effects of a sharp increase in oil prices. A significant demand for sterling resulted from OPEC countries who once again invested part of their surplus in sterling, and from the general shift in the composition of investors' portfolios into sterling (BEQB March, 1980). More important at this time was the monetary and fiscal policy being pursued by the government in its attempt to curb inflation. The monetary policy stance at the beginning of the 1980s was intended to be a gradualist one. In practice because the monetary targets adopted ignored the impact of the abolition of the Supplementary Special Deposits (which resulted in the reintermediation of funds which had moved offshore after the abolition of exchange controls)[55] and because of the difficulties of using £M3 as a target,[56] the policy was much tighter than admitted. Both nominal and real exchange rates rose dramatically, with the result that international competitiveness worsened by some 30 per cent.[57]

4.5.3 Impact of Exchange Controls

Exchange controls in the UK were on outward movements of capital. Such controls had three important consequences:

Table 4.4   Mean and standard deviation (sd) of the differential between
Eurosterling and the LA rates

	mean	sd	
1967–Oct 1979	−1.43	1.64	$n = 153$
Oct 1979–Aug 1984	−0.03	0.32	$n = 57$

where; n = number of observations

i)   Domestic residents could not purchase foreign currency for overseas investment and thereby take advantage of interest rate differentials against their own currency:

ii)   limits could be placed on the ability of non-residents to borrow domestic currency;

iii)   domestic residents were unable to switch from the domestic to the Eurocurrency sector of their currency's market since there was a need to stop conversion of sterling into foreign currency through the use of the Euromarkets.

The first effect of exchange controls which inhibit outflows is the likely appearance of large covered interest differentials against domestic assets. In the case of the Eurosterling – domestic sterling arbitrage, the Eurosterling rate could not fall significantly below the domestic rate. If this were to occur, then banks would borrow in the Eurosterling market to finance domestic bank lending. However, the Eurosterling rate could rise above the domestic UK rate, because domestic residents were unable to switch into Eurosterling deposits.

The case of Eurodollar – domestic UK arbitrage is similar. Exchange controls limited the ability of banks and individuals in the UK to deposit in the Eurodollar market when the covered differential was in favour of Eurodollar assets. When it was in favour of UK domestic assets, banks were able to borrow in the Eurodollar market to deposit in the UK domestic markets. Thus as before, a covered interest differential against sterling was sustainable, and was indeed evident through most of the period of exchange controls, as we can see in figures 4.5–4.8 and table 4.4.

The mean deviation from interest parity between Eurosterling and the UK domestic market has been − 0.03 per cent since October 1979, compared with − 1.43 per cent before. Arbitrage is now almost perfect between the two markets. The graph of the relation between the Eurodollar and the UK domestic market shows the same result (figure 4.5). The abolition of exchange controls strikingly enhanced the ability of the UK banks to arbitrage between the two markets.

Table 4.5   Sterling Liabilities of BIS Reporting Banks
billions of US dollars

1978	September	9.8	1980	March	19.5
	December	10.4		June	23.2
1979	March	12.2		September	23.5
	June	13.2		December	24.4
	September	15.0			
	December	15.3			

Source: BIS (1984) International Banking Statistics

The second major effect of exchange controls was on the growth of the Eurosterling market. This required both a supply of sterling to use and a demand for sterling to hold. Controls on UK capital outflows affected the supply side of the market. The sterling supply originates from both residents and non-residents of the UK. Exchange controls restricted the amount of sterling that could be directed to this purpose. The abolition of the controls led to a noticeable increase in the size of the Eurosterling market, as the supply constraint was released. The size of the market as measured by the amount of deposits increased by 40 per cent in the first half of 1980 (table 4.5).

The increase in the size of the Eurosterling market was not due only to the ending of exchange control. Oil exporting countries were once again adding to their holdings of sterling, mainly because their surplus revenues were high in the wake of the second oil price shock. High interest rates in the UK and increasing confidence in sterling also played a part. In addition, at this time, the removal of exchange controls led to substantial disintermediation to the Euro-sterling market, because of the operation of the Supplementary Special Deposits Scheme.[58]

Thirdly, we can identify the effects of the abolition of UK exchange controls on the operation of UK monetary policy. The controls imposed on outflows implied a separation of the UK domestic capital markets from the international markets. In many ways, this situation was paradoxical. London was a major financial centre especially for Eurodollars, yet exchange controls allowed the authorities to maintain a separation and implement internal credit policy with a greater degree of independence.

Llewellyn (1979) identifies two monetary implications for the abolition of exchange controls. The first concerns the monetary effects of capital flows, and the implications for the Supplementary

Special Deposits scheme in particular. Llewellyn considers three cases – an outflow of non-bank funds into foreign currency assets, a switch from a domestic to a Eurosterling bank account and a switch by UK banks from sterling to foreign currency assets. He differentiates each case between fixed and flexible exchange rates, and also between the liquidation of interest bearing eligible liabilities (IBELs) and public sector debt.

We look first at the case of a switch by non-banks from UK public sector debt into foreign currency assets, under floating exchange rates. There are two considerations here:

i) The PSBR financing after the sale of the public asset. Llewellyn makes a crucial assumption; he assumes that the PSBR is refinanced through the banking system, thereby excluding the case of the purchaser of sterling using the funds to acquire public sector debt. In the case where banks purchase the public sector debt, the supply of reserve assets increases and there is a rise in £M3. If the new holder of sterling buys the public sector debt, then there is no effect on £M3.

ii) Who buys the sterling which is for sale? IBELs increase if the funds (formally invested in public sector bonds) are purchased by a resident/non-resident who maintains his deposit in IBEL form. If the new holder of sterling is a UK resident, then £M3 will rise also.

Secondly, in the case of a switch from UK public sector debt to a Eurosterling bank account. Any rise in £M3 will again be the result of PSBR financing through the banking system, and not because of the transfer to the Eurosterling market *per se*.

These two examples give us some idea of the mechanisms involved.[59] The capital flows generated by UK residents can have a significant effect on the money supply.

Llewellyn also notes that removal of exchange controls could have undermined the efficacy of the corset, as we noted in section 4.5.3, because of the possibility of disintermediation through the Eurosterling market. Offshore sterling flows through the Euromarket will either add to the volume of credit (with the money supply unchanged) or may cause a rise in the money supply given the assumption about PSBR financing (with the volume of credit constant). In either case, monetary restraints are relaxed, because of the ability to move offshore. The conduct of monetary policy becomes more difficult through the abolition of capital controls.

The second monetary implication of abolition of exchange control concerns the use of foreign currency within the UK, as Eurocurrency deposits can now be freely held. Llewellyn (1979) remarks that 'there is no legal reason why purely domestic transactions could not be conducted in foreign currency through the transfer of current bank deposits in London'.[60] The main reason for moving to a Eurodollar account is that a greater return can be earned. Borrowers would also benefit from lower lending rates. These narrower margins are the result of the competitive advantage of the Euromarkets over their domestic counterparts. The effect of this would be that transactions within the economy would go outside the control of the monetary authorities, causing them to lose some leverage over the volume of credit.

4.5.4 Conclusion

This section has sought to analyse the changing nature of the Eurosterling/Eurodollar arbitrage relationships with UK domestic markets. We initially examined the graphs prior to the abolition of UK exchange controls on 23 October 1979. It was clear that exchange controls played a key role in the arbitrage relation and lent support to domestic monetary policy. The data supported the analysis of the implications of the existence of controls and their subsequent removal. Britain now has neither exchange controls nor reserve requirements on foreign currency deposits. The control of the authorities over international banking – which also affects their domestic monetary policy position – has become minimal.

4.6 INTERDEPENDENCE AND MONETARY POLICY IN THE UK, 1974–1984

4.6.1 Background

This section considers the extent to which UK monetary policy was affected by external influences in the period 1974–84. In particular, to what extent were UK interest rates forced to change by the movement of interest rates abroad, particularly in the US? Specific episodes will be examined, picking up some of the factors which were shown to be important in chapter 3; namely, the removal of exchange controls, exchange rate policy and adjustment of the forward exchange rate in response to a change in interest rates abroad.

Monetary policy in this period was more prominent than in earlier years. The main economic objective of the Conservative government was the control of inflation. Concern for its level was always to the fore, and policies to contend with other problems such as unemployment were always assessed by reference to their effect on the battle for price stability.

The value of the pound varied widely over period. In the first half of the period (1974–79), the pound was subject to many speculative attacks, which put downward pressure upon it. With the impact of North Sea oil and tighter monetary policy being felt in the second half, the pound was generally stronger although still subject to much volatility.

The period witnessed many policy changes. Initially there was much intervention in the foreign exchange markets to influence the level of the pound. This, at times, had major implications for interest rates (see p. 99). At the end of October 1977, a decision was taken to allow the pound to float more freely.

The change of government in 1979 led to more weight being given to monetary policy, although there had been publicly announced monetary targets since 1976. Firstly, as noted in section 4.5, exchange controls were removed and this had implications for the behaviour of both interest rates and the exchange rate. Secondly, following the 1980 Green Paper on Monetary Control and discussions between the Treasury and the Bank of England, several modifications to the existing system of monetary control were suggested.[61] Market forces were allowed more influence on short term interest rates. Greater emphasis was put on open market operations rather than on lending through the discount window to relieve liquidity pressures.

4.6.2 Exchange Rate Policy

At the beginning of the period, the quadrupling of oil prices caused prospective problems for the exchange rate. The current external account worsened substantially. Policy under these circumstances was aimed at maintaining interest rate competitiveness with other major financial centres, so that further pressures should not be put on the exchange rate. Interest rates rose. On the 13 November 1973, the Minimum Lending Rate (MLR) was raised from 11.25 per cent to 13 per cent.

During 1976, the exchange rate fell by some 20 per cent over nine months for several reasons.

i) Inflation, although it had slowed somewhat by November, continued to be high relative to other countries. Moreover, monetary growth had been 9 per cent in the first half of the 1976/77 financial year, well outside its target of 12 per cent for the year as a whole.

ii) The current account deficit deteriorated further through the first three quarters of 1976: 'one reason for this protracted period of pressure on the [exchange] rate has been the continuing large current account deficit'.[62]

iii) In May, uncertainty developed regarding the wage restraint policy. Several trade unions criticised the agreement between the government and the TUC and some settlements had exceeded the guidelines of 3 per cent.

These problems reduced confidence regarding the lowering of inflation, putting downward pressure on sterling. This was compounded in October with reports circulating that the IMF viewed the sterling exchange rate as overvalued. The resultant heavy downward presure on the pound led to the need for the MLR to rise several times in the last six months of the year. On 21 May, the MLR was increased from 10.5 per cent to 11.5 per cent, on 10 September to 13 per cent and on 7 October to 15 per cent. Confidence was finally restored to the markets early in 1977.

On 31 October 1977, the authorities announced their decision to let the pound float more freely. The current balance of payments had improved and there had been upward pressure on sterling and an increase in UK exchange reserves in the several months preceding the decision. It was feared that the money supply would not be controllable if intervention continued to prevent the rise in the pound that had been resisted. Intervention, henceforth, would be undertaken only to smooth short term fluctuations and maintain an orderly market.

These episodes illustrate the difficulty of pursuing both an exchange rate and an interest rate policy. A policy to maintain some stability in the exchange rate, to hold it at a level that is thought to reflect the underlying competitiveness of the economy, implies that at some time interest rate policy may have to take second place. The fact that exchange controls were still in operation helps to account for the few periods in which this incompatibility was manifested, relative to the post 1979 period (see below), when the authorities intervened frequently to support the exchange rate. Exchange controls allowed the policy of maintaining exchange rate stability to have some impact, without completely undermining monetary policy.

4.6.3   Adjustment of the Forward Rate to allow some Independence

In chapter 3, it was argued that a measure of independence with regard to interest rate policy could be maintained when the forward premium adjusted to absorb the pressures from arbitrageurs arising from a change in, say, US interest rates. The period under consideration witnessed frequent occasions when forward premium adjustment allowed some independence. We examine here two such episodes.

The first occurred in November 1976–January 1977. The confidence crisis of earlier in 1976 had abated as monetary growth was brought under control, lessening fears regarding inflation. Renewed confidence in exchange markets led to appreciation of the pound. Market interest rates in the UK decreased, whilst those in the Eurodollar market remained steady. The forward discount on sterling narrowed to allow the decrease in interest rates that was appropriate given the situation in the economy. Arbitrage possibilities, which might have caused pressures for the fall in interest rates to be halted were absorbed by the forward premium adjustment. Exchange controls also helped, in the sense that they allowed some differential against domestic sterling assets to be maintained.

The second instance occurred in March–April 1981. Sterling was stable on the foreign exchanges helped by North Sea oil, tight money and a strong current account. Interest rates in the US were volatile (from December 1980–March 1981) and the dollar was weakening. The Eurodollar rate, reflecting US domestic conditions, fluctuated widely, falling from 17 per cent in December 1980 to 14 per cent in March 1981, before rising again to 16 per cent in April 1981. Interest rates in the UK, however, were able to remain steady at around 12.5 per cent, because the forward premium on sterling varied between 1 per cent and 4 per cent maintaining interest parity even in the face of very volatile dollar interest rates.

Both these episodes indicate the nature of financial and exchange rate markets when the forward premium adjusts to a change in interest rates. Confidence in the UK economy and the government's policy prevailed on the foreign exchange markets, leading to a lack of volatility in the sterling/dollar exchange rate, which allowed forward premium adjustment. Adjustment of the forward premium to changing interest rates allowed appropriate policy for the domestic economy to be maintained in the light of divergent policies being pursued in the US. As we shall observe below, it is when speculative pressure on sterling was great that the forward premium would not adjust to absorb all the arbitrage pressures arising from interest rate changes abroad.

4.6.4 Interest Rate Changes in Response to Arbitrage Pressures

At other times, UK interest rates were forced to change in response to changing interest rates abroad. We can identify two general reasons for this, other than the existence of an exchange rate policy.

Firstly, changes in US interest rates had expectations effects in the UK – for example, a decline in the US interest rate would lead to expectation of a decline in the UK interest rate. Such expectational effects occurred mostly after 1979 and were the result of the abolition of exchange controls and the realisation that as arbitrage became more efficient, interdependence would become stronger. Since the end of 1979, numerous instances can be identified where interest developments in the US caused expectations and subsequent realisation of interest rate changes in the UK. By way of illustration, we shall examine one of these episodes.[63]

During the second half of 1982, conditions in the economy – firm exchange rate, prospects for low inflation, as well as depressed output – pointed to the appropriateness of lower interest rates in the UK. However, external influences dictated the speed and timing of the fall and in mid-November actually caused a reversal of the policy.

The UK economy would not have been adversely affected and indeed would have benefited from a fall in interest rates. Inflation, which was 12 per cent in the year to end-December 1981, had declined to 8 per cent (annual rate) by August 1982 and the monetary authorities expected it to continue to fall. The exchange rate had been steady since the end of 1981, as a result of the severe monetary contraction and the success of monetary (and fiscal) restraint in reducing inflation. However, the economy was still in a major recession. The index of industrial production had declined from 107 at the beginning of 1979 (1975 = 100) to 90 by mid-1982. Thereafter, it remained steady. A fall in interest rates was clearly possible and, given the low level of economic activity, had been warranted since April.

Two factors delayed this fall. Firstly, the political uncertainty generated by the Falklands (Malvinas) War. Secondly, conditions in the US, where monetary growth rates were giving cause for concern and this led to expectations of increases in dollar interest rates on several occasions. UK interest rates remained steady at around 13 per cent despite the indications in the economy that they should fall. At the end of June, it seemed likely that the US money supply growth was not excessive, as had been feared, and indeed the money supply figures published in the first week of July were better than expected. Interest rates began to fall allowing UK ones to follow. The US Treasury bill rate fell from 15.23 per cent (week ending 25 June) to 11.32 per cent (week ending 30 July). The UK Treasury bill rate declined from 13 per cent to 11.87 per cent over the same period. The downward movement in short term interest rates continued until the end of August in the US when interest rates levelled off at around 8 per cent. In the UK, however, the decline was slower to around 9 per cent by the middle of October.

By mid-November, uncertainty in US markets about monetary growth led to less optimism about future further declines in US interest rates. Sterling came under downward pressure as a result, and this was compounded by a weakening of international oil markets. Despite the continued appropriateness of lower interest rates in the UK, they were forced to rise again from around 9 per cent in November to 10 per cent in December and 11 per cent in January 1983.

The general conclusion emerging from this example, which is typical of many other instances, is one where expectations and market sentiment in the UK were largely determined by conditions in the US. An aspect of interdependence that emerges from this episode is that even with stable conditions in the UK economy, conditions abroad can affect confidence in this country so leading to changes in interest rates – changes that are not warranted by purely domestic considerations.

A second type of situation in which interest rates rather than the forward premium are more likely to change, because of changes in interest rates abroad, arises when speculative pressure on the pound is strong. The usual pattern of events is that the sterling exchange rate is very volatile and subject to pressures other than those of interest rate changes. One example of several which could be cited will illustrate the principles involved.

From March to October 1976, sterling was weak and subject to many periods of downward speculative pressure, because of problems with the Trade Unions about wage restraint, the continuing problem of inflation and excessive monetary growth and the continued existence of the current account deficit (see section 4.5.1 for a fuller account of the pound's weakness at this time). Interest rates in the

US were fairly steady at around 5–5.5 per cent from March (Euro-dollar rates were around 5.5–6.5 per cent). As a result of the downward pressure on the sterling exchange rate, the forward discount followed a downward trend from 4 per cent in March to around 7 per cent in July and further to 13 per cent in October. The covered interest differential against sterling rose to around 5 per cent in October. UK interest rates rose sufficiently to halt the fall of sterling. The UK Treasury bill rate increased from 11.20 per cent in August to 14.94 per cent in October. The covered differential against sterling improved to 1 per cent which was sustainable with exchange controls in operation. In this case, dollar interest rates had not altered, but sterling interest rates had to rise because of the increase in the sterling forward discount *vis-à-vis* the dollar.

We can see from this example that the existence of speculative pressure on sterling can lead to a very volatile forward discount or one that will not adjust to maintain interest parity. Interest rates then have to adjust, whether domestic conditions warrant their movement or not, so leading to greater interdependence with respect to monetary policy. Since financial markets are prone to changing levels of confidence, which seriously affects the price variables in these markets, it is important for a government to create conditions in which confidence can be maintained regarding the performance of its economy.

4.7 CONCLUSIONS *VIS-À-VIS* INTERDEPENDENCE

The results of the chapter generally point to the existence of a highly efficient arbitrage network between domestic and Eurocurrency markets. The accepted view that arbitrage between Eurocurrency markets is institutionally determined seems to have been borne out. Similarly, arbitrage between domestic and Eurocurrency markets, in the absence of capital controls, is very efficient. In the case of the US and the Eurodollar market, high variability of interest rates tended to produce wide fluctuations from parity; but these deviations did not last long. In the case of the UK, the existence of exchange controls had significantly affected arbitrage efficiency with large covered differential against sterling being maintained: exchange controls appeared to offer some degree of insulation and, therefore, some freedom of policy choices.

As regards monetary policy, three points emerge from our analysis. Firstly, before 1977 exchange rate policy was important and tended frequently to dominate monetary policy, as attempts to halt a falling pound would lead to rises in interest rates whether domestic monetary conditions warranted them or not. Exchange controls helped to allow domestic interest rates to remain to some extent below those abroad (or to remain below what they would otherwise have been), and enabled exchange rate policy to be more easily implemented. After exchange control abolition, the forward premium adjustment mechanism became more important in principle if a measure of insulation was to be maintained. In practice, however, it failed to assume this role on many occasions because of expectations effects and speculation.

Secondly, stability of financial markets is an important factor in determining the insulation offered to a country from interest rate changes abroad through movements in the forward discount. By contrast, when there was speculative pressure on sterling, and the forward discount fluctuated a lot, interest rates in the UK generally responded to a change in the US interest rates.

Thirdly, since the removal of exchange controls, monetary policy has been conducted within a framework of greater interdependence. Expectations of a change in UK interest rates have frequently been generated by a change in US interest rates. Such expectations were less evident (although not wholly absent) before 1979, because it was felt that the authorities could choose between several responses to such a disturbance.

Part II
Competition, Efficiency and Stability in Financial Markets: The Case of the International Credit Markets

The first part of this book showed how removal of exchange controls in the UK had increased the interdependence between financial markets in the UK and those in other industrialised countries. This led to increased difficulty in controlling monetary conditions when pursuing a policy different from the other industrialised countries.

As we noted in part I, the UK was not the only country to remove exchange controls during the 1970s. The period witnessed a general dismantling of controls on capital and a growing interdependence between the financial markets of the industrialised nations. Alongside the Eurocurrency markets there was a growth in other kinds of international banking activity – floating rate notes, international banking facilities, etc. Two common features of these instruments are the high degree of competition involved in their production and the tendency for those instruments to fall outside the supervisory control of central banks.

In the second part of the book, we look at a question raised by these developments; the effect of growing interdependence of international capital markets on the stability of the international monetary system.

In chapter 5, I examine the effect of competition on the efficiency and stability of international banking in an informal model, which highlights the shortcomings of orthodox neoclassical models, especially on the policy side.

Chapter 6 considers the various attributes of the international capital markets (that is, maturity mismatching, the risk-return relationship, the interbank market, etc.) in the light of the informal model of chapter 5. This provides an insight into the role of the banks in the international debt crisis of the 1980s.

Finally, chapter 7 outlines the policy implications for the industrialised countries in general and the UK in particular, given the importance of the City of London in international financial markets.

5 Competition, Stability and Efficiency in International Banking

5.1 INTRODUCTION

The purpose of this chapter is to develop an informal model which investigates the effect of competition on aspects of efficiency in banking. This model is applied to the international capital markets, focusing on the role of banks in the international debt crisis. I argue that greater competition in financial markets increases the propensity for instability and crisis, because of failures in the neoclassical market mechanism some of which are common to all markets and others of which are specific to financial markets.

There are two main approaches to financial crises in the literature, as identified by Kettell and Magnus (1986):

i) The orthodox, monetarist approach of Friedman and Schwartz[1] argues that financial crises are unrelated to previous movements in economic activity. Rather they are the result of factors which are 'exogenous' to the economic system: that is, man-made. For example, Friedman and Schwartz argue that the crisis of the 1930s was the result of the inappropriate monetary policy pursued by the Federal Reserve. The implication of this view is that a financial system in which crises would not occur requires merely firstly the adoption of a fixed monetary growth rule to ensure that the monetary authorities cannot induce financial crises through monetary mismanagement and secondly the existence of deposit insurance to prevent confidence crises.

ii) The alternative approach has its roots in Fisher, Keynes and Kalecki and has been expanded further by Minsky and applied to the history of Western Europe by Kindleberger.[2] This approach stresses the interconnections between behaviour of financial institutions and the business cycle. It argues that the capitalist system has an inherent tendency to instability in economic activity. Cumulative upward movements in economic activity are halted by the level of over-indebtedness,[3] which becomes unsustainable and causes crisis. The economy then moves into a downward spiral, which is checked by the intervention of the monetary authorities carrying out lender-of-last-resort functions.

There is some literature which views the Euromarkets as a phenomenon which generates instability in economic activity. Metais (1982) argues that there is a tendency towards overindebtedness by less-developed countries. The other side of this coin is the large build-up of claims on developing countries by international banks. By contrast, McClam (1982) considers the view that these markets are potentially explosive to be an exaggeration, although he admits that at times they do 'involve disturbances or inconveniences for individual countries'.[4]

The present chapter concentrates on the theoretical arguments concerning the stability of the financial system. Their applicability to the international credit markets will be examined in chapter 6.

The chapter is organised into four sections. Section 5.2 presents the neoclassical model. The third discusses the assumptions of the model and shows that competition is unlikely to maximise efficiency. The fourth section argues that a high degree of competition in financial markets may also lead to instability. This part presents a descriptive model of instability in financial markets, which draws on the discussion in the earlier sections.

5.2 NEOCLASSICAL MODEL

The orthodox position argues, on the basis of standard general equilibrium theory, that competitive markets will distribute resources efficiently and evenly, through a process of exchange between individuals, firms or countries who relate to each other as autonomous and formally equal agents.

Let us examine the terms 'competitive' and 'efficient' and their relationship to each other. 'Efficiency' is usually defined in allocative terms. Markets that are allocatively efficient establish prices which encourage the economy's capital (savings) to flow to those individuals, firms or organisations with the most promising investment returns, thus ensuring that the capital is used where it will do the nation or world economy 'the most good'. This means producing returns such that those who are sacrificing present consumption will receive the greatest possible command over future consumption in return for their investment. Tinic and West (1979) argue that in the financial sector allocative efficiency has two aspects. First, operational efficiency ensures that buyers and sellers of the product can purchase transaction services at prices that are as low as possible given the costs involved: in other words, those providing the services of an intermediary between end-users and end-depositors do not earn abnormal profits.

Secondly, pricing efficiency means, in the case of banking, that the prices of loans and deposits should reflect the value of the investment to society. This requires that all information of relevance to the investment as well as a risk premium be included in the price.

What market structure will ensure that resources are allocated efficiently? The textbook principle is that, under perfect competition, profit maximisation by producers and utility maximisation by consumers lead to an efficient allocation of resources. Firstly, the price of the financial services (that is, the difference between the deposit and loan interest rates) is equal to the marginal cost of providing them, thus ensuring operational efficiency. Secondly, the interest paid on the loan, or the inducement offered for the deposit is only the expected yield plus a risk premium (that is, pricing efficiency). The two conditions together ensure an efficient allocation of resources, given allocative efficiency in all other (commodity) markets.

As regards dynamics, the ability of entrepreneurs from outside the industry to enter, tends to maintain profit levels for each firm at the long run rate for the industry as a whole. If a new profit opportunity becomes available in banking, the excess profits accruing to existing firms will attract new entrepreneurs. Individual firms' profits will fall as supply of the product and demand for the factors of production increase. The former reduces the price of the product and the latter increases the cost of producing it.

Authors (Griffiths (1970), Meltzer (1967)), who argue that competition in the banking system will lead to a stable and efficient equilibrium, are generally critical of regulation in the banking sector and/or of collusion between the banks, claiming that this has negative effects on allocative and operational efficiency.[5] Competition is held to be the optimal market structure.

Our discussion of the perfectly competitive paradigm has made only brief mention of uncertainty and risk. Given that an important function of banks is to assume the risk inherent in financing investment, we need to discuss the approach of neoclassicists to this issue. Tinic and West (1979 p. 156) define any investment as risky if it has more than one possible real return. The measurement of risk involves a determination of the dispersion of these possible returns. It is usual to divide the risk of an investment into two sections:

i)   Systematic risk, which is the portion of the variability in returns associated with movements in general economic activity and therefore affects the capital market as a whole;

ii) unsystematic risk, which is associated specifically with an individual investment.

All loans which a bank undertakes will contain elements of both risks. However, a bank (like any other portfolio holder) is able to diversify away the unsystematic component of risk. To understand this, we may look at the widely accepted 'market model' (see Bernoulli (1954), Blume (1971) and Tinic and West (1979), p. 171);

$$Rit = ai + bi(Rmt) + eit$$

where:

Rit = return on the bank's *ith* asset at time, t

ai = $rf(1-bi)$: rf = risk-free rate of interest

Rmt = return on the market (that is, all banks' financial assets)

eit = random error which embodies elements of unsystematic return on asset i at time t

bi = measure of systematic volatility of asset i (dependent on the degree to which returns on asset i are correlated with the return on the market (all assets held by banks)).

The variance of return on the *ith* asset, $s^2(Ri)$, can be represented as the sum of two components;

$$s^2(Ri) = bi^2s^2(Rm) + s^2(ei)$$

where the first term on the right hand side is the systematic risk element $(bi^2s^2(Rm))$ and the second term the unsystematic risk element $(s^2(ei))$.

If a bank holds a portfolio of assets, then we can calculate the variance of returns on the portfolio, $s^2(Rp)$ which tends to;

$$1/N^2(b1 + b2 + b3 + \ldots\ldots + bN)^2s^2(Rm)$$
$$-> ba^2s^2(Rm) \text{ as } N -> \infty$$

where ba = average b for all assets in the portfolio.

As N (the number of randomly selected assets) increases, ba tends towards 1 (that is, towards the risk of all assets in the market combined) and hence the variance of the portfolio tends to approach the variance of all assets in the market. Thus the risk on the whole portfolio converges on the value of the systematic risk of that portfolio.

Nonetheless, there still exists the systematic component of risk, and, given that the bank is risk averse,[6] the expected return the bank receives from each investment should be enough to compensate the bank for the degree of systematic risk each loan entails (that is, the sensitivity of each loan to general economic conditions, bm).[7] This model implies that the bank distinguishes between loans on the basis of price charged (that is, the interest rate plus any spread).

5.3 COMPETITION AND MARKET FAILURE

Having outlined the neoclassical model, I now turn to the question of market failure in general, and examine its consequences for banking in particular. We will show that a competitive system may be partly inefficient in terms of resource allocation and secondly, when combined with attributes that actually characterise banking markets, may lead to instability. The stability aspect will be tackled mainly in section 5.4.

We shall examine the following assumptions of the competitive model:

i) There are no externalities: social costs and returns are equal to private costs and returns;

ii) there are no economies of scale in production;

iii) there are no information deficiencies;

iv) the product produced is homogeneous;

v) there are a large number of buyers and sellers.

5.3.1 Externalities

The assumption behind the perfectly competitive market model is that a producer will make a profit only by selling useful products or services and thus benefit himself only by benefiting the consumer. Fulfilment of this assumption requires markets to be characterised by both the exclusion principle and the rival principle. The exclusion principle argues that only those who pay the market price for a product can partake in its consumption with those not paying that price being excluded: or only those who create the cost actually pay for it. The rival principle argues that A's consumption of a good reduces the benefits derived by all others. However, there are many cases where these conditions are not satisfied and either members of a community do things which are of benefit to others for which they receive no return or their actions impose costs on others and involve no commensurate cost to themselves. In such cases, economic activity is said to involve 'externalities'.

Efficient use of resources requires that price (P) is equal to marginal cost (MC). In the case of non-rival goods, where A's consumption does not reduce the benefits available to all other people, the cost of another consumer benefiting from consumption of the good is equal to zero. That is, the *MC* of adding an additional user is zero which implies that the Pareto optimal price is zero. Clearly, however, the total cost of production of this non-rival good is greater than zero and this raises the question of providing facilities for production and this will not be achieved efficiently through the market mechanism. On the other hand, non-excludability causes market failure because consumption of the good in question is not dependent on payment and therefore people are not forced to reveal their preferences. This may lead to a 'free rider' problem, where people opt out of purchase because they derive the benefits even when they do not purchase the good in question. If a significant number of consumers act in this way, then market demand for the good is suboptimal and the correct amount of the good is not provided.

In the case of the banking industry, there exist both social goods and social bads (costs), which prevent the free market solution from being optimal or efficient. This essentially stems from the key role of banking and finance in the determination of investment demand. Firms rely on banks (amongst other mechanisms such as the equity market and retained profits) to make investments which are central to a healthy and growing economy. Investment may generate social returns which are greater than the private returns that the businessman receives, because investment is to some extent non-excludable. For example, the investment may be in a new plant, which will employ workers thus raising the local level of demand which helps the various providers of services and entertainments in the area who benefit from people having more money to spend. Not only does the businessman not get the social returns of his investment, neither does the bank which made the investment possible. Investment may therefore be 'underproduced'.[8]

More important, consider the question of bank failure. When any company fails, there is some risk of it triggering a decrease in the local level of aggregate demand and thus depressing the local economy (or indeed a wider area if large firms are involved). The costs of closure are then not fully internalised – the social costs are much greater than the private costs. In the case of a bank such risk is amplified because of the interlocking debt structures which are the essence of any banking system. Three elements of this interlocking debt structure can be identified. Firstly, the bank may be unable to pay back all its depositors' money, so that the depositors lose and not just the bank's shareholders. Secondly, a failed or failing bank will be unable to roll-over some loans which the borrowers, under normal conditions, might have expected to be renewed. Those in debt to the bank, who expected their overdrafts, for example, to be renewed, will have to repay sooner than expected and may have to realise some of their assets to do so. If the numbers affected are large, then this may result in the quantity of assets for sale being sufficient to cause a fall in their price thus making it more difficult for those in debt to the bank to acquire the money to repay. Bankruptcy of either corporate or individual debtors could result, further increasing the social costs. Thirdly, other banks may be affected either if they had deposits with the failed bank or if the failed bank had deposits with them through a loss of confidence leading to a run on banks unconnected with the failed bank. These other banks will experience a liquidity crisis.

Thus the costs of a banking failure are not confined to the shareholders of the bank. The social costs are far higher than the private costs, the effects of the failure being felt by other banks and by the economy as a whole, which due to a liquidity crisis may spiral into recession.

These social costs are liable to be heightened in the wholesale banking markets because two institutional features of these markets make for a greater degree of interdependence within the banking sector. The first feature is the interbank market. This adds to the efficiency of distribution of liquidity in the market, but also increases the interdependence of the international system. If one bank gets into difficulty, then it may have to repudiate its debts not only to its depositors, but also to other banks, who may in turn have problems paying back their deposits, and so on leading to a chain reaction. Whilst this can occur in the domestic banking market, the extent to which it could occur in the wholesale market is greater because rumours spread much faster in these latter markets.

Secondly, syndication allows larger loans to be put together while still maintaining individual bank portfolio diversification but it also increases interdependence. If one borrower defaults, more banks are going to be affected at the same time. Syndicated loan agreements usually carry a cross-default clause on sovereign loans, such that if the country asks for a rescheduling of one sovereign backed loan, it must reschedule all the others. Thus if the country is facing a problem on repayment of several of its loans, then the problem will be made greater in that all of its sovereign borrowings must be put into the rescheduling agreement.

These two features of the wholesale Euromarkets may be seen as innovations in the credit system. It is argued that greater competition has produced a more innovative environment, which in turn leads to greater efficiency. However, there is liable to be a trade-off between greater efficiency through innovation and greater risks associated with interdependence. Minsky (1982b, p. 66), moreover, argues that such innovations, in conditions of euphoria where steady growth is expected to continue, skew the bank's loan portfolio in a more speculative direction, leading to greater risk of instability. Thus there may be a further trade-off between innovation and stability.

5.3.2 Information Deficiencies and Uncertainty

Probably the most significant type of market failure within credit markets is that of information deficiencies. When uncertainty is assumed to be a feature of the economic system, acquiring information becomes of paramount importance in order to try to reduce that uncertainty. Moreover, because the information gathered is imperfect and is costly to acquire, the uncertainty is never totally removed. I outline here the various concepts that arise in markets with imperfect and costly information. The consequences for financial markets are examined in later sections.

Firstly, imperfect information leads to the moral hazard problem. This principle is most clearly visible in insurance markets (see Shavell (1976)). The probability of having your car stolen, for example, is dependent on the care taken to prevent theft: for example, in locking it securely, etc. If the insurance company could observe the care taken, then each premium would be determined by the risk of the insured contingency and therefore the insurance company would break even.

However, assume now that the insurance company cannot observe the level of care exercised by individual agents and sets its premiums on the basis of how many times the event insured against occurred in the past. If the owner of the car is now fully insured, then there is no incentive to take any care because there will be no personal loss, if the car is stolen. But the insurance company will lose; and given that all its clients have no incentive to take any care, the company will lose money overall. In the long run, this position is clearly infeasible. Either the insurance company will cease trading or some incentive to take care must be introduced (for example, no claims bonuses).

The same dilemma may apply to central bank lender-of-last-resort activities in the case of banking. This is discussed in chapter 7.

The second problem associated with markets characterised by imperfect information is that of adverse selection which results directly from asymmetry of information. This principle was identified by Akerloff (1970) with reference to the used car market (the market for 'lemons'). The used car market exhibits asymmetries of information because the seller of the used car knows more about the quality of the car than the buyer. However, both good and bad used cars must sell for the same price since the buyer cannot tell the difference. In equilibrium, therefore, we would expect to find 'lemons' (that is, bad quality used cars) dominating the market, because fewer people with good used cars will want to sell them. However, the equilibrium is inefficient. The buyer would be willing to pay more if he could be sure of getting a good used car and the seller of a good used car would prefer to make that transaction. However, such trades cannot occur because of asymmetries of information. Section 5.3.4 examines the consequences of this principle for banks.

The third problem occurs where the incentive to gather information is restricted by cost even though the market does offer a signal *vis-à-vis* the quality of the product. Grossman and Stiglitz (1976) examine the case of the stock market. The argument runs as follows. If the price of a stock supposedly reflects aggregation of information which differs across individuals, then a paradox will arise. If the market aggregates information perfectly, then the market price, acting as a signal, would convey all the information investors require to know and thus there would be no incentive to gather information. But if there is no incentive to gather information, there is no market and therefore the price cannot aggregate all the different information. We will address this problem in section 5.3.4.

The foregoing summary indicates some major ways in which the market mechanism either breaks down or becomes inefficient under conditions of imperfect information. Financial markets, as we shall show in the next sections and chapter 7, suffer acutely from information failures which affect the way in which banks deal with risk and the way in which central banks deal with supervision.

5.3.3 Economies of Scale

The existence of economies of scale in various aspects of production in banking may imply that the efficiency criterion will not be met by a competitive structure. Economies of scale arise when a firm's average costs decrease as the scale of production increases. For output to be established at either minimum average cost or a low average cost (where average costs decrease beyond the level of output demanded), the industry must be characterised by a few large firms or even a monopoly.

The main difficulty encountered by studies of economies of scale in banking is the question of how best to define bank output. Early studies (for example, Alhadett (1954) and Bell and Murphy (1968)) mainly used an unweighted stock variable such as total assets or earning assets. The problem with such an approach is that it assumes a bank product to be homogeneous. To overcome this weakness, Bell and Murphy (1968) and Benston (1972), for example, recognise the multiproduct nature of bank output by using a different production function for each service. But in doing so they ignore the jointness of production of various bank activities. Greenbaum (1967a) attempts to deal with both these criticisms by using a weighted index of bank output. From data derived from the income statement, a weighted[9] index of the sum of the earning assets plus non-earning activities which contribute to welfare[10] is calculated.

The results of the various studies have proved inconclusive. Greenbaum (1967b) reviews all the previous literature on economies of scale and concludes that small banks (that is, less than $10 million assets) are 'grossly inefficient' (Greenbaum (1967b) p. 473). Beyond the size of $10 million, economies probably exist on a small scale. But the evidence for larger banks (that is, greater than $300 million assets) is mixed. This inconclusiveness is also a feature of later studies. Brucker (1970) finds no evidence of economies. Clark (1984) firstly finds no practical difference between the various output measures, and secondly finds evidence of only small economies of scale. Thus the optimal bank size is still unknown.

Baltensperger (1972) uses an approach, of particular interest here, because it examines the possibility of a relationship between economies of scale and uncertainty or informational deficiencies. Financial institutions generally arise because they are able to reduce the costs of raising finance for end-users, by acting as an intermediary between the end-users and the end-sources of finance. Baltensperger argues that over and above this comparative advantage, there exist economies of scale in intermediation, because of uncertainty and the costs of information gathering. The two main sources of uncertainty about which information is difficult to gather are firstly the risk of deposit withdrawals and therefore the level of reserves that should be held to cover the bank; and secondly, the risk of loan losses and therefore the amount of capital the bank should hold. Both a lack of reserves and a lack of capital are assumed to lead to costs because they require the portfolio to be rearranged.[11] At the beginning of the period, the bank is unaware of the inflows and outflows that will occur through the period. The only information the banker has about this is a probability distribution based on past experience. What has to be determined is the optimal level of reserves, given that it is costly to run out of reserves and also costly to hold reserves (because they have zero return).

Baltensperger argues first that the optimal percentage of reserves varies with bank size. As the number of independent depositors increases, there is a relative decline in likely reserve loss in any one period. Secondly, because of adjustment costs, optimal reserves will not always be held; rather there will be a fluctuation of reserves around the optimal level. Adjustment to the optimal level takes place only when the decrease in the costs of uncertainty associated with the move to the optimal level of reserves outweighs the cost of adjustment itself. The presence of adjustment costs accounts for the existence of a range around R^* (the optimal level of reserves) within which the bank allows reserves to fluctuate without adjustment. If increasing size of bank implies diminishing variability of reserves, then a larger bank will have a smaller range of reserve fluctuations than a small bank and hence the cost of adjustment will decline with increasing size.

Baltensperger claims that his hypothesis can be examined empirically if we look at the relation between the degree of uncertainty of any category of liability or loan and the extent to which concentration occurs in the provision of these different services. For example, the withdrawal of bank demand deposits is more uncertain than that of time deposits; so one would expect a higher degree of concentration in the provision of services for demand deposits. In the Swiss banking system he finds this to be so.

Whilst this analysis is incomplete (it does not actually suggest the optimal size for a bank) and also suffers from some problems (concentration may exist for reasons other than uncertainty), it is intuitively appealing and does point to one of the consequences of information deficiencies which play such a large role in the banking industry.

Stillson (1974) offers another intuitively appealing argument *vis-à-vis* information and economies of scale. He argues that the costs of gathering information about alternative assets are dependent on the size of the portfolio only to a limited extent. Initial information costs are extensive as expertise is acquired in one area. Unit costs therefore decline as the portfolio of assets increases, and once past the crucial point where expertise is acquired, even out.

In conclusion, whilst studies of economies of scale have produced mixed results, the existence of informational deficiencies within financial markets has spawned some interesting intuitive arguments which suggest a role for economies of scale within banking.

5.3.4 Homogeneity of the Product

A further important assumption of the neoclassical model is that the product sold by each firm in the industry should be homogeneous. The degree to which a product is homogeneous depends on the extent to which buyers regard the products of all sellers as identical and on the extent to which sellers have no preferences as to the buyer to whom they sell. With respect to one of the products of the banking system, deposits, there are definite preferences on the part of depositors for certain banks, preferences based on political as well as economic decisions.[12] With regard to the other banking product, loans, banks also have definite preferences about whom they wish to lend to. Because there are different risk categories of borrower, the construction of an efficient portfolio requires a bank to distinguish between different borrowers. Different terms are offered on different types of loans to cater for the preferences of different borrowers; this diversity of preferences causes product differentiation.

Thus, each bank or borrower is liable to be assigned to one of numerous different risk categories. In the case of deposits, the depositor may assign a bank to one of several risk categories dependent on the political or economic risk factors he attributes to each bank. In the case of loans, each borrower represents a different risk to the bank, because of uncertainty about the return profile of the investment that the borrower wants to undertake. In short, risk leads depositors to discriminate between banks and banks between borrowers. Such discrimination implies that the products are non-homogeneous. Given the familiar analysis above (section 5.2), of the relationship between risk and return, we should expect the non-homogeneity of the products to be reflected in price discrimination, with greater risk compensated for by greater return.

Many authors have claimed that in practice the variation in price between loans does not properly reflect the variation in risk. Instead, product differentiation leads to a role for credit rationing in the determination of loan portfolios. This phenomenon is discussed by (among others) Hodgman (1960), Freimer and Gordon (1965), Jaffee and Modigliani (1969), Kindleberger (1975), Kapur (1977), Eaton and Gersovitz (1981) and Stiglitz and Weiss (1981).

Credit rationing is defined as the situation which occurs when banks are unable or unwilling to allocate funds between borrowers purely on the basis of price; instead they ration the quantity available to each borrower.

Hodgman (1960) notes the tendency for credit rationing to be ignored in the main body of economic theory, even though those of a more practical persuasion have long recognised its existence. Early attempts attributed credit rationing to sticky interest rates associated with oligopoly and to interest rate ceilings imposed by usury laws. Such a view denies credit rationing any rationale, independent of market structure or social pressures. Hodgman himself seeks an explanation for credit rationing that does not rely on either oligopolistic market structures or interest rate ceilings. He defines the risk of a loan as a ratio EY/EZ, where EY is the expected value of the actual repayment to the banker (that is, the amount the banker does not expect to lose) and EZ is the banker's expected value of possible repayments below the contract payment (including interest payments), that is, the expected value of possible losses. This measure is used because Hodgman argues that EY and EZ are the two aspects of the payoff distribution which the lender regards as relevant. However, the measures are only 'suggestive rather than definitive' (Hodgman (1960), p. 264). Given risk measured by EY/EZ, and a bank policy of keeping this ratio above a predetermined level, Hodgman shows that as the amount loaned increases the risk ratio can be kept above a predetermined figure by increasing the interest rate. However, the supply of loanable funds from the banker which each borrower faces, will become completely inelastic above a certain size of loan, the size depending on the probability function which the lender attaches to the borrower repaying what he has promised to repay (including interest). If the borrower promises to pay more back (that is, a higher interest on the loan) this will not affect the maximum size of loan offered to him (given market conditions and the lender's preferences for risk and return) because of the lender's perception of his capacity to repay. The expected value of losses (EZ) will be greater than the expected value of repayment (EY).

Therefore, given some risk ratio requirement, a banker will refuse to extend credit beyond a certain level, regardless of the interest rate.

Freimer and Gordon (1965) argue that Hodgman did not provide a rationale for the optimality of a policy of minimum risk ratio. In their view, Hodgman was concerned only with so-called weak credit rationing. According to them, 'a banker who practises weak credit rationing will vary the amount he is willing to lend a borrower with the interest rate up to a limit. Only beyond that limit will he refuse to extend credit regardless of the interest rate.' (Freimer and Gordon (1965) p. 398). They define strict credit rationing as existing when the banker sets an interest rate (the 'customary rate') and lends to borrowers up to a limit, at that interest rate. They demonstrate that credit rationing will occur often, 'under fairly common circumstances' (Freimer and Gordon (1965), p. 398) and when a banker seeks to maximise profits. It occurs because the interest elasticity of the amount a profit maximising banker is willing to lend above the customary rates is very low and borrowers are not willing to borrow such small increments at such large cost.

Jaffee and Modigliani (1969) approach the rationality of credit rationing by examining the three elements of loan demand, loan supply, and the determinants of the commercial loan rate. Earlier authors, they suggest, discussed the supply of loans and ignored the other two elements. They argue that conclusions *vis-à-vis* credit rationing require all three elements to be considered. They begin by generalising Freimer and Gordon's work to derive the supply curve of loans. They show that the optimal size of loan is finite regardless of how high an interest rate is offered. As the loan rate increases, the size of the optimal loan will eventually decline because, as the repayments become sufficiently large, default becomes almost certain; as loan rates tend to infinity, so the size of the loan required to make default almost certain tends to zero.

Thus the optimal loan offer curve, or the bank's supply of loans curve looks like SS in figure 5.1.

However, because Jaffee and Modigliani are discussing the possibility of equilibrium rationing, we need to include the demand curve for loans.[13] This is because equilibrium rationing is defined as credit rationing which occurs when the loan rate is set at its long run equilibrium level by the intersection of the demand and supply curves (Jaffee and Modigliani, p. 851). The demand curve is shown as DD which is assumed to be downward sloping. If the bank chooses an interest rate less than Ri^* then rationing will occur, since loan size is

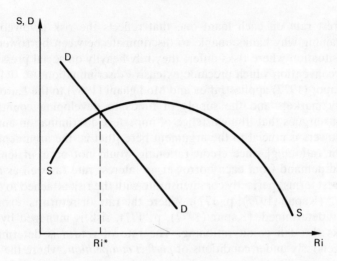

Figure 5.1   Equilibrium Rationing in the Market for Credit

less than that demanded. Rationing will not occur, however, if the bank chooses an interest rate greater than Ri^*.

What determines Ri^*? Jaffee and Modigliani argue that the crucial factor determining the existence of rationing will be the nature of market competition. *In theory*, if the bank acts as a discriminating monopolist, or if all banks act collusively to maximise joint profits, then credit rationing is not profitable. Credit rationing will be rational where the bank has to charge all customers the same rate, although it can choose that rate freely and can also choose the quantity of the loan. *In practice*, banks will not be able to discriminate freely between borrowers and can best exploit their market power by classifying customers into a small number of classes, within each of which a uniform rate is charged, despite considerable diversity in terms of the optimal interest rate that each should pay. Usury laws and social mores would, on this view, compress a potentially wide structure of interest rates within limits far narrower and less differentiated than they would be if chosen on the basis of risk considerations. Thus even a monopolist would find it difficult to discriminate freely between borrowers, and credit rationing is likely to occur even in a monopolistic banking system.

The key to credit rationing in Jaffee's and Modigliani's opinion is thus the extent to which a bank is able to discriminate freely between borrowers, that is, the degree to which a bank can charge a different interest rate on each loan, one that reflects the risk involved. In explaining why banks unable to discriminate between borrowers in the situation where risks differ, they rely heavily on social pressures and convention which preclude extensive discrimination.

Kapur (1977) applies Jaffee and Modigliani (1969) to the Eurocurrency markets and the supply of funds to developing countries. Kapur argues that 'the existence of imperfect discrimination among borrowers is crucial to the argument here [that is, the argument for credit rationing] since credit rationing would not occur if lenders could demand from each borrower an interest rate (as well as non-interest terms) perfectly commensurate with the risk attached to each loan.' (Kapur (1977), p. 177). Where the rate of return is 'exogenously determined' (Kapur (1977), p. 177), risk is managed by the banks through credit rationing. The rate of return is determined exogenously under conditions of *perfect competition*, where the rate of interest will not vary enough between borrowers to account for the differences in risk of potential borrowers.

Kapur's account does not explain why perfect competition under conditions of risk (resulting in non-homogeneous products) cannot discriminate on the basis of price. If capital markets are efficient, then perfect competition will be compatible with the existence of different risk classes. In applying his theory to the international capital markets, Kapur argues that the maximum quantity lent to any borrower, which is the bank's exposure level, is a function of the perceived creditworthiness of the borrower in question. This is true in Kapur's model because of his assumption that the interest rate is exogenously and uniformly determined. However, in neoclassical competitive markets, one would expect that the perceived creditworthiness of the borrower would be reflected in the price charged by the bank for the loan, and that as borrowing increased, the price of any further loans would rise. The key point that we need to explore further is why banks cannot protect themselves from risk through the price mechanism, and whether the degree of competition has an impact on their ability to do so.

Stiglitz and Weiss (1981) set out to show that equilibrium in the market for loanable funds is liable to be characterised by credit rationing. The explanation they give for this derives from recognition of information imperfections within credit markets. Thus we are looking at one of the consequences for financial markets of the problem of imperfect information which we discussed earlier (see section 5.3.2). Credit rationing occurs because higher interest rates will have an unfavourable impact on the riskiness (or quality) of the loan through two distinct effects. The first is an *adverse selection* effect (explained above in relation to the market for used cars). In the case of credit markets, the borrower is likely to have more information about the prospective investment than the lender (that is, the bank) and thus we have a situation of asymmetric information. The lender is aware that the quality of potential borrowers differs: in other words, that different borrowers have different probabilities of repaying the loan. Given that the expected return to the bank is dependent on the probability of repayment, the bank would prefer to identify borrowers who are more likely to repay. Various screening devices are therefore used. If the interest rate is used, then those who offer to pay a high interest rate are likely on average to be worse risks; they are willing to pay such an interest rate because they are unworried by the prospect of being unable to repay. Thus as the interest rate offered by the borrower rises, so will the average riskiness of the loan, possibly resulting in a lowering of expected bank profits.

Secondly, the *incentive effect* (in Stiglitz and Weiss' terminology) means that as the interest rate rises, firms are likely to switch to more risky projects, because higher rates lower the return on all successful projects, so that the least risky projects cease to be profitable at high rates.

As Stiglitz and Weiss argue, if information were perfect and costless, then the bank would be able to control all the actions of the borrower which might affect the return on the investment project. The adverse selection effect and the incentive effect arise in the case of costly and imperfect information, because the bank is unable to assess and monitor borrowers in sufficient depth. Hence, it is in the interest of a profit maximising bank to practise credit rationing. The expected return to the bank increases at a rate smaller than any given rise in the interest rate, and beyond some point, call it r', expected returns may actually decrease. However, at r', demand for loans may exceed the supply; in other words there is credit rationing. In traditional neoclassical analysis, the existence of excess demand would cause potential borrowers, who had not received loans, to increase the interest rate that they were willing to pay. However, this would produce a worse risk, as a result of the two effects mentioned above, which is not compensated for by the rise in expected return. Thus, the bank is unwilling to make such a loan, because the expected return to a loan at an interest rate above r' is lower than the expected returns which the bank is making at the current interest rate, r'. Hence credit is rationed.

How does this model fit in with Jaffee and Modigliani's explanation? Jaffee and Modigliani do not recognise the importance of information costs but essentially their analysis is compatible with Stiglitz and Weiss. Their explanation that credit rationing results from default being almost a certainty as the loan rate rises is essentially the same as Stiglitz and Weiss' incentive effect. Stiglitz and Weiss add to our understanding of credit rationing by drawing attention to why this 'common sense implication' (as Jaffee and Modigliani call it) is applicable in realistic circumstances – that is, because of costly and imperfect information. If it were not for this information problem, then the bank would know as much as the potential borrower and could impose conditions on the loan and monitor it effectively.

Stiglitz and Weiss' arguments also show that it is likely that there will be some combination of credit rationing and a spread of interest rates which will compensate for risk within credit markets. Some borrowers will face both risk premiums and exposure limits, because of the banks' inability to ensure that the expected return reflects risks *fully*.

The question which arises now is how banks choose the exposure limit for each borrower. Stiglitz and Weiss say nothing about this problem, although when there is imperfect information regarding the use to which the borrower will put the funds, then it is not clear how much should be lent. Eaton and Gersovitz (1981) suggest that the amount lent should be such that the costs of default to the borrower are exactly equal to the benefits of default to the borrower. However, these benefits and costs are continually changing. They vary with the general level of economic activity (as reflected in income) and political mood. The existence of uncertainty makes it very difficult for a bank to estimate a safe ceiling which will also maximise its return. Thus the ceiling and risk premium (assuming both to be used by the bank to protect it from taking excessive risks) are dependent to a great extent on the attitude of the financial market towards the particular type of investment at any one time. Each individual bank has neither the time nor resources to investigate, and the herd instinct tends to replace risk assessment. Minsky (1982b) argues that in conditions of euphoria (that is, where steady growth is expected to occur), there is 'a willingness to assume liability structures that are less defensive, and to take on what would have been considered in earlier times, undesirable chances' (Minsky (1982b), p.121). In other words, risks that would have been unacceptable in more pessimistic times, will become more acceptable as optimism grows. In this sense acceptable[14] credit limits, or risk-return relationships, under conditions of uncertainty and imperfect knowledge are dependent on the 'mood of the market'.

I shall argue in section 5.4 that increased competition in the presence of informational problems has resulted in both the exposure limits becoming too loose and the risk premiums too small, thus weakening the banks' ability to deal with the risk of default, in spite of their use of credit rationing. Such an argument has implications for the stability of the system. What we have argued here is that although imperfect information makes perfect discrimination through price discrimination impossible, acceptable exposure limits, along with whatever price discrimination is possible[15] would allow risks to be kept within safe levels. However, where it is not clear what exposure limits will maintain a safe level of risk, increased competition and/or increasing (but unfounded) confidence could lead to an unacceptable deterioration in the quality of a banks' portfolio and thus threaten the stability of the system.

5.3.5 Number of Buyers and Sellers

Retail banking markets typically have many customers on both sides of the balance sheet; wholesale or international financial markets tend to have a small number of customers whose transactions are very large.[16] The implications of this for retail banks is that they can invoke insurance principles to determine the size of reserve holdings required to 'insure' against the risk of deposit withdrawals. Wholesale banks, on the other hand, cannot – or at least not always – utilise the law of large numbers to determine the level of reserves they should hold.

The BIS argue that the implications of this have led to the theory[17] that wholesale banks do not produce liquidity but only ensure that it is more efficiently distributed throughout the global system.[18] The implication of this view is that wholesale banks do not engage in maturity mismatching (which would create liquidity).

Maturity mismatching or transformation occurs when the maturity structure of assets and liabilities differ. Financial intermediaries usually engage in positive maturity transformation; they borrow short and lend long. However, where there is a small number of depositors, the law of large numbers cannot be employed to determine the likely amount of withdrawals over a certain time period. There is therefore the danger that a bank will not be able to fund the loans that it is making for longer periods than the deposits have been placed for. This is known as the funding risk, or the inability of the bank to refinance a loan at any price.

A second risk associated with maturity mismatching is the interest rate risk. Interest rates may alter; in this case a bank can refinance loans but at an interest rate which may be greater than that on the previous financing of the loans, to which fixed earnings (that is, the interest rate) from the loans are related. Recognition of this risk led to the development of roll-over loans. However, even if the banks eliminate this risk through perfect matching of the roll-over periods of loans and deposits, the interest rate risk associated with mismatching is passed on to the borrower and if interest rates rise sufficiently, the borrower is liable to default. Thus the development of roll-over loans may have reduced the risk to banks only superficially; they now face greater risk of default on the part of the borrower.

If wholesale banks should not engage in maturity mismatching, what is their *raison d'être*? According to one theory – the BIS view expounded, for instance, by Hewson (1975) and Niehans and Hewson (1976) – it is the existence of transactions costs. In the absence of banks, prospective borrowers would have to employ significant resources in the search for a lender – search costs, communication costs, administration costs etc. Similarly, the prospective lender would have to engage in a costly analysis of the creditworthiness of potential borrowers. These costs drive a wedge between the net return to lenders and the net cost to borrowers. Essentially, the financial intermediary minimises this cost, achieving economies of scale through specialisation and reducing search costs. The profits of the international banks derive, therefore, from their ability to reduce the costs of distributing funds internationally and there is no need to indulge in maturity transformation.

The only case to be made for wholesale banks engaging in maturity transformation in the foregoing analysis is where movements in longer run interest rates relative to shorter run rates make it profitable (Niehans and Hewson (1976) and Niehans (1978)). Such behaviour is usually undertaken by the Treasury department of a bank. This explanation of the possible existence of maturity transformation relies on the fact that a bank may take a view on interest rate changes and organise its maturity profiles accordingly. If the bank expects interest rates to rise, then it will want to fund a loan with a deposit of greater maturity; in which case it will engage in negative maturity transformation and the economy's liquidity will be reduced. Similarly, if interest rates are expected to fall, then the bank will fund a loan with a succession of shorter term deposits and thereby engage in positive maturity transformation. In both cases, if the bank's expectations are fulfilled, a greater return will be made. However, both Niehans and Hewson (1976) and Niehans (1978) argue that because the term structure of interest rates is close to parity, there is little tendency for maturity transformation to occur.

Artis and Lewis (1981) offer a second view concerning maturity transformation, based on their belief that the manner in which transformation occurs in the wholesale market differs greatly from that which occurs in retail banking. Their argument is that banks do engage in positive maturity transformation, but that the presence of the interbank market allows individual banks to maintain a lower level of positive maturity transformation than that which exists in the system. They illustrate their theory with two examples, one of which will suffice here to understand their contention. Bank A receives a large deposit for three months, which it distributes between borrowers in the following way: some percentage of the deposit is lent to a non-bank at a maturity of greater than three months; the rest is lent to Bank B as a three-month interbank deposit. Bank B then lends some proportion of this deposit that it has just received to a non-bank, for more than three months and lends the rest in the interbank market for three months; and so on. We can see that, in terms of the amount of transformation in the system, the whole of the initial deposit will eventually be lent out for more than three months. However, each individual bank has less maturity transformaion because only a proportion of each deposit has been lent out for a period of greater than three months.

A third (and final) hypothesis argues for the existence of positive maturity transformation in the markets in the following manner. The level of competition in the wholesale markets is high and has increased in recent years (see chapter 1.4). This has led to two trends. Firstly, borrowers have obtained increased power to determine the conditions in the market. This has lengthened maturities, thus inevitably increasing positive maturity transformation, given that the maturities of deposits remain the same. Secondly, greater competition among the banks has led to reduced profits from liquidity spreading activities. Banks may have moved, therefore, into other areas, such as liquidity creation (as opposed only to mere distribution), in order to boost returns and profits on their wholesale Eurocurrency activities. The question that arises is whether the returns are commensurate with the risks involved.

The issue of maturity transformation is important because of the problem of determining the level of liquid reserves that should be held by banks operating in such markets. Even if the law of large numbers holds in wholesale markets, the safe level of maturity transformation is something which banks have to determine, and competitive pressure can still force the degree of transformation to dangerous levels. Clearly, however, if there is a high degree of concentration among depositors, then the level of transformation which can be considered safe is lower, because the law of large numbers no longer holds. In chapter 6, we shall be testing each of the above hypotheses by looking at Bank of England quarterly data on maturity transformation in the Eurocurrency markets.

We have discussed the implications of possible depositor concentration in the wholesale markets. We now turn to the implications of possible concentration in the numbers of borrowers.

In markets where the size of loans is very large, there is a tendency for the number of borrowers wanting such amounts to be much smaller than the number of potential borrowers in the retail side of bank lending. The consequences of such possible concentration are, firstly, that it becomes more difficult for an individual bank to diversify its portfolio to get rid of the unsystematic component of risk discussed in section 2 of this chapter; and secondly, that this diversification problem encourages a form of collusion or co-operation among the banks, namely syndication. Syndication is a technique that allows large loans to be put together for borrowers by many banks forming a syndicate and participating in the financing of the loan. If such a loan were financed solely by one bank, then the bank's portfolio would be too concentrated and therefore inefficient. When many banks participate in each loan organised, this allows each bank to maintain a well (or at least better) diversified portfolio. However, the diversification of loans in the whole system will not be improved by such a method of collusion, and there could still be overconcentration in certain types of financing (for example, less-developed country balance of payments financing) in the system as a whole.

A further aspect is the number of banks in the international markets. This is far greater than the numbers involved in retail banking (see chapter 1.4). There are three kinds of banks which operate in the wholesale markets;

i) Retail banks based in the major industrialised countries which have diversified their portfolio internationally, partly as a result of a shortage of domestic business relative to their growth targets, and partly as a result of the desire to escape regulations in their own countries, as we saw in part I. In London, there are representatives of most major industrialised countries which compete with the British clearers mainly in the wholesale Eurocurrency markets but also increasingly in retail markets.

ii) Smaller banks, which specialise in wholesale business and which finance most of their loans in the interbank market. These include consortium banks, although there are only a few left now.

iii) Subsidiaries or branches of banks from developing countries which have set up in the major financial centres in order to promote their country as a candidate for loans from the private international capital markets and to take part in some of the syndications that are set up.

All these kind of banks seek business in the wholesale markets. However, whether this signifies intense competition in the markets depends on the extent of collusion and co-operaton. There is no evidence of any cartel type of arrangements like those which existed, for instance, among the UK clearing banks prior to 1971. However, as noted above, syndicated financing of large loans is to some extent a form of collusion. In addition, there is a herd instinct in financial markets which is in some ways tantamount to collusion – the safety in numbers argument. However, such an instinct does not altogether destroy competition, even though it distorts it; and it tends to result in too many banks moving into new profitable opportunities, thus reducing returns for any one bank. It can also be dangerous in that it encourages banks to move in quickly after the initial bank's move, without proper analysis of the avenue. Where analysis occurs, it tends to be coloured by both a sense of euphoria at the new opportunity and by the need to get into the new area and not let competitors steal a march.

5.4 CRISIS THEORY AND INTERNATIONAL FINANCIAL MARKETS

This section, using the concepts discussed above, outlines a dynamic theory of crisis for application to the international credit markets in the following chapter. The elements of the theory will be related to relevant literature on both competition in international banking and crisis theory in general.

The concept of a tendency towards crisis suggests that market determined equilibrating forces do not exist, are too weak, or fail to come into action quickly enough (that is, to avoid the need for government intervention to forestall collapse). Clearly our theory needs to depart in some way from the equilibrating mechanisms customarily postulated in neoclassical analysis.

There has been considerable focus on this issue in recent years.[19] However, the subject is not new and discussion dates back at least to Bagehot (1878), Fisher (1932) and Kalecki (1971). The common underlying theme of all these authors is the inability of the neoclassical model to explain real and financial instability in advanced capitalist economies.[20] Dissatisfaction with the neoclassical model is summarised by Minsky (1982b):

> The major theorems of the neoclassical synthesis are that a system of decentralised markets, where units are motivated by self-interest, is capable of yielding a coherent result and, in some very special cases, the result can be characterised as efficient. These main conclusions are true, however, only if very strong assumptions are made. They have never been shown to hold for an economy with privately owned capital assets and complex, ever-evolving financial institutions and practices. Indeed we live in an economy which is developing through time, whereas the basic theorems on which the conservative critique of intervention rests have been proven only for 'models' which abstract from time.
>
> (Minsky (1982b), p. xii)

I concentrate here on financial aspects of the international economic cycle, which can be divided into four phases. Let us begin, in Phase I, with a situation where a new profit opportunity has appeared for banks in the international sphere as the result of an exogenous change in the macro-economic system (for example, the increase in oil prices in 1973–4). The extent to which banks move into this new area depends on the level of confidence in the banking sector and on the intensity with which banks are looking for new ways to expand their balance sheets. The level of confidence of the bankers is a key variable throughout this analysis and is essentially dependent on the stage of the financial cycle in which we find ourselves. Confidence is important initially, because it determines how risky the new profit opportunity is viewed as being. Minsky (1982b p. 121) argues that 'expected gross profits after taxes reflect the expected behaviour of the economy, as well as expected market and management developments'. Where the banks' management is confident about the prospect for growth, the riskiness of the new investment will seem less and banks are more likely to view the new investment opportunity as a profitable one, in which they should get involved. Let us assume that this is the case here. Banks looking for new avenues to expand their balance sheets feel confident enough to move into the new area produced by the exogenous shock to the world monetary system.

However, the new business may still be considered more risky than traditional banking pursuits (for example, domestic retail banking). New borrowers therefore face both a risk premium and some credit rationing, because of the adverse selection effect and the incentive effect. As more banks move into the area, confidence increases and the opportunity begins to be viewed by banks still outside the new area as one which should not be missed. Competition intensifies as the number of banks chasing the new profit opportunities expands.[21] This is especially so if there is an increasing internationalisation of banking and the numbers of banks based in the major financial centres is increasing;[22] and this produces a greater incentive for banks to be seen in the new and fashionable area.

We now enter Phase II, where balance sheets are validated. Profits are being made and reinforce the banks' decision that this area was and is a good profit opportunity. Confidence increases further. So does competition, as more banks get involved in the new lending.

Four consequences follow, however, from this increased confidence and competition. Firstly, as Barclay (1978) argues, there is a tendency for too many new entrants to be attracted to the market, because not all entrants know about each other (information problem) and because it is not clear how many new entrants the market will support. This problem was discussed by Richardson (1960) in the general context of investment decisions. He argues that without information regarding the investment plans of competitors entrepreneurs cannot formulate their own investment plans – because they do not know by how much total supply is liable to increase unless they know their competitors investment plans. The competitors face the same problem. The result is that the adjustment mechanism under perfect competition is an illusion.

Although supply is increasing, demand will probably be increasing for some time, as borrowers learn of the existence of the new market.

If demand does not increase as fast as supply, profits will fall, causing an important margin of safety to come under pressure. Profits can be described as a margin of safety because they bolster reserves, which combined with capital, cover any bad debts and defaults that the bank may have to face (see Minsky (1982b, p. 74). Given the attraction of too many entrants because of increasing confidence under conditions of imperfect information, there is a tendency to overproduction. Too many suppliers are chasing too few demanders. Is the resulting profits squeeze a short-run phenomenon or something more fundamental? There are three reasons why it should be considered more fundamental.

Firstly, as Pitman (1985) argues, there may have been a need for large investment in expertise, which has to be maintained at a certain level to reap economies of scale in banking information. Although I argued earlier that the herd instinct in financial markets is to some extent a substitute for genuine information, there will be some attempt on the part of banks to set up a department dealing with the new lending market, even if its effectiveness, in the initial stages, is to be doubted. Given possible economies of scale, it may be cheaper to have a larger proportion of assets in the area,[23] and withdrawal may be difficult and protracted.

Secondly, if prospects worsen, many banks may not consider withdrawal appropriate in the first instance. They may even engage in an aggressive pricing strategy to enlarge their share of the business (see Group of Thirty (1982b)), taking losses in the short run in order to obtain the profit available from opportunities when competitors have withdrawn. Price warfare will, of course, reduce profits further.

Thirdly, supply may increase further as new nationalities of banks join the market, who were previously prevented through regulations within their respective countries of origin.[24]

The second consequence of increased competition is that both the risk-return relationship will deteriorate and the credit exposure limits will be increased. We argued in section 5.3 that some combination of risk premiums and credit rationing is likely to exist in credit markets. The impact of increasing competition on risk premiums is two-fold: firstly, to decrease them (given the overall balance between the demand and supply of liquidity in the market); secondly, to decrease the spread of premiums (where the spread is the difference between the highest and lowest premium) as banks compete amongst one another and try to maintain, if not increase, their individual market shares. Many argue[25] that, with greater competition and the need for banks to maintain their market share, individual lenders cannot stop the erosion of risk premiums, if their competitors are not making sufficient provision for risk. Methods that usually prevent this erosion in the quality of the banks' balance sheets may be rendered ineffective (Barclay (1978)). Shareholders are not in a position to judge the soundness of loans made and face the general problem of shareholder authority. Borrowers are unlikely to complain, because they are benefiting from the reduced prices and increased amount of credit available and, in some cases, probably believe that they will repay the money.[26] Finally, the depositor is interested only in his deposit, not in the general prosperity of the bank; this leads to a discontinuity in attitude such that in normal circumstances he does not bother, but when the risk becomes great he is inclined to withdraw his deposit, causing a run on the bank, by which time it is too late to improve loan quality and the bank is liable to fail.

Increases in the amount of credit to which a borrower is deemed to be entitled (that is, a loosening of the credit rationing which he faces) is also likely to arise as a result of increased confidence and competition. This leads to a greater concentration of loans within a particular risk class than might be advisable for risk diversification reasons. Innovations may have the effect – or intention – of decreasing the apparent concentration for individual banks. Syndication in the medium term Eurocurrency markets is said to reduce the risk involved in large loans because any one bank finances only a small part of each loan. This ignores the fact that concentration of borrowers for the system as a whole may increase. In conjunction with the increased interdependence that results from such an innovation, this means that systematic risk has probably not decreased (see Angelini *et al* (1979)).

Thirdly, increased competition results in an increase in the maturity which banks are willing to offer borrowers (Group of Thirty (1982b) and Saade (1981)). This is part of the package of better terms available to borrowers which also include lower risk premiums and higher credit limits.

Fourthly, the increase confidence and competition, combined with the decrease in profits, causes the banks to move into greater risk areas in order to try to maintain or increase earnings.[27] Valentine (1973) and Revell (1980) suggest that speculative maturity mismatching will increase, with an associated increase in the interest rate and funding risk. Minsky (1982b) describes this as a feature of what he terms a speculative finance unit. Long positions in assets are financed by short run liabilities, which implies interest rate risk (see section 5.3.5. above). Together with greater maturity mismatching, banks also speculate on interest rate changes and foreign exchange rate changes. However, where exchange rates and interest rates are very volatile (for example, as during the 1970s), it is difficult to guess the correct movements and very costly to guess wrong. The effect of such behaviour is thus to increase the volatility of profits (Revell (1980)).

These four consequences of increased confidence and competition signify increased risk both to individual banks and to the system as a whole. Some brief comments are in order before we move on to consider what happens when the crisis occurs. Firstly, why are banks able and willing to sacrifice short run profit considerations? A partial answer is presumably that they are interested not so much in immediate profit maximisation, as in increasing market share and the size of their balance sheets. If their competitors move into the new area, there is strong motivation for them to follow, otherwise they will lose their relative position. Moreover, each bank hopes that if it can become well-established in a market and force out some of its rivals, greater profit will be available.

Secondly, why is a deterioration is the risk-return relationship allowed to happen? That is, why do banks not recognise that this will be damaging in the future? Firstly, growing confidence and an improving economic situation will result in banks assessing risk on the basis of good economic conditions,[28] where there is a smaller probability of default than under worse conditions. This point reflects Minsky's view on the economics of euphoria (Minsky (1982b), p. 120–5). The second possible reason (Revell (1980) and Barclay (1978)) is that retribution for bad banking (that is, for undue risk taking) seldom occurs immediately. The banker who is underproviding for risk and engaging in speculative activities will probably earn greater profits in the short term than his prudent rival. In many cases, the new entrants are the first to involve themselves in such activities; but as confidence increases, the more established become involved.[29]

These various elements combine to produce a situation of increasing fragility and and we enter Phase III of the cycle. Risks have not been properly assessed or provided for, speculative activity may be playing a prominent role and declining profits may have affected the degree to which banks have provided reserves against bad debts. A crisis is increasingly possible. We can identify several factors that might act as the spark:

i) As Fisher (1932) recognised, investments made for speculative purposes (for example, foreign exchange speculation) are a likely cause of the crisis.

ii) A default or need for rescheduling on the part of a major borrower or borrowers can spark off a crisis because it implies that the quality of some of the banks' assets is low. Moreover, because competition and aggressive pricing has reduced capital ratios and reserves,[30] the ability of the banks to deal with possible loan losses is reduced. Defaults or reschedulings may occur because of factors exogenous to the banking system, for example, a decline in economic activity or the collapse in the price of an important export commodity, but may also be encouraged by factors endogenous to the banking system. For example, the roll-over loan innovation in the Eurocurrency markets is thought to reduce the interest rate risk inherent in maturity mismatching. However, the risk of interest rate increases is passed on to the borrower and it is possible to conceive of a situation where an increase in the interest rate in the Eurodollar market (for example, due to US monetary policy, see chapter 4.3) causes the borrower severe repayment problems resulting either in the need for rescheduling, or in default.

The sequence of events during the crisis period, Phase IV, is dependent on the initial spark but even if only one bank is affected initially, interdependence within the system as a result of the inter-bank market and syndication is liable to generate a domino effect and many banks may subsequently get into difficulties. As McMahon (1985) argues, the interbank market is more fragile and susceptible to shocks than other forms of funding and could cause a failure of the system. In the event of rescheduling or default, many banks will be affected because of the process of syndication. Moreover, reschedulings or defaults may be bunched, as Revell (1978) and Barclay (1978) argue is likely, because the economic problems that affect one borrower have a high probability of affecting many; this is the element of risk that cannot easily be diversified away (see section 5.2 above).

The characteristics of the crisis period are:

i) Liquidity in the market, in this case mainly the interbank market, dries up so that banks are unable to refund their loans;

ii) other assets, which the banks consider to be liquid under normal (non-crisis) circumstances either become illiquid or must be sold at well below their non-crisis value, resulting in losses for the banks;

iii) confidence gives way to pessimism and banks as yet unaffected will try to bring a halt to dealings with those that have been affected.

Such a process increases the fragility of the situation by adding to domino effects;[31]

iv) rescheduling forces banks into involuntary lending[32] and greater maturity mismatching. They may be unable to write off the losses without severely weakening or exhausting their reserves which because of falling profits may have fallen as a percentage of their assets (see earlier in this section);

v) the decline in confidence may not be confined to the wholesale banking system and may reach the general public, sparking off a run on the retail banks.

Bank runs have been analysed within a model with a unique equilibrium with the bank run occurring under some states of nature:[33] within a multiple equilibria model where one of the equilibria is a bank run:[34] and within a catastrophe theory framework.[35] The common element running through all these approaches is that depositors face information imperfections: they are either uncertain of when they will require liquidity (see Diamond and Dybvig (1983)) or are uncertain about the safety level of the bank in which they have placed deposits (see Batchelor (1986)). This literature relies on the information imperfections which were crucial to our analysis in section 5.3.

In most of the models,[36] the bank's role in society and its susceptibility to a run arise from the fact that the bank is a provider of liquidity: it transforms illiquid assets into liquid liabilities. To highlight the importance of this characteristic of banks, Diamond and Dybvig (1983) assume that the asset in which the bank invests has a certain return. There are three periods in the model (0, 1 and 2). Assets yield a return equal to R if production is allowed to run until period 2. If production only runs until period 1, then there is no return – only the initial amount lent can be recovered.

Risk in the model arises from the fact that depositors can either be of type 1 (an agent who wishes to consume in period 1) or of type 2 (an agent who wishes to consume in period 2), something which only becomes clear to the depositor in the second period of the model. Because this risk of being a type 1 agent (and thus requiring liquidity in period 1) is only privately observable and not publicly verifiable (the information problem), competitive markets cannot provide agents with insurance.

The bank offers depositors a contract which provides liquidity for the depositor and guarantees a return should the deposit be withdrawn before maturity. In this way, the bank provides insurance against being a type 1 agent (whose consumption opportunity is in period 1). Each depositor gains (that is, has a higher expected utility) as a consequence of this risk pooling.

The problem with this contract is that it has (at least) two equilibria. The 'good' equilibrium occurs where those agents of type 1 withdraw their deposits in period 1, whilst those who are type 2 agents wait. The 'bad' equilibrium is characterised by all agents seeking to withdraw their funds in period 1 because they believe that others are seeking to do the same whether or not they are type 1 agents. In this situation the bank is insolvent – the face value of its deposits is greater than the value of its assets following liquidiation.[37] Why do agents withdraw their deposits early? Diamond and Dybvig (1983) argue that this could arise due to a number of factors which cause depositors to lose confidence in the bank – for example, bad loans, a run on another bank, or sunspots.[38] Chari and Jagannathan (1984) and Postlewaite and Vives (1984) attribute the bank run to signals which arrive in the model and which give information to depositors regarding, for example, the imminence of a consumption opportunity. Is such action rational? Diamond and Dybvig (1983) argue that it is rational for agents to deposit their funds with a bank, even if there is a positive probability of a bank run, so long as that probability is small enough. This is the case because the contract offered by the bank (a return on the asset plus liquidity if required) is superior to what individual wealth holders can derive if they hold the productive assets directly.

Diamond and Dybvig (1983) show that a government deposit insurance which guarantees that any depositor who withdraws will receive the return promised in the contract dominates any contract which the bank itself could enforce to prevent runs (for example, withdrawal of convertibility if too many deposits are withdrawn).

In this model, the bank's role as a transformer of illiquid assets into liquid liabilities is the key reason why banks are susceptible to runs. The question of whether the risk associated with bank lending may play a role in bank runs is not addressed (the return on assets is known with certainty). Risky loans thus do not provide a rationale for deposit insurance within this model.[39]

In contrast, Goodhart (1987) argues that a lengthening of the maturity of deposits (that is, a reduction in the degree of liquidity transformation) would simply slow down the bank run rather than prevent it. He argues that the factors characterising banks which lead to the possibility of bank runs are the 'combination of uncertain "true" bank asset valuation, and fixed nominal value deposits' (Goodhart (1987), p. 77).

To highlight this point, he examines the case for central bank support when the value of an investor's deposit is allowed to fluctuate with the underlying value of the assets which the bank holds in its portfolio. In this situation, bank runs would not arise, firstly, because the liquidity of a bank would be assured since the bank would hold marketable assets; secondly, because solvency would be guaranteed since the value of the bank's liabilities varies with the value of its assets.

Would this policy solution, (that is, allowing the value of liabilities to fluctuate with banks' assets) remove the need for central bank provision of lender of last resort facilities? The issue of how easy it is to value a bank's assets is crucial to this question. Uncertainty regarding the 'true' value of a banks' assets, which Goodhart recognises in the above quote, is the reason why we cannot do without a lender of last resort even if the value of deposits were allowed to fluctuate. Banks deal primarily in non-marketable assets whose 'true' value is difficult to assess (these assets do not have a market price). Thus banks would still be vulnerable to runs on the time deposits which finance these loans. There is still a case for a lender of last resort.

Nonetheless Goodhart's insights allow him to argue that it would be possible to remove the means of payment function from banks. If this were done, and the value of demand deposits fluctuated with the underlying value of the marketable assets in which these deposits were invested, the need for a lender of last resort would not arise with respect to deposits acting as means of payment. In this way, the externality of disruption of the payments mechanism associated with banking failure would be removed. However, banks, whose business now is to extend non-marketable loans financed by time deposits and CDs, would still require a lender of last resort because, since it is optimal for loans to be extended on a fixed nominal value basis,[40] it is optimal for their deposits to be extended on this basis as well (Goodhart (1987), pp. 86–87).

Banks would therefore still be susceptible to runs which now have a damaging impact only on bank borrowers and thus on investment in the productive sector of the economy. That this is the main damage associated with bank failures is also the view of Diamond and Dybvig (1983): 'our results . . . imply that the real damage from banking runs is primarily from the direct damage occurring when recalling loans interrupts production' (Diamond and Dybvig (1983) p. 404).

Both these models give support for government intervention via a lender of last resort in the banking industry – this support arises from the role of banks in providing liquidity and from the fact that their assets are non-marketable and thus of uncertain value.

In this chapter we have stressed the fact that one bank failure can often lead to contagion effects on other parts of the banking system. Neither of the above authors, whilst recognising that contagion effects can occur, explicitly modelled the dynamics of this process. Batchelor (1986), who analyses the dynamics of a bank run within a catastrophe theory framework, explicitly examines the relationship between the degree of insolvency of one bank in the system and the degree of insolvency of the banking system as a whole.

Where depositors have complete information, a fall in the value of the assets held by one bank in the system would have no impact on other banks. The perceived degree of solvency of the system would decrease by the same amount as the degree of solvency of the one bank alone. Where, however, investors have less than complete information about each individual bank's balance sheet, it is optimal for them to use information from other sources to calculate the degree of solvency of the bank in which they hold their deposits. In particular, Batchelor suggests two sources of importance (Batchelor (1986) pp. 63–5). Firstly, it will be optimal to use the solvency levels of other banks in the system. In this case, if one bank fails, those who deposit with other banks will revise their perceptions of their bank's degree of solvency downward. The perceived solvency of the whole system therefore falls by a greater amount after the failure of one particular bank than under full information. The extent of a bank run thus depends on the degree to which individuals are informed about their own bank's solvency position. The less information, the more widespread the bank run is likely to be.

The second source of information is a bank's past record on solvency. A depositor may use past values of solvency, either giving roughly equal weight to each past value or using only information from the recent past. This determines the length of time between a shock to bank i, say, and the subsequent bank run (the severity of which depends on the value of information in the system). If only recent solvency values are used, the bank run will occur relatively quickly.

To generate the catastrophe (where system moves from one state to another), we have to envisage a shock to the system which causes depositors to forget the past record of a bank. For example, evidence of insolvency of bank i could be so strong that past solvency levels are ignored. We then move to a state where confidence in the system is low. The size of the shock which is required to move the system from optimistic state to the pessimistic state depends on the level of information available in the economy. The less well-informed depositors are, the more they use information on other banks when calculating the solvency level of their bank and hence the smaller the shock to confidence which could trigger collapse.

Analogously, once we are in a situation where a bank run has taken place (that is, the pessimistic state), the system may require another shock to move it back towards recovery. Such a shock could involve an asset endowment to the original bank (and perhaps others which have been affected) such that confidence recovers in bank i and in the system.

Batchelor (1986) recognises that whilst the generation of a bank run within this model results from optimising rational behaviour in the face of imperfect information, the generation of catastrophe (that is, a switch from one state to another) depends on the rather arbitrary assumption that a shock to the system causes a sudden switch in confidence. Nonetheless this model along with the analyses of Diamond and Dybvig (1983) and Goodhart (1987) provide a case for government intervention in banking as a result of the possibility that imperfect information can lead to a bank run, the consequences of which are potentially enormous (section 5.3.1). At the international level, the free market notion of capital flowing to underdeveloped regions, where the return is higher, is distorted as new lending is halted because of the problems which such regions are experiencing in servicing existing debt. At the domestic level, the shrinkage in liquidity may cause a sharp decline in economic activity, with companies failing as they cannot meet obligations which they expected to refinance when they were due.

5.5   CONCLUSION

This chapter began with an outline of the neoclassical view of financial crises and with the model espoused by its proponents to justify their position of no government intervention in banking. This model argues that competition ensures that resources are allocated efficiently. Both pricing efficiency and operational efficiency are guaranteed. The presence of risk leads the bank to distinguish between loans on the basis of price charged, thus making sure that the expected return is commensurate with the risk involved.

Having outlined the neoclassical model, we went on to examine sources of market failure and suggested that the promotion of competition would not invariably lead to efficiency. Firstly, the existence of external costs associated with banking failure imply that it may not be desirable to allow the normal market retribution for bad banking to operate.[41] Secondly, information asymmetries lead to the problem of adverse selection. This prevents the bank from using the interest rate charged on loans as an effective screening device. As a consequence, credit rationing is likely to be favoured by banks as a method of controlling risk. Thirdly, there may be economies of scale associated with banking production. We argued that uncertainty regarding deposit withdrawals and the cost of gathering information associated with financial intermediation provides a theoretical case for the existence of economies of scale. Evidence on their importance in banking is mixed, but this may partly reflect the difficulties of measuring bank output. Finally, we argued that banks have to determine the extent to which they can engage in maturity mismatching or equivalently the level of liquid reserves they should hold to meet their deposit withdrawals. This is especially a problem in wholesale markets where the law of large numbers may not hold.

Using some of the ideas generated by our discussion of market failures, we further argued in section 5.4 that competition in financial markets may generate instability. Competition at times of increasing confidence may lead to falling reserves (used to meet bad debts), a deteriorating risk-return relationship, greater maturity mismatching and greater speculative activity. These factors combine to generate increasing fragility leading possibly to crisis, with the associated external costs of bank failure should government action not prevent it.

6 Maturity Transformation, Risk-return Analysis and Credit Rationing in the Euromarkets

The purpose of this chapter is to examine the informal model in chapter 5 in relation to the international financial markets. Whilst the model is applicable to these markets generally, I focus on the Eurocurrency markets in particular in this chapter, firstly, because of the availability of data, and secondly, because these markets form a large and representative section of international financial activity.

The outline of the chapter is as follows. Section 6.1 looks at the extent to which maturity transformation has been practised by the London banks involved in the Euromarkets.

Sections 6.2 and 6.3 examine the risk-return relationship in the market. 6.2 discusses the methods of country risk assessment. Sections 6.3.1 to 6.3.4 look at the extent to which the risk premium (spread) has deteriorated over time. Section 6.3.5 examines credit rationing in the markets.

The final section, 6.4, seeks to bring together the results of the previous analysis and to relate them to the model of chapter 5. Does the model as a whole represent a good description of the workings of the Eurocurrency markets, or does the evidence suggest a different set of mechanisms at work?

6.1 MATURITY TRANSFORMATION

6.1.1 Hypotheses and Existing Literature

The informal model (chapter 5.4) posited three possibilities with regard to maturity transformation. Firstly, as competition increases at a given level of demand, borrowers find that conditions in the market improve for them. This improvement includes a decrease in spreads, an increase in the volume of funds available and an increase in the average maturity of loans. Given that there is no reason to

142

expect a comparable increase in the maturity of the bank's liabilities, this implies greater positive maturity mismatching.

Secondly, an increase in competition may decrease profit from intermediation services offered by banks and cause them either to move into the speculative activity of taking a view on the expected future movement of interest rates or to seek profit recovery through increasing the maturity of the loan. The effect of the former on maturity transformation may be either positive or negative depending on the direction in which interest rates are expected to change. The impact of the latter attempt to enhance profit by increasing loan maturity, would clearly be an increase in positive maturity transformation.

Finally, we argued that rescheduling on 'soft' terms may result in longer loan maturities and hence more positive maturity transformation.

The following pages survey the existing literature on maturity transformation in the market over the period 1973–85 and indicate the hypotheses we consider later. Thereafter (sections 6.1.2–4) we attempt a comprehensive examination of maturity mismatching during this period because the literature focuses only on selected dates between 1973 and 1985.

Existing literature on maturity transformation in the Eurocurrency markets is classified here according as it looks at one or other segment of the market. Four categories can be distinguished.

i) Firstly, many authors have commented on the general extent to which maturity transformation occurs in the market. Conclusions vary partly because of differences over time and partly because, where the figures are ambiguous, the theory propounded by each author dominates the interpretation of the findings. Thus, Hewson (1975), Niehans and Hewson (1976) and Niehans (1978) argue that the extent to which general maturity transformation occurs is very limited. Their evidence is based on the work of Hewson (1975), who looks at Bank of England data on maturity transformation as of September 1973, with a view to determining the extent to which Eurobanks engage in liquidity creation.

McKenzie (1976) notes that there was a move from negative maturity transformation in 1969 to positive maturity transformation in 1974. Bank of England data shows that in 1969 assets of less than three months maturity were greater than the amount of liabilities in that maturity; in the over one year maturity category, the value of liabilities was greater than that of assets. However, 1969 was a year of very tight credit conditions in the US resulting in heavy market borrowings by US banks which probably accounts for the large volume of assets of less than three months maturity. In November 1974, the situation was the opposite of this with positive maturity transformation in evidence. Weston (1980) notes an increase in positive maturity transformation for the period 1973–7, also using Bank of England data.

More recent evidence is provided by Pecchioli (1982), Ellis (1981) and Dennis (1984). Pecchioli (1982) looks initially at BIS data on the maturity distribution of international banks' claims, which shows that the international banks are heavily involved in long term lending (that is, greater than two years) to residents of countries outside the BIS reporting area;[1] about 37 per cent, on average, of Euroloans made by reporting banks in the period 1978–82 had a maturity of over two years. However, this data does not indicate the maturity structure of these banks' liabilities. An analysis of Bank of England data on maturity structure of assets and liabilities of London Eurobanks for December 1975 and February 1982 shows that the level of mismatching has shown 'remarkable stability' (Pecchioli (1982), p. 36). Ellis (1981)[2] and Dennis (1984) find evidence of positive maturity transformation; the largest percentage liabilities are in the maturity category of less than three months, whereas the largest percentage of claims are for over three years. Dennis (1984) looking at mismatching of London Eurobanks between 1975 and 1981[3] finds a sharp rise in mismatching between 1975 and 1978 which was only partially reversed over the next three years.

Finally, Davis (1980) interviewed senior management of 40 Eurobanks. Many of these banks engaged in deposit dealing, arranging the maturities of liabilities to profit from changes in interest rates. The extent of the profit margins from taking a view on interest rate movements are expected to be only modest; otherwise, too much risk would have to be assumed. Hence usually a maximum quantitative exposure level is set by senior management.

The conclusion with respect to the general degree of maturity transformation in the Eurocurrency market is thus mixed. Evidence for earlier dates shows less maturity transformation than for later. However, the extent to which detailed work on historical trends has been carried out is not great.

ii) With respect to the interbank market, Ellis (1981) finds only slight mismatching in the London interbank market for the period 1974–1981. Johnston (1983) notes that there is a problem with the

interpretation of data on the London interbank market: by definition, the total assets and liabilities in each maturity category should
match, because one bank will report the transaction as a liability,
whereas another will report it as a claim. Thus it is better to look at
the different categories of banks. Ellis' conclusions remain, however,
that on balance there is little interbank maturity transformation: the
American banks have some positive transformation, the British and
consortium banks, some negative transformation. Dennis (1984)
confirms these results for the end of 1981.

iii)   Artis and Lewis (1981) look at banks' claims on and liabilities to
non-banks, and find a relatively significant degree of mismatching
compared to interbank business (for February 1980, Bank of England
data).

iv)   Weston (1980) and Dennis (1984) both examine the difference
between the different categories of banks in the London Eurocurrency market. The greatest positive maturity transformation is undertaken by the consortium banks; their importance has been declining
since 1977 (figure 1.2). Dennis (1984) notes that US banks have the
highest net liabilities in the maturity category of less than eight days.
He argues that they can afford to be less liquid than other categories
of banks, because of the ease with which they can obtain dollars from
their parent banks in New York. Dennis also finds that Japanese
banks had a strong demand for liabilities of more than one year,
something uncommon elsewhere in the market. This resulted from an
official requirement that claims of more than one year be matched by
liabilities of more than one year.

The literature surveyed above shows that most authors look at the
levels of maturity transformation at a given date. There has been
little systematic work on changes in these levels including changes
which may result from exogenous shocks. It is interesting to ask
whether any of the major events during the 1970s and 1980s have had
any discernible effect on the level of mismatching. The major event
of the 1970s was the oil price rise in 1973. The subsequent need for
recycling of petrodollars had a profound impact on the Eurocurrency
markets as we saw briefly in chapter 1. This would be expected to
increase maturity mismatching for two reasons. Firstly, as OPEC
surpluses increased, there was a large rise in the volume of short term
deposits placed in the Euromarkets. The deposits were mainly short
term because OPEC countries, being relatively unsophisticated investors and suddenly swamped with large sums of money, needed
time to consider where best to employ these funds. On the other

hand, the deficit countries required longer term finance to allow smooth adjustment to the change in the cost of energy and to maintain growth in the face of a less favourable global environment. Hence, mismatching is expected to be a natural development of the recycling procedure.

The major event of the 1980s, which is expected to be of critical importance for mismatching, was the debt crisis of 1982. The rescheduling agreements represented an attempt by the banks to recover the funds they had lent in the past. To do so, banks were required to lend at far more realistic and therefore longer maturities. We might expect to see, therefore, an increase in mismatching in the post-1982 period.

If changes over the period 1973–86 can be identified and explained, we may learn something with regard to the attitudes of banks to mismatching and the effect of changing market conditions upon mismatching. In sections 6.1.3 and 6.1.4 I examine developments in the period 1974–1985, paying particular attention to possible causes of the changes in maturity transformation that have taken place.

6.1.2   Data and Methodology

Pecchioli (1982) discusses the data that is available on maturity transformation in the Euromarkets. The BIS publishes data in its semi-annual press release. This is a reliable source, but includes a maturity breakdown of claims only. We require figures on the maturity structure of both claims and liabilities in order to examine maturity transformation.[4]

The Bank of England produces some of the most comprehensive data on the maturity of liabilities and claims in foreign (that is, non-sterling) currencies of banks in London. Although this does not cover the whole of the geographical spread of the Euromarkets, it is commonly assumed that London is representative of the international credit markets as a whole because of its dominant position. Pecchioli argues that Bank of England figures contain a disproportionate amount of interbank data, because of London's importance as an interbank centre. If there is less maturity mismatching in the interbank market then mismatching in the whole of the Euromarkets (that is, not just London) would be underestimated.

The interbank data can be separated out, because the Bank of England gives figures for both the London interbank market and London banks' claims on and liabilities to overseas banks. These figures give us the best idea of the level of interbank maturity transformation, and therefore they are used here. Nonetheless, even adding the London interbank data to the overseas interbank data, we still face the problem highlighted by Johnston (1983) (see point *ii*) in the literature survey on p. 145) that such figures may understate the degree of maturity transformation in interbank trading by London based banks.

In so far as there is data for interbank transactions, so there is data for non-bank transactions. Looking at the data for non-bank transactions of London-based banks should give us some indication of the level of maturity mismatching that exists in the *system* as a whole (that is, end-sources and end-uses of funds).

Bank of England data has been collected from September 1973 on a quarterly basis, for seven maturity ranges. The analysis here focuses on the period 1973–1985. Aside from being classified into bank and non-bank transactions, the data is also divided into five sections based on the nationality of London-based banks. These sections are British banks, American banks, Japanese banks, consortium banks and foreign banks. The latter section includes banks from Commonwealth countries as well as overseas banks other than American or Japanese.

The main problem faced in assembling the statistics is to categorise the loans by maturity. This is because of the variety of grace periods and redemption features that affect the average maturity of a loan. The main question is whether the appropriate period for the maturity of a claim is the roll-over period or the time left until the ultimate maturity of the loan. The Bank of England data is mainly presented on a final maturity basis rather than by interest rate commitment period. Hewson (1975) argues that in 'more normal times Eurobanks can realistically consider (say) a 10-year loan with six-month roll-overs as a succession of 26 month loans, especially if a new promissory note is issued at each roll-over date' (Hewson (1975) p. 40). Thus, in Hewson's view, the Banks of England data overstates the extent to which maturity transformation occurs in the market.

This line of argument has three faults. Firstly, the interest rate roll-over period is usually designed to protect the bank from the risk of interest rate changes and does not necessarily allow for the possibility that the deposits funding the loan may be withdrawn. Secondly, the uses to which the borrowers have put funds does not suggest that they anticipate that the banks will call in the loan before the final maturity date of the agreement. This is clear in the case of project funding which is likely to have a much longer gestation period than the usual three–six month roll-over period. Finally, the phrase in 'more normal times' precludes periods where the level of maturity transformation is likely to cause problems. In normal times, refunding of loans is not usually a problem, but when there is a crisis of confidence banks will have difficulty in refunding loans and may at the same time be unable to call them in. It seems therefore that the Bank of England's choice of classifying claims on the basis of the period remaining till final maturity is a more defensible way of allowing an assessment of the problem which maturity transformation could cause.

Several possible methods are available to analyse these statistics. The first method is simply to examine the raw statistics, either comparing the total claims and liabilities in each class or examining the net figures (that is, the difference between liabilities and claims in each class of maturity).

The second method (Johnston (1983), Dennis (1984)) calculates a maturity transformation ratio (TR) for each maturity range;

$$TR = \text{(net position)/(total liabilities + total asssets)}$$

where, total liabilities and assets is the total over all maturity ranges.

Using *net* positions makes it more difficult to determine on which side of the balance sheet any change in maturity transformation has occurred. It is preferable to look at some comparison of liabilities and claims when determining the degree of mismatching.

A third method (Dennis (1984)) calculates the proportion of foreign currency liabilities in any one maturity category that is covered by assets of an equivalent maturity. However Dennis found this method not very sensitive to changes, which the TR method had shown to have occurred.

The final method, and the one to be used here, allows us to examine any changes in the proposition of liabilities or assets in each maturity category and provides a graphic presentation of the degree of maturity transformation at each point in time. This method, used by Hewson (1975), employs a statistical tool – the Lorenz curve – commonly employed to measure income inequality. Whilst it does not allow us to measure the exact quantity of maturity transformation that has taken place, it does make for easy quantitative and visual comparisons through time. The first step is to calculate the percentage of total liabilities and total assets in each maturity class. These percentages are then cumulated. The Lorenz curve plots the cumulated percentages of liabilities in the various maturity classes against the cumulated percentages of claims. If there is a perfect matching of maturities, the plot follows the 45° line. To the extent that it deviates from the 45° line, the banks are engaging in maturity transformation; the greater the deviation, the greater the degree of mismatching. If the plotted curve is below the 45° line, there is positive maturity transformation (that is, banks are borrowing short and lending long); if above, negative.

Whilst the Lorenz curve presents a useful summary measure of the degree of mismatching, it is also useful to look at changes in the percentages of assets and liabilities in each maturity class in order both to confirm our graphic findings and to examine more closely changes which are not clear from the graphs.

6.1.3 Results

We now turn to the statistical results on sections *i)* to *iv)* above. The results are presented in figures 6.1–6.8 and in Appendix II (p. 227). For ease of exposition, I number the maturity categories as follows:

Category I   =   less than eight days
Category II   =   eight days to less than one month
Category III   =   one month to less than three months
Category IV   =   three months to less than six months
Category V   =   six months to less than one year
Category VI   =   one year to less than three years
Category VII   =   three years and over.

i)   General Trends in Mismatching

Figure 6.1 shows the extent to which general maturity transformation occurred for the period 1973 to 1985 in London Eurobanks. Over the whole period maturity transformation increased. The increase was not continuous but occurred in two particular phases. During the first period, 1973–75, the mismatch curve moved out substantially each year. There was then a period from 1975–1982 with little change. This was followed by another increase, although smaller than either of the yearly increases 1973–4 and 1974–5. As table 1 (Appendix II) shows, increased mismatching after 1982–3 reflected a rise in the percentage of total claims in category VII, from 13.3 per cent in 1982 to 16.4 per cent in 1983 and 17.4 per cent in 1985.

ii)   The Interbank Market

To calculate the mismatching curves for interbank claims and liabilities. I have included claims and liabilities of the London-based banks

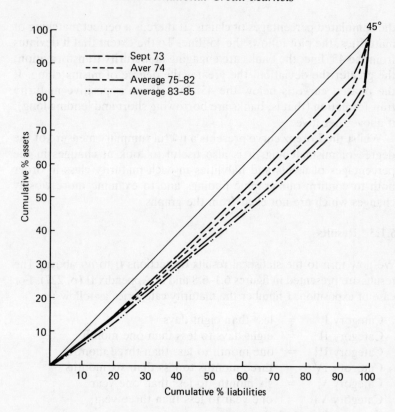

Figure 6.1　Maturity Mismatch Curves, 1973–85 All Banks

not only to each other but also to banks abroad. Thus the problem identified by Johnston (see section 6.1.1) is minimised.

As Figure 6.2 shows, there was little mismatching over the whole period. Before 1977, there was almost none. In 1977 positive mismatching emerged reflecting developments at the shorter end of the maturity spectrum. From 1978–83, there was a slight increase in positive mismatching, affecting almost all maturity classes. Subsequently, mismatching decreased back to 1979 levels. In short, the level of mismatching for interbank transactions by London-based banks has been very low and showed little net change over the period. A gradual increase was followed by a falling off towards the end of the period.

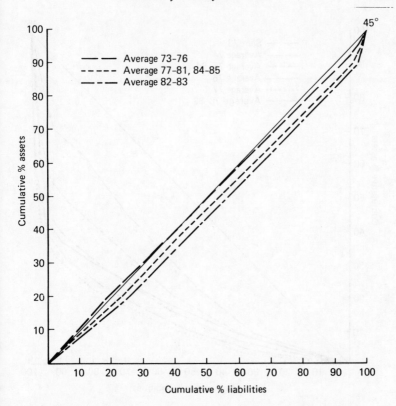

Figure 6.2   Maturity Mismatch Curves, 1973–85 Interbank Market

iii)   Non-bank Claims and Liabilities

In contrast to the interbank market, mismatching of maturities in the London-based Eurobanks' claims on and liabilities to non-banks was positive and substantial throughout the period. As figure 6.3 shows, mismatching increased at a decreasing rate in every year from 1973–77. From 1978, it declined slightly on balance, notably in maturity category I; at the longer end of the maturity scale, it actually rose slightly. Hence the averages for 1979–83 have tended to be pivoted around the 1975 curve.

iv)   Differences Between the Various Country Groupings of Banks

We have noted the changing importance of the different nationalities of London-based banks in an earlier section (6.1.1; Figure 1.2).

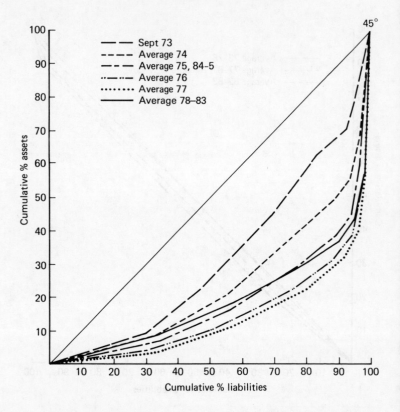

Figure 6.3   Maturity Mismatch Curves, 1973–85 Non-bank Customers

To what extent is each of these categories of banks responsible for maturity transformation?

The British Banks

Figure 6.4 shows the extent of maturity mismatching by British banks during the period 1973–85. These banks have engaged in positive maturity transformation throughout the period 1973–85. Examination of movements in the percentages of total liabilities and of total claims in the different maturity categories sheds light on the fluctuations in mismatching shown in figure 6.4 and table 2 (Appendix II, p. 229). In 1974, there was a general increase in mismatching right across the range of maturities excluding category I. The share of liabilities increased and that of claims declined in the maturity categories I to V; the opposite was true of categories VI and VII. In category VII, the percentage of total claims almost doubled, from 7.5

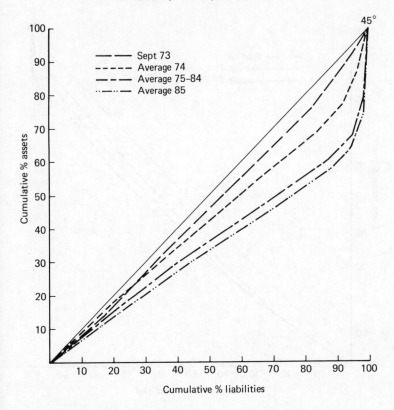

Figure 6.4   Maturity Mismatch Curves, 1973–85 British Banks

per cent in Sept 1973 to 13.9 per cent in 1974. In the years 1975–6 the level of mismatching continued to increase but at a decreasing rate. The percentage of total claims in category VII climbed to over 20 per cent. This is in line with the impact of the rise in the price of oil on mismatching which we discussed in section 6.1.1 above.

From 1977 to 1982, the degree of mismatching remained much the same, decreasing slightly in 1978 and 1981.

In 1983 the second phase of greater positive mismatching began. The percentage of total claims in category VII rose by some 6 per cent to around 26 per cent in 1985. This rise seems attributable to rescheduling in the wake of the international debt crisis.

American Banks
Maturity mismatching by American banks has for the most part been less than by British banks, although it followed a similar pattern of

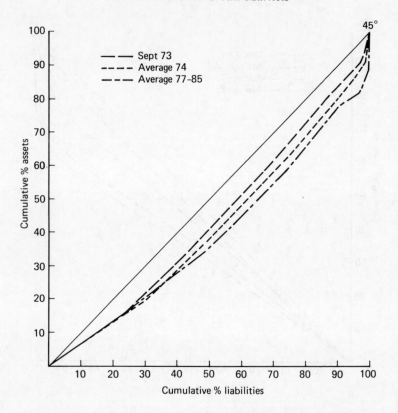

Figure 6.5   Maturity Mismatch Curves, 1973–85 American Banks

fluctuations (see figure 6.5 and table 3). The two periods in which mismatching increased were 1973–5 and 1981–5 as in the case of British banks. This again supports our arguments about the effect of the rise in the price of oil in 1973 and rescheduling after 1982 (see section 6.1.1).

The Japanese Banks

Looking at figure 6.6, it appears that the Japanese banks are the most conservative of all the banks. In the early part of the period, from 1973 to 1977, there was very little maturity transformation. Moreover, unlike the cases of both British and American banks, the degree of mismatching did not increase at all during the period 1973–7. What was notable in this period was the level of claims in category VII; 21 per cent of claims were in this range (see table 4, Appendix II),

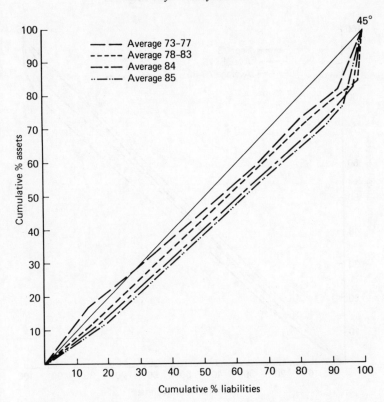

Figure 6.6   Maturity Mismatch Curves, 1973–85 Japanese Banks

much greater than either for the British or for the American banks. However, the percentage of liabilities in category VII was also much greater than the other banks, at around 8 per cent.

In 1978, positive mismatching emerged and this continued at the same level until 1982. In 1983–5, as in the cases of the British and to a lesser extent the American banks, mismatching increased again.

Other Foreign Banks
The changes in mismatching over the period in question for other foreign banks are shown in figure 6.7 and table 5 (Appendix II).

In September 1973, the degree of mismatching was very small. It then increased in 1974 and in 1975 by similar amounts. From 1976–85, there was no change in the level of mismatching and very little change in the percentage of total liabilities/claims in each of the

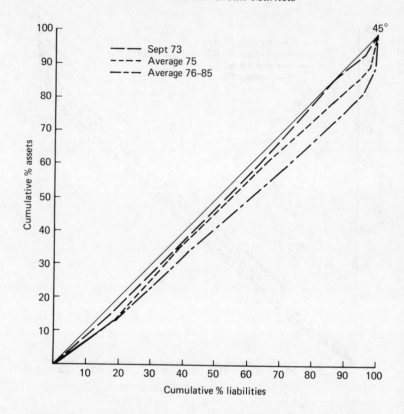

Figure 6.7　Maturity Mismatch Curves, 1973–85 Other Foreign Banks

maturity classes. The stability of the level of mismatching from 1983–5 is in contrast to the other groups of banks examined. We argued in section 6.1.1 that increased mismatching in the period 1983–5 would be expected as a result of a lengthening of loan maturities. The absence of such an increase in the percentage of claims in category VII suggests that the banks in this group have been less involved with the international debt crisis than banks in the other groups.

Consortium Banks

The level of maturity mismatching by consortium banks throughout the whole period is by far the largest of all bank groups (see figure 6.8 and table 6, Appendix II). Moreover, the extent of mismatching increased almost continuously throughout the period under discussion.

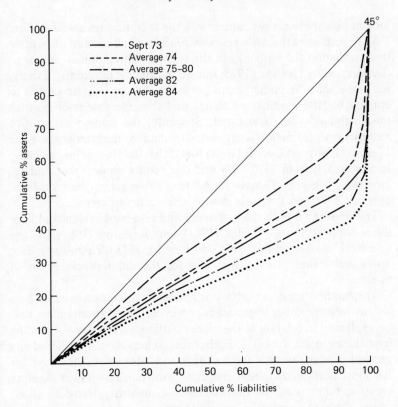

Figure 6.8   Maturity Mismatch Curves, 1973–85 Consortium Banks

Table 6 highlights the large extent to which consortium banks rely on short term funds which they lend out for much longer periods, reflecting their greater dependence on interbank deposits. The percentage of total claims in category VII increased from 17 per cent in September 1973 to 29 per cent in 1975, the largest rise of any group of banks. This reflects a response to the increased demand for medium term funds by deficit countries after the 1974 price rise. As with other groups of banks (except 'other foreign banks') there was an increase in mismatching from 1981 reflecting the increased maturities which accompanied reschedulings.

6.1.4   Analysis of Results

Our data suggests that the London-based Eurobanks have almost always engaged in positive maturity transformation. Let us briefly look at how these results concur with the literature reviewed earlier.

With respect to the early years we found a small amount of positive transformation for all banks in the market. This result is similar to that derived by Hewson (1975) but we interpret it differently. Firstly, we argue that the commitment period is the appropriate period to employ for the maturity of claims and thus the extent of positive mismatching is not overstated. Secondly, the finding of positive maturity transformation is supported by data for the later years. Both Weston (1980) and Dennis (1984) found that the level of mismatching had increased from 1975–1977 and our results support that finding. However, whereas Dennis found that mismatching had declined between 1978 and 1981, our results show little difference.

The finding on both the interbank and non-bank claims and liabilities support those of Ellis (1981) and Johnston (1983) for the interbank market and of Artis and Lewis (1981) for non-bank liabilities and claims. This is true also for the different categories of banks.

The method used to derive our results thus appears broadly consistent with the other approaches surveyed. These results must now be explained in relation to the model outlined in chapter 5.4 and the hypotheses in section 6.1.1. Earlier researchers have not offered any general explanations for the results found. Moreover, they have for the most part been content simply to ascertain how much liquidity creation takes place in the market, via maturity transformation, rather than to assess the potential risk of crisis because of the problem of funding risk.

The suggestions put forward in section 6.1.1, that both the oil price rise of 1973 and subsequent recycling and the reschedulings of 1982–5 should have increased maturity transformation at those times, are supported. Firstly, mismatching was found to have increased substantially from 1973–5 both generally and for all groups of banks with the exception of the Japanese, which can be explained by regulations imposed by the Ministry of Finance (see chapter 1.4). Secondly, the effect of the international debt crisis on mismatching appears to be consistent with our model of chapter 5.4. As crisis conditions are approached banks become more tied into their positions and the authorities forced them to remain involved (see chapter 7). This was seen by the involuntary increases in loan maturities associated with rescheduling. These involuntary increases were the result of the attempt by the authorities to forestall a crisis.

It is interesting to note that the oil price rise of 1979 did not have the same effect on mismatching which remained fairly stable between 1977 and 1982. A possible explanation for this is the greater maturity of the market. There was much less of an increase in competition which was already at a high level in 1979.

Aside from these exogenous influences on the Euromarkets, we can also examine the role played by the internal dynamics of these markets in influencing the level of mismatching. In this respect, the new recycling opportunity attracted many banks into the markets especially at a time when domestic loan demand was somewhat slack (the number of foreign banks in London was growing, see chapter 1.4). Increased numbers of banks and increased competition within international capital markets resulted and banks faced a borrowers' market (Goodman (1980); see note 24). This point was emphasised by bankers during interviews (see Appendix III, p. 239). They felt that competition had been instrumental in increasing mismatching at that time. The reason for the anomalous position of the Japanese banks was the fact that they had been ordered by their Ministry of Finance to withdraw from the market, because of Ministry fears that the market would produce unsound activities (see chapter 1.4, for more details of Japanese supervision throughout the period).

During the period 1977–82, the trend towards increased mismatching halted. This may have occurred because banks became more conservative in the face of increased volatility of interest rates and the high (real) levels of market rates, which would increase the interest rate risk associated with mismatching.

The period under discussion also witnessed two crises of confidence because of bank failures. These were Herstatt and Franklin National in 1974; and Continental Illinois in 1981. The 1974 failures were caused by excessive foreign exchange speculation. Continental Illinois' failure was due to bad US domestic loans. Both precipitated a crisis of confidence and the drying up of interbank funds. But although confidence decreased as a result of these events, mismatching did not appear to be affected and the events proved to be short term setbacks. This is especially true of the first failure; mismatching actually increased, as the underlying factors discussed above played a more dominant role.

In conclusion, it would seem that the factors of competition and involuntary lending which I examined in the informal model in the previous chapter have combined to offer a possible explanation of the movements in mismatching of maturities over the period under consideration.

6.2   THE RISK-RETURN RELATIONSHIP – COUNTRY RISK ASSESSMENT

Most of the risks faced by international banks engaged in lending in the Eurocurrency markets are those associated with lending to countries. The banks' approach to assessing country risk may help to explain movements in spreads which we analyse in section 6.3.

Nagy defines country risk as 'exposure to a loss in cross-border lending, caused by events in a particular country'.[5] Country risk arises when the borrower is unable or unwilling to service its foreign currency loans. Where the borrower is the government of a sovereign nation, country risk is sovereign risk.

Banks are used to dealing with commercial risk in their domestic portfolios, but country risk must be distinguished from this. A default caused by mismanagement of a company is defined as commercial risk; country risk defined similarly is the possibility of default due to government mismanagement of the economy. Within country risk, however, there is the added possibility that the country may be able to repay but has deliberately decided not to. In lending to a company in another country both these elements will be present. Here, however, we are concerned with the banks' ability to deal with country risk and not commercial risk. The events which generate country risk can be of a political, social or economic nature; in the event that they cause debt servicing problems, these problems will be experienced typically by all borrowers in that country.

There is some debate about whether banks should spend the resources required[6] to assess this risk, that is, to assess the extent to which events which lead to debt servicing problems might arise. One body of opinion represented by Haegele (1980) argues that if the international financial market for cross-border loans is nearly perfect, then information will be efficiently and quickly reflected in interest rate spreads. Any individual bank can use the spread to gauge the risk involved in lending to a particular country, so there is no need to engage in costly country analysis. Nagy (1984) argues, in contrast, that the market is not so perfect and thus an individual bank can ensure better performance by investing in country risk analysis.

This argument relies on the existence of imperfections in the financial market. There are, however, two far more powerful arguments for engaging in country risk analysis, which arise from our discussion of the theoretical aspects of international financial markets in the previous chapter. The first is the argument of Grossman and

Stiglitz (1976) that the prices of financial assets will reflect all the relevant information only if costs have been incurred by some market participants to gather that information. That is, if everyone relied on the market spread to determine the risk involved, the market spread would not reflect the risks, because nobody would be engaged in gathering the information. The efficient market hypothesis, when taken to its logical conclusion, thus produces a paradox; hence, there is something lacking in the ability of this approach to explain the behaviour of these markets. The second argument arises from the consequences of credit rationing. If banks are unable to reflect the risk of a loan adequately through the spread, then they will resort to quantitative exposure limits for each borrower in order to manage their exposure to country risk. However, country exposure limits are not published and therefore if a bank seeks to control risk, it is important to engage in country risk analysis to determine its exposure limits.

A fundamental problem of assessing country risk is that of information. Even in the case that the factors most important for assessing country risk are well understood, banks generally find up-to-date published information difficult to come by. The main sources are the IMF, the World Bank, OECD, BIS and UN. These sources became available only after lending had begun, primarily because they are not designed specifically for the banks but rather for the use of the international agency which produces them, mostly to monitor events in the international capital markets. The World Bank, for example, in its debt tables published only government or government guaranteed loans until 1982–3 when it included private debt; the IMF concentrates on its own members and their drawings and borrowings; the BIS includes private as well as government debt, but only that which is reported by banks in the Group of Ten plus Switzerland and some offshore banking centres.

No less important than the information problems is each bank's ability to make effective use of the information that is available. Initially, banks were unprepared for the expansion of cross-border lending. It would appear that they went into country lending without much knowledge of the countries they were financing;

> They [the banks] were, therefore, confronted by a loan demand that was profitable, attractive from a marketing point of view, and yet they were dealing in activities and areas with which they were not familiar. Would they turn away this business, or would they try

to become more acquainted with the necessary information and background to be able to assess and take advantage of this increased market demand?

(Friedman (in Ensor (1981)))

In some prominent cases it was initially thought by banks that sovereign lending was relatively low risk, because of Walter Wriston's celebrated dictum that 'countries cannot go bankrupt'. Countries *can* go bankrupt; but the problem arises that this bankruptcy cannot be treated like commercial bankruptcy because assets cannot be seized in an attempt to recover losses. Why was this exercise in self-delusion allowed to occur and the usual cardinal rule of banking (that is, 'know your customer') ignored? Kettęll and Magnus argue that it was the result of the financial culture at that time; 'the allocation of bank credit was driven primarily by marketing considerations i.e., increased revenues based on an everexpanding volume of loans sold'.[7] This view complements that of Friedman presented in the quote above. Banks, although unprepared for assessing the risks of this new area of banking, could not afford to turn down the opportunity of expansion and had to 'learn-by-doing' the art of country risk assessment.

Initial attempts among those banks who realised a need to assess risk included both in-house analysis and the use of consultants. However, during the 1960s and early 1970s, the lack of information combined with the absence of any systematic framework of country risk analysis, led commonly to the phenomenon of 'headline banking'[8] or a dependence on what was currently fashionable in banking circles – a manifestation of the herd instinct. Whilst this was especially popular with those who had no in-house facilities for assessing risk, it was true even of those who did have the ability and capacity to judge creditworthiness for themselves.[9] This type of banking occurs when sensational headlines immediately have a negative or positive impact on the credit rating of a country, without any analysis of the effect that the event might have on the country's debt servicing capacity. At the extreme, this implies that headlines related to wars, violence, civil unrest, strikes etc would immediately result in a decline in the country's perceived creditworthiness. Discoveries of natural mineral wealth would lead to immediate increases in the perceived creditworthiness, without regard to either the ability of the country to exploit these resources successfully, or the likely volatility of their price (given that most primary commodities suffer from extreme price volatility). There was a tendency therefore for banks to divide events into two kinds – positive or negative, regardless of the particular country involved. There was little recognition that the same event may be a disaster for one country but only a minor inconvenience for another. Events have to be assessed relative to their impact on a particular country.

The developments of syndications allowed herd banking to manifest itself in another way. Those who were ill-informed could free-ride behind the larger banks which they (correctly or otherwise) assessed as being better informed. For example, Ipsen (1983) argues that the US regional banks were guilty of free-riding in the late 1970s when they became heavily involved with the international syndication markets due to declining loan demand at home. The Group of Thirty (1982a) found, in answer to their questionnaires, that whilst 90 per cent of all banks preferred to have an independent risk assessment scheme, 36 per cent of the smaller banks disagreed; they preferred to rely on other banks. In many cases, at least in the early years, the larger banks, although attempting to introduce some form of country risk analysis, were no better informed than some of the smaller banks who were seeking to rely on their judgement. Moreover, the question of exposure limits would still have to be decided by the smaller banks – which implies that they ought to carry out their own risk assessment to enable them to develop a portfolio compatible with their type of bank.

Gradually during the second half of the 1970s, a literature began to emerge dealing with questions of how to ensure a more systematic assessment of country risk. Historically, such assessment began with a description of the country in terms of a few key economic and socio-political indicators; moved on to simple assessment of the country's structural characteristics and past performance; and eventually graduated to attempt at evaluating a country's debt servicing ability. Nagy (in Ensor (1981)) argues that an adequate country risk analysis system should enable a bank to make a distinction between different kinds of risk within each country, and to monitor and predict risk changes. Moreover, in terms of the banks' initial portfolio decisions the analysis should give some indication of risk rating as well as ranking.

The distinction between ranking and rating is of some importance. Ranking is a purely relative procedure, designed to produce a certain limited consistency within the bank's portfolio. Countries are put in order of creditworthiness. Rating is a more absolute form of risk analysis. It is required to determine at what spread the bank is willing to consider lending to each country and how much (that is, the level of its exposure limits). Ranking merely ensures that, for example, country A which is ranked below, say, country B has a greater spread and/or a smaller exposure limit. The ideal system used by each bank is therefore required to judge two questions. With respect to pricing, the system should allow the bank to decide whether the market price is right (that is, the spread and fees) and therefore whether the bank should lend or not. Secondly, where the bank decides to lend, the risk rating along with factors like diversification requirements and market potential determines the exposure limit for each country.

To achieve these aims, we require firstly a picture of the country's resources and how effectively they have been exploited. Physical resources require development programmes in order to ensure they are optimally exploited. Human resources also require organisation and education before they can be effective in contributing to the wealth of the country.[10] Secondly, the government and the quality of its economic and financial management must be assessed. This should allow the bank to determine the ability of the government to react to any exogenous economic crisis and minimise debt servicing problems. Thirdly, possible financial restrictions on the ability to service debt need to be examined. This includes investigation of ratios indicating debt service burden, the balance of payments including composition of imports and exports, the term structure of existing debt and the ability of the country in question to draw on funds from either the IMF or commercial banks at a time of difficulty. Finally, a view may usefully be taken on political factors relating to the stability of the regime and the degree to which any change that may possibly occur will take place in an orderly fashion, without disruption to external commitments. Factors affecting political risk became prominent in the late 1970s and early 1980s, especially after the Iranian crisis. However, some bankers had been arguing earlier that political issues were important; history had shown them to be so (*cf.* for example, the pre-revolutionary debt of Eastern Europe) and there were signs that they would be important in the present climate as new governments were threatening to renege on international agreements on the grounds that they were contracted by a previous regime.[11] By the early 1980s, some banks were incorporating a crude form of political analysis into their country risk analysis systems.[12]

Within the literature we can identify several approaches to assessing country risk which attempt to produce a system approaching the ideal one outlined above. The first approach is that of *judgemental risk rating* where there is little structure to the approach, but a haphazard attempt to produce some idea about a country's rating. There are many problems with this approach, which was widely practised in the early 1970s. Firstly, crucial variables could be omitted. Among variables included, some may be overemphasised and others underemphasised. Secondly, the lack of a structure leads to inconsistencies between different countries' ratings. Nagy (1984) argues that only a very experienced team could make use of this approach and produce results of any value. Moreover, such a team would produce better results using a more structured approach.

The second approach is that of *quantitative risk rating*. At its lowest level of sophistication, this approach includes a checklist of variables, usually ratios, which appear to be intuitively important in analysing a country's ability to repay any loans granted. Customary indicators of this type include domestic savings/GNP (to give some indication of ability to finance long run growth internally), export product concentration (to show vulnerability to export price changes), debt service/value of exports (to indicate the ability to generate foreign exchange to service debt), and imports of non-essential commodities/ total imports (to show ability to cut imports in a crisis). These are in addition to general macro-economic indicators such as growth of GNP, growth of the money supply, inflation etc.

During the early 1970s, these ratios came to be given a weight and combined into a total score for each country on which each country's ranking would be based. However, there was no standard scheme and there was much argument about what indicators should be included and much effort was expended in refining various ratios.[13] There are four problems associated with ratios and the quantitative approach.

i) The first shortcoming of ratios is the question of unquantifiable variables which are important in determining the risk rating of a country. Puz (1977) identifies a variety of non-quantifiable items influencing the cultural, political and social life of a country. Typical ones are the degree of education, stability of the political system, the strength and types of political opponents, the quality of management of the economy and international relations with both the major world powers and countries close to home. Recognition of the importance of such variables led to the adoption of approaches where a quantitative checklist of mainly economic variables was supplemented by qualitative analysis of political and social life within the country – the *quantitative/qualitative* approach.[14]

In many cases these variables (that is, both quantitative and qualitative) are given some weighting and value to produce an index. Whilst such an approach is an improvement on the mainly economic indices that were used initially, the system still suffers from two drawbacks. Firstly, weights were for the most part uniform across countries, whereas in reality each variable would be expected to take on different importance in each country. Secondly, even if it is possible to capture political or social factors in ratios, the interaction between the political and economic factors at a time of crisis certainly cannot be captured in indices or individual ratios. Field (1980) argues that this is one reason why the more qualitative system of risk assessment (without indices), common to the European banks (Field (1980)) is preferable to the strict quantitative systems that tend to dominate the North American banks. Qualitative systems without indices allow for such interactions to be spelled out and included in any risk assessment; but the basis for doing so becomes highly subjective.

ii) The use of quantitative methods and ratios involves a second problem. There is the question of identifying critical or excessive levels of the ratios. History appears to give us little guidance. In the past there were no simple relationships between, for example, individual ratios and debt servicing difficulties.[15] Implicit in many of the banks' analyses is the assumption that if they rank each developing country relative to other developing countries, and pick the top five, six, or whatever, they will produce a portfolio of relatively safe assets. There seems to have been little attempt to question the degree to which developing countries should be in the portfolios of the majority of banks. This is partly the result of the difficulty of defining critical levels for the ratios.

iii) The third problem with ratios and purely quantitative methods of risk assessment is that although ratios give us a clear picture of the past, they are not necessarily the best possible guide to the future. The bank is interested in possible future debt servicing problems; attempts to predict the variables that produce the ratios have tended to be very poor.[16] For example, the debt service/exports ratio is highly sensitive to movements in interest rates. Interest rates in the Euromarkets are greatly influenced by those in the US (see chapter 4.4). Thus, the prediction of future debt servicing problems requires not only the prediction of variables which are endogenous to the country in question but also variables over which the country has no control.

A more sophisticated quantitative approach which attempted to overcome the forecasting problem, whilst at the same time offering (so it claimed) complete objectivity, is the *econometric approach*, pioneered by Frank and Cline (1971) and further developed by Feder and Just (1977). This attempts to identify factors that were important in explaining reschedulings from 1957 onwards with the help of various econometric techniques. For example, Frank and Cline (1971) using discriminant analysis found that two key variables were the debt service ratio and the average maturity of existing debt. The debt service ratio (that is, the debt service to exports ratio) is included because debts are serviced either out of export earnings or out of foreign exchange reserves. A high ratio is thus indicative of a higher risk of default because the burden on the country's resources is greater. Similarly, if the average maturity of existing debt is high, the risk of default is higher because the debt service burden cannot be alleviated in the short run by reducing the amount of borrowing. However, it could be argued that debt is more likely to be repaid if a realistic maturity is associated with a loan. Thus it may be desirable to have a longer average maturity of debt if loans are for development purposes.

Feder and Just (1977), using possibly a more powerful econometric technique (logit analysis), extended the number of key variables which affected debt servicing capacity to six – namely the two identified by Frank and Cline plus the imports/reserves ratio, export growth, per capita income and capital inflows/debt service. The imports to reserves ratio indicates the ability of the country to cope with foreign exchange earnings fluctuations through a relative measure of reserves. The growth of exports and per capita income provide an indication of the resources that will be available for repayment. Finally, higher capital inflows are associated with lower default probability because they represent a source of foreign exchange reserves. The inflows/debt service ratio captures this. Once the key variables have been identified, they can be incorporated into an econometric forecasting model. Statistics can then be collected and predictions for the key variables computed. The weights given to each variable are produced by the model (the coefficients) and hence the problem of subjectivity is supposedly eliminated.

Whilst such models are appealing and were widely used in the late

1970s by the larger banks, they do suffer from a number of problems. Firstly, they exclude the unquantifiable variables which have already been identified as being important in the determination of debt servicing problems. Secondly, they suffer from the problem of all econometric forecasting models, namely that future predictions are made using coefficients derived from past relationships. Structural and exogenous institutional changes result in changes in the coefficients and the model becomes increasingly inaccurate as a forecasting tool. This was found by those who invested heavily in this method.

iv)   The final problem which a purely quantitative approach and also a mixed quantitative/qualitative approach face is that within the same country different risk levels could exist dependent on the maturity of the loan, the type of borrower, and the purpose of the loan. Thus assigning only one risk level to each country is misleading. Uncertainty tends to increase with maturity, so unless there exist present circumstances which preclude lending short term but are expected to clear up over the longer term, loans with longer maturities are riskier. As regards the type of borrower, the government is generally a better risk than the private sector because there is no transfer risk. Exchange controls, for example, do not apply to governments. Within the private sector, banks may be better risks than non-banks. In some countries banks can count on the assistance of the central bank if they get into trouble. Also interbank loans tend to be for a shorter period than non-bank private sector loans, and this may facilitate withdrawal if signs of trouble appear.[17] Finally, the purpose to which the loan is put is important.

The following risk categories can be identified in theory, if not always in practice (in descending order of risk); budget finance to governments to finance current consumption, balance of payments financing, development financing, project financing. Within project financing a project that generates foreign exchange earnings is a better risk than one which improves the infrastructure of the economy and the productive capacity designed to serve the domestic economy. Quantitative methods of risk analysis do not allow such discrimination between economic sectors. The bank has to approach all sectors within one country as if they were rated according to its overall perception of the country's risk rating and there is no room for selectivity. In practice, cross-default clauses in all government guaranteed loans of the 1970s and 1980s reduced the need for banks to discriminate between different risks within a particular country.

Quantitative approaches do not exclude judgemental factors. In determining an index for one country, there is a need to take judgemental decisions with regard to the weighting of factors which make up the index. As already mentioned, the implicit assumptions in the econometric forecasting model that the weights are constant over time is a subjective judgement. So subjective assessment should enter into the purely quantitative approaches too.

Whilst most banks presently use a qualitative/quantitative approach, this is by no means ideal. Nagy (1984) argues that the *structured qualitative* method is the most comprehensive. This method is based on recognition that risk comprises two components: the size of the loss and the probability of its occurrence. The system produces a risk rating which is the probability of a certain kind of debt difficulty occurring during a period, weighted by the size of the potential loss. Different probabilities can be attached both to the different types of borrower, loan etc and to the different types of debt servicing difficulties for example, rescheduling, a moratorium and a technical default. Moreover, the size of the loss varies according to when the risk occurs (that is, how many payments have already been collected).

To conclude this section with a historical résumé:[18] the banks in the early 1970s employed a purely judgemental approach to risk assessment, lacking in structure and highly subjective. Recognition of this brought a swing towards quantitative approaches – either use of ratios or the econometric forecasting model – in the later 1970s. However, these approaches excluded a lot of valuable non-quantifiable data and so banks began to reincorporate qualitative variables into their quantitative analysis. This is the technique most widely used today. For example, the Group of Thirty found that a majority of respondents to their questionnaires now had a system of risk analysis where 'political and social conditions carried the greatest weight . . . followed by quantitative analysis of economic data'.[19]

What does all this imply for movements in the risk-return relationship and exposure limits? The historical approach to looking at country risk analysis has shown us how underdeveloped the approach was both academically and practically. In the early 1970s, the question of how to assess country risk was only beginning to be raised, yet lending to developing countries had already begun and was growing at a phenomenal rate. Evidently, bankers did not want to think about what they did not know how to tackle properly. They therefore relied on the idea of sovereign borrowers being low risk and the fact that they (the banks) were all in the same boat (the herd instinct). Improvements in the banks' approaches to risk assessment were only just beginning to be incorporated when the debt crisis emerged. Once these problems were evident, banks resorted to headline banking once more. Some, such as the merchant banks, got out as quickly as they could.[20] The majority were tied into the markets and had limited room for manoeuvre. Why did the banks not ensure that they were prepared for complex analysis when history had proved that lending to countries was risky (*cf.* the 1930s) and required careful analysis? A partial answer lies in the fact that the 1970s generation of bankers had no historical perspective in which to think about the question of lending to countries. Banks were therefore not used to assessing medium term loans which involved sovereign risk.

If credit rating and ranking systems became better over the period in question, then one would expect spreads and certainly the dispersion of spreads to have increased. In addition, given the importance of credit rationing, exposure limits should have decreased over the period 1970–1986. Four factors may help to explain why this may not have occurred. Firstly, given the extent of banks' existing commitments, there was little room to introduce these improvements in risk assessment because there was little new lending. Banks could only conclude that they should not have lent as much in the first place. Secondly, the analysis was not fully implemented in practice. Thirdly, there was much competition within the markets and the resulting borrowers' market which appeared after mid-1977 (see section 6.3.1) made it very difficult for a bank to impose higher spreads on the market. Fourthly, spreads and exposure limits are influenced greatly by confidence which varies over the 'financial cycle'. The subjective factors implicit in all of the approaches will also vary over the cycle. Improvements came when confidence was at a high level and were therefore less likely to affect spreads and exposure limits. We examine these influences on spreads in the next section.

6.3 EMPIRICAL INVESTIGATION OF THE RISK – RETURN RELATIONSHIP

6.3.1 Hypotheses and Existing Literature

I now turn to the specific hypotheses which are to be tested in sections 6.3.2 to 6.3.4 below and examine the existing literature on the topic. I focus on movements in spreads as a measure of returns and seek to determine whether these movements can be explained in a manner consistent with the model presented in chapter 5. Here we determine whether spreads are a good measure of the relative return within the market.

A bank's return on a loan is determined by two sets of factors: the elements which comprise the price of the loan and the cost of funds. The price of the loan consists of the interest rate, the spread and fees. The question of interest rate determination in the Euromarkets is complex and we touched on it briefly in section 1. There we argued that the Eurodollar rate is influenced by US domestic policy. Non-dollar Eurocurrency interest rates are institutionally determined with reference to the Eurodollar rate. Therefore, for the purposes of this section, a good first approximation is that Euromarket interest rates are exogenously determined by the economic system and economic policy. Here we focus on spreads and fees and attempt to highlight the factors which have influenced them.

If interest rates in the Euromarket are determined by exogenous factors along with the demand for and supply of funds within the syndicated credit market, then we can argue that spreads and fees represent the price of the intermediary services offered by the Euro-banks (balancing the demand for and supply of these services). The price includes administration costs, the opportunity cost of syndicated lending (that is, the return that could be achieved in another market for the given level of risk) and a risk premium (either positive or negative depending on the relative riskiness of Euromarket lending).[21]

The cost of funds is the second factor which determines the bank's return. If, for example, spreads and fees have remained constant, yet the cost of funds has been decreasing, then spreads and fees are not a good measure of the relative return which would have increased in this example. A crucial assumption of the following analysis which uses spreads and fees to measure relative returns is that the cost of funds has not decreased over time. Evidence on the appropriateness of this assumption is difficult to come by. Revell (1980, p. 53) in his study of costs and margins in banking argues that it is difficult to identify the cost of funds associated with any type of bank business. In interviews with bankers (see Appendix III, p. 238), it was clear that at any point in time smaller banks had to pay more than LIBOR for funds, whilst larger banks could attract funds at a rate below LIBOR. However, there was no evidence of a systematic decrease in the cost of funds over the period 1977–86 for any group of banks. Moreover, the syndications departments of banks usually use LIBOR as a measure of the cost of funds irrespective of whether the Treasury has acquired funds for less. Loans granted by the syndication department are therefore made on the assumption that LIBOR is the cost of funds. Thus whilst we cannot be completely confident that the cost of funds has not systematically influenced the return on syndicated lending, it seems reasonable to work with this assumption.

Given these two assumptions – that the interest rate is exogenously determined and that the cost of funds has not systematically decreased over the period 1977–86 – interest rate spreads plus fees can be taken as a good indication of a bank's relative return on syndicated loans. To determine whether spreads alone (on which there is more data) are a good measure of returns, the relationship between spreads and fees is examined in the next section (6.3.2). If movements in fees compensate for movements in spreads (that is, there is an inverse relationship) then both must be considered in any analysis of relative return. Fleming and Howson (1980) find that fees tend to move with spreads, implying that spreads alone are a good indicator of the relative return in the market from different categories of borrowers.

We can identify four factors which determine the price of the intermediation services (that is, spreads and fees) offered by banks.
i)   The interest rate may play a role in determining spreads and fees. Literature on this question offers two explanations of why interest rates may influence spreads. Goodman (1980) and Fleming and Howson (1980) argue that interest rate *levels* are important in determining movements in spreads. When interest rates are relatively high, spreads tend for two reasons to be low. Firstly, given that banks are expected to equate the marginal cost of all sources of funds, and given that in periods of high interest rates the opportunity cost of reserve ratios is higher than in periods of lower interest rates, we expect more funds to move from domestic financial markets to the Euromarkets, where there is no requirement to hold reserves. Given the demand for funds from the Euromarkets, this will tend to reduce spreads. Secondly, when nominal interest rates rise, the marginal (nominal) rate of return on capital rises as less profitable projects get dropped. If the banks wish to maintain a given rate of return, so spreads may fall. Why should the banks seek to maintain a constant nominal rate of return on capital? Neither of the authors offer an

explanation. A possibility is that the bank sees its rate of return on capital as a constraint in its attempt to maximise other factors such as market share. It thus attempts to reduce spreads to become more competitive in the market whilst still attaining its rate of return on capital constraint.

Secondly, greater *volatility* in interest rates might be expected to increase the spreads on loans because the roll-over period of assets (usually six months) is not perfectly matched with the roll-over periods of liabilities (which vary from overnight to greater than six months). In so far as greater volatility of interest rates increases the risk associated with this mismatching, so the spread would be expected to increase.

How do the abovementioned determinants of spreads fit into the view expressed above that the spread and fees represent the price of intermediation in the Euromarket? The volatility of interest rates and the maturity of the loan represent different aspects of the risk of the loan. The level of interest rates is not so easily integrated. Evidence is somewhat ambiguous. Goodman's empirical work suggested that a 1 per cent increase in LIBOR leads to a 0.07 per cent decrease in spreads.[22] Fleming and Howson (1980) found that the three-month Eurodollar rate was not significant in *explaining* spread movements,[23] although the two variables did have an inverse relationship.

ii) The price of the intermediation services might be expected to include a risk premium to distinguish between the risk of different borrowers in the market. Previous research on the relationship between risk and return has concentrated on determining whether various factors indicative of a borrower's risk category are important determinants of spreads. Fleming and Howson (1980) found that a country's reserve adequacy was a good predictor of spreads. Sargen (1976) found that per capita income, the debt service ratio and the rate of inflation were all significant explanatory variables. Angelini *et al* (1979) maintained that different explanatory variables were significant in the two quarters which they analysed. In the second quarter of 1975, export growth, the growth of per capita GNP and the ratio of GNP to external debt appeared to explain spreads. In the fourth quarter of 1976 the debt service ratio and the ratio of imports to reserves were significant. The authors offer no explanations for the changes in significance of the variables. Their results may point to some inconsistency in the method of risk analysis practised by the banks. Indeed, a problem with this whole method is that over time banks may have altered their approaches to country risk. Further-more, at any one point in time there is considerable variety among the banks in their approach to assessment, which this method does not capture.

If banks are assessing risk well and spreads are a good indicator of risk, then we might expect spreads to increase prior to a crisis. If however, spreads increase only after the crisis has struck, then this is suggestive of headline banking, and an inability to assess risk correctly. These competing hypotheses are examined in section 6.3.4. Section 6.2 has already provided some evidence on the role of risk in determining spreads. It concluded that country risk assessment was poor. This suggests that risk played little role in determining spreads.

We argued in chapter 5 that banks may seek to control risk through credit rationing because the price mechanism was unable to adequately reflect risk differences between borrowers. Section 6.3.5 examines the role that credit rationing has played in controlling risk.

iii) The third factor which may determine spreads and fees is the competitive structure of the syndicated credit market. In chapter 5 we argued that increased competition between banks supplying Euroloans is likely to produce a deterioration in the risk-return relationship. Whilst spreads have been shown to move cyclically,[24] a long term downward trend is consistent with this hypothesis. Moreover, the range of spreads and fees between low and high risk country groups might also be expected to decrease when competition is particularly intense.

There is some support for this hypothesis from market commentators.[25] They argue that competition between banks has resulted in spreads which no longer reflect the risk of syndicated lending.

iv) The final factors important for the determination of spreads and fees are shocks to the market. The period under examination (1977–86) may be divided into two main subperiods with the international debt crisis in 1982 as the watershed. In the pre-1982 period, the market was functioning freely without regulatory intervention. In the post-1982 period, the effect of the international debt crisis and the various initiatives presented, should have exerted an important influence on spreads and maturities. Two other events might also have been expected to influence spreads and maturities – the 1979 oil price rise and the Polish debt crisis of 1980–81.

There have been no attempts to examine the influence of these events on spreads and fees. Section 6.3.4 seeks to do this.

6.3.2　The Spreads – Fees Relationship

In order to examine our hypotheses, we need to ascertain the importance of fees in the total return. If spreads are to be a satisfactory
indicator of relative returns in the market, then we require either that
fees vary directly with spreads or that there be no relationship
between the two. If, on the other hand, fees vary inversely with
spreads, then spreads alone will not indicate the relative return in the
market. Spreads alone may indicate an improvement in conditions
for the borrowers, but fees could be increasing such that the overall
return to the bank remained the same.

It is important to examine the relationship both cross-sectionally
and over time. Looking first at the time-series, it is useful to distinguish three possible scenarios. Firstly, fees may vary inversely with
spreads and movements in them may be explained by movements in
spreads. A possible explanation for this would be that borrowers like
to be seen to be obtaining a good (that is, low) spread, because this
acts as an important indicator of risk to other banks in the market and
puts pressure on them to offer similar terms. Thus the borrower may
be willing to pay increased fees, which are not usually advertised, to
enable the bank to offer a lower spread. This is a cosmetic exercise to
attempt to fool other banks into lowering spreads. If the other banks
also insist on increased fees in return, the exercise is fruitless.
However, such practice implies spreads are no longer a good indicator of relative returns in the market. We would have to include fees
in the analysis, which would severely restrict the sample available.[27]

The second possible scenario is that fees vary directly with spreads,
with both being determined by market conditions (that is, by the
supply of and demand for intermediation services, risk etc – see
section 6.3.1). In such a case, we would expect to find a positive
correlation between the two variables. This scenario has less of an
effect on our proposed methodology; movements in spreads would
still indicate movements in relative returns, although in the case that
spreads are decreasing, the absolute return will be decreasing by an
even greater amount and vice versa.

The third possibility is that movements in fees are unrelated to
movements in spreads. In this case, fees are clearly not determined
by risk considerations, but by some other factor. In the interviews
conducted (see Appendix III, p. 238), one suggestion made was that
fees tend to cover administration costs and as such may come under

some pressure from competition between banks for the supply of intermediation services, but are unrelated to changes in the assessed risk of borrowers over time.

These three scenarios may also occur cross-sectionally. An inverse relationship would indicate that countries considered a higher risk at any point in time would prefer to have much of that risk reflected in the fee, in order that the spread remain attractive. A positive relationship would imply that the absolute return is underestimated when spreads are rising and overestimated when they are falling. Such a situation could be explained in two ways. Firstly, fees could reflect administration costs, with those costs being higher for higher spread groups of countries because risk assessment in their case is more difficult. Secondly, fees might include some risk assessment element, such that high risk countries pay not only greater spreads but also greater fees.

Methodology

The World Bank has published data on spreads, maturities, volume and, where available, fees for the period 1978 till the first half of 1981.[28] Whilst it is possible to disaggregate the data into observations for each month, it has been left in its published quarterly form, in order that a reasonable number of observations for each time period could be obtained.

Several different kinds of fees are received by banks in the syndicate. The World Bank distinguishes four types:

i) The management fees, paid to the bank (occasionally banks) acting as lead manager (or co-managers);

ii) the commitment fee, which is charged at an annual percentage rate on the undrawn proportion of the loan, compensating the banks for keeping the funds available;

iii) participation fees, paid to each member of the syndicate. These have several levels, dependent on the extent of the participation. For the purposes of this analysis an average of these levels was taken to be the participation fee for each loan. This did not appear to bias the sample;

iv) other fees, which include the agents' fees for administrating the loan annually.

Analysis is undertaken using not only these four categories of fees, but also the total percentage fee on each loan. This total does not relate to any sum that a bank in the syndicate would actually receive. That amount depends on the nature of each bank's participation in the loan. The total, however, should give us some indication of the way in which fees vary with spreads both over time and at any point in time.

The observations of spreads are confined to loans where the spread is quoted over LIBOR and to loans where data for fees is present.

With respect to the time-series relationship, country data was divided into five groups – OECD major (the Group of Five), OECD minor (other OECD countries), oil importing developing countries, oil exporting developing countries and centrally planned economies. These five groups form the basis for our analysis of spreads in section 6.3.4. We discuss them in more detail there. For each group the average spread and the average of each type of fee as well as total fees were calculated quarterly over the period 1978–I to 1981–II. Correlation coefficients between fees and spreads were then calculated together with the following regressions, one for each country group;

$$Yit = b0 + b1(Xit) + eit$$

where:

Yit = the average fee for group i in period t
Xit = the average spread for group i in period t
$b0, b1$ = the regression coefficients
eit = the error term for group i in period t.

This regression presupposes that fees are dependent on spreads.

For the cross-sectional relationship correlation coefficients and a regression equation were again used. For each quarter, we examine the relationship between total fees and spreads. The regression equation for each quarter is of the form;

$$Yt = b0 + b1(Xt) + et$$

where:

Yt = the total fees in period t
Xt = the spread in period t
$b0, b1$ = the regression coefficients
et = the error term.

The number of observations varied between quarters, depending on the number of loans with published fees and spreads. The equation likewise postulates that the fees are dependent on the spreads.

Results and Analysis
A   Time-Series Analysis
The results of the time-series analysis are generally statistically insignificant and show great instability. No significant relationship between

spreads and total fees was identified either for all countries taken together or for each of the individual groups of countries. In addition, there would appear to be no *a priori* reason why the correlations between spreads and fees for each of the groups of countries should have different signs; yet three out of the five groups (OECD minor, oil importing developing and oil exporting developing) show a negative correlation between spreads and fees, whilst the other two (OECD major and centrally planned economies) show a positive correlation. The correlations and regressions between the individual fee categories and spreads exhibit a similar degree of instability and insignifance except in the case of the commitment fee. This tends to vary positively with spreads over all country groupings and is statistically significant in three out of the five (OECD major, OECD minor and oil importing developing).

We are thus driven to reject the hypotheses that argue for either a positive or a negative relationship between fees and spreads and accept (at least provisionally) that there is no systematic relationship.

B. Cross-sectional analysis

Tables 6.1 and 6.2 show the results of the cross-sectional analysis.

The correlation coefficients indicate a small positive relationship between fees and spreads. This is confirmed by the regression analysis ($b1$ is always positive). However, this relationship is neither stable nor always statistically significant at the 5 per cent level. It is significant in seven out of the 13 quarters.

These findings, enable us tentatively to reject the hypothesis that fees are inversely related to spreads. Indeed the regression analysis suggests that fees are not strongly dependent on spreads either directly or inversely. Movements in fees are rather poorly explained by movements in spreads, as the R^2 in particular indicate. There is just the hint of a positive relationship between spreads and fees. Without more comprehensive statistics on fees, we can go no further.

In terms of our attempt to assess the risk-return relationship in the medium term Eurocurrency market, fees may contain some element of risk premium such that the variation of returns is higher than would be indicated by the variation in spreads alone. We may be reasonably confident, however, that at any point in time, observed differences in spreads will reflect differences in relative return to the banks from the loans in question. If a country has a lower spread then it will also give a lower return; the fees will not be higher to compensate.

Table 6.1 Correlation Coefficients (*r*)

Quarter	r	Quarter	r
1978(1)	0.181	1980(1)	0.149
1978(2)	0.449	1980(2)	0.230
1978(3)	0.448	1980(3)	0.312
1978(4)	0.251	1980(4)	0.159
1979(1)	0.306	1981(1)	0.354
1979(2)	0.306	1981(2)	0.502
1979(4)	0.092		

Table 6.2 Regression Results

Quarter	Regression Equation		
1978(1)	Y = 0.360 + 0.183X	$R^2 = 0.033$	
1978(2)	Y = −0.055 + 0.431X	$R^2 = 0.202$	*
1978(3)	Y = 0.317 + 0.422X	$R^2 = 0.201$	*
1978(4)	Y = 0.317 + 0.422X	$R^2 = 0.063$	
1979(1)	Y = 0.092 + 0.484X	$R^2 = 0.094$	*
1979(2)	Y = 0.219 + 0.563X	$R^2 = 0.094$	*
1979(4)	Y = 0.627 + 0.138X	$R^2 = 0.008$	
1980(1)	Y = 0.439 + 0.178X	$R^2 = 0.022$	
1980(2)	Y = 0.480 + 0.274X	$R^2 = 0.053$	
1980(3)	Y = 0.345 + 0.480X	$R^2 = 0.097$	*
1980(4)	Y = 0.657 + 0.222X	$R^2 = 0.025$	
1981(1)	Y = 0.433 + 0.372X	$R^2 = 0.125$	*
1981(2)	Y = 0.172 + 0.635X	$R^2 = 0.252$	*

* = $b1$ significant at 5 per cent level.

C. Conclusion

These results suggest that we are able to go ahead with our analysis of movements in spreads as indicators of the risk premium in the market. Fees do not on the evidence appear to be systematically over time related to spreads. It appears that fees are not determined by considerations such as the supply and demand for intermediation services, risk etc. The idea that fees reflect administration costs appears to have some support. The slightly positive cross-sectional relationship between fees and spreads may conceivably indicate that those countries which tend to be high risk also tend to be more costly to evaluate than lower risk countries. This conclusion can only be tentative, however, especially in view of the lack of comprehensive data on fees.

Nevertheless we have some grounds for not feeling compelled to include fees in our analysis of the risk-return relationship in the market. An analysis of movements in spreads should be sufficient.

6.3.3 Spreads – Data and Methodology

Leaving fees aside, we focus on interest rate spreads and loan maturities. Extensive data is available on this aspect and was gathered from the *Amex Euromoney Syndication Guide* and the World Bank publication, *Lending in International Capital Markets*. Monthly data from 1977 and July 1981 to December 1986 was drawn from the Amex source. The World Bank was used for data from 1978 to June 1981. The reason why data was drawn from the Amex Guide after June 1981 was that the World Bank ceased its publication. These sources are not a totally comprehensive guide to Eurocredits because not all Eurocredits are published. FRN issues are also included in the Amex guide and I have retained them here.[29]

An observation was included in the sample if it had a value for both the spread over LIBOR and the maturity. Since 1980, the use of LIBOR as a base for the loan has decreased. Borrowing over US prime became more popular (Curtin (1981)). For the lender it was generally more profitable and attracted the US regional banks into the market, whose cost of funds is usually better represented by US prime. The borrowers gained (or were thought to gain) from lower published spreads because the published spread was thought to have cosmetic value (see Appendix III, p. 237, for confirmation of this view in interviews with various bankers).

The data was published by country for the majority of the period. Where it was not, it was published according to borrower and each borrower was therefore assigned to its country. This allowed us to divide the data into the same five groups of countries as before, representing crude risk categories:

i) Major OECD countries, which comprises the Group of Five (US, UK, West Germany, Japan and France);

ii) minor OECD countries, which include all OECD countries except for the Group of Five;

iii) oil importing developing countries;

iv) oil exporting developing countries (including OPEC countries);

v) centrally planned economies (Eastern European countries plus China and Cuba).

The major OECD category represents the prime risk category. It was felt necessary to divide OECD countries into two groups as some of these countries, especially the Mediterranean countries, were being offered spreads considerably above those of the prime risks. The minor OECD category includes some countries which arguably belong in the prime risk category, such as the Scandinavian countries, but it was not clear where the line should be drawn and thus the separation of the Group of Five appeared reasonable.

Developing countries have been divided into two groups depending on whether they are considered to be major oil producers or not. Countries with substantial oil reserves, who were oil exporters, were thought by the banks to be good risks firstly, because the price of oil in the 1970s was high, thus producing foreign exchange for the exporting country; and secondly, because oil exporters did not experience the balance of payments deficits which oil importers did in 1974 and 1979. The debt service capacity of these countries appeared to increase as their trade surplus grew. Debt accumulation was therefore encouraged (Allsopp and Joshi (1986), p. xi). In view, however, of later debt servicing difficulties of Mexico, Algeria and Venezuela, for example, the banks' confidence in this group of countries was misguided.

The final group is that of the centrally planned economies which were quite prominent in the market until the Polish crisis of 1980–81.

Goodman (1980) and Howcroft and Solomon (1985) argue that spreads are influenced by the maturity of the loan. A longer maturity is associated with a greater spread because loans with larger maturities are more risky. If at any point in time a borrower has to pay a larger spread because he/she requires a longer maturity, then average spreads could differ across time because of maturity differences rather than underlying differences in risk assessment.

In order to remove any bias in the data arising from a cross-sectional relationship between spreads and maturities, the spreads were weighted by maturity. The weighted average for each group of countries for each month can be defined as;

$$aver(Sit) = \sum_j (Sjt.Mjt) / \sum_j Mjt$$

where:
$aver(Sit)$ = the average spread of group i in month t
Sjt = spreads of observation j in month t (where observation j is from a country in group i);

Mjt = maturities of observation *j* in month *t*.

In the case of individual loans with a split spread (the first four years may be at *x* per cent above LIBOR whilst the last four years are at *y* per cent above LIBOR), a weighted average spread was taken as the observation for that loan.

The spread varies not only between countries but also between loans to any country. As we argued in section 6.2, there is a hierarchy of risks from the lowest risk – loans to government for project purposes – to the highest – loans to private companies. As we are taking the average of all acceptable loan observations without division into these risk categories, we are implicitly assuming that each monthly average observation is not biased because of the predominance of any one type of loan.

The average spreads and maturities were calculated for the following categories:

i) The quarterly weighted average spread and the quarterly average maturity *for all countries* for the period 1977 to 1986 allow us to get a general picture of the movement in spreads and maturities over the period.

ii) The three-monthly moving averages for spreads (used to smooth monthly fluctuations) for *each country group* for the period 1977 to 1986 allow comparisons of potentially different risk groups to be made.

iii) The monthly weighted average spreads for individual countries who are among *the top debtors* of the developing countries allow further insight into the effect of the 1982 crisis on individual countries. This will enable us to determine the extent to which spreads anticipated the debt servicing problems which most of these countries now face.

6.3.4 Results of the Risk-Return Analysis

The trend in average quarterly spreads over all countries was generally downward over the whole period 1977–1986 (see figure 6.9). The downward trend was especially pronounced from 1977 until the middle of 1980, when spreads decreased from an average of over 1.5 per cent to around 0.8 per cent. Towards the end of 1982, they increased sharply to around 1.1 per cent. After 1982, the downward trend resumed with spreads falling to below 0.5 per cent. The years 1982 to 1984 were marked by much volatility, even in the quarterly averages.

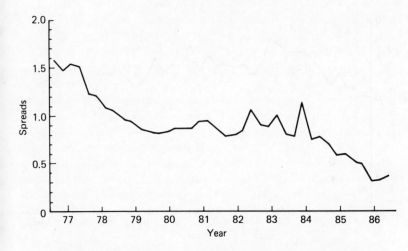

Figure 6.9   All Groups – Quarterly Average Spread, 1977–86

Movements in the average quarterly maturities tended to mirror changes in spreads although not to the same extent as they had done from 1972–77.[30] It is to be expected that movements in maturities mirror movements in spreads because the market tends to move in cycles from a borrowers' market to a lenders' market. Borrowers' markets are associated with low spreads and long maturities and *vice versa* for lenders' markets. Maturities increased from six years at the beginning of 1977 to nine years at the end of 1979. Since 1980, there has been a slight downward trend to an average of 7.5 years in 1982 and just under seven years thereafter.

The main events of the period which would be expected to have an effect on maturities and spreads are the oil price rise, in 1979, the Polish debt problems of 1980 and the Mexican and Brazilian crises of 1982 which developed into a more general crises with some 30 developing and Eastern European countries having to reschedule between 1982 and 1986. The aftermath of the 1979 oil price rise differed in several ways from that of 1973–4. In 1973–4, not only did demand for funds from the market for balance of payments financing increase, but the supply of funds to the market were less than they might have been because of the crisis of confidence in the market after the collapse of Herstatt in 1974. The fact that spreads rose at that time was therefore not surprising.[31] In 1979, however, there were different factors at work. The BIS (1980) argued that three main supply-side factors help to account for the continuing borrowers'

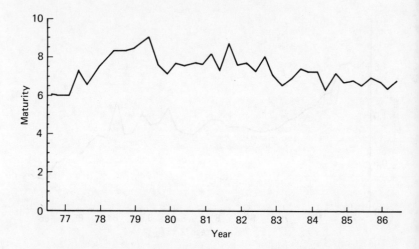

Figure 6.9a   All Groups – Quarterly Average Maturities, 1977–86

market. Firstly, the OPEC surplus resulted in oil exporting countries' deposits rising from $6 billion in 1978 to $38 billion in 1979. Secondly, rising interest rates in national markets increased the competitive advantage of the Euromarket as the real cost of holding reserve requirements in national markets increased. Thirdly, banks were still eager to expand their international business. The resulting intense competition between banks together with no shortage of liquidity ensured the continuance of a borrowers' market.

The Polish debt problems became evident in 1980 and rescheduling first took place in 1981. The downward trend in average spreads was halted at this time. This event may account for this pattern. We shall examine this event in greater detail when we look at the group of centrally planned economies to determine whether spreads among this group of countries anticipated the problems.

The other event which we might expect to be reflected in spreads is the international debt crisis of 1982 which was first reflected in the inability of Mexico and, shortly afterwards, Brazil to continue to service their debt. The subsequent spreading and proliferation of debt servicing difficulties has pointed to some fundamental problems in the international lending markets. However, spreads increased only slightly to 1.0 per cent on average during 1983 and 1984. By the middle of 1984, it appeared that spreads were decreasing again. What is noticeable about the period 1982 to 1984 is the increased volatility of spreads, perhaps reflecting increased uncertainty.

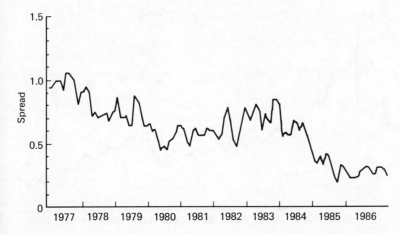

Figure 6.10   OECD Major – 3-monthly Moving Average Spread, 1977–86

We now look in more detail at these results, examining the three-monthly moving average spread for each group of countries. The OECD major group (see figure 6.10) of countries represents the prime risk spread. The cyclical tendency of this group of countries followed the average, but to a lesser extent. Spreads decreased throughout 1977 to the middle of 1980, falling from about 1.0 per cent to just over 0.4 per cent. From the middle of 1980 to the middle of 1982 spreads averaged around 0.55 per cent. By the end of 1982 they had increased slightly again to 0.7 per cent where they remained through 1983. In 1985–86, they fell to just over 0.2 per cent. It appears, therefore, that the debt crisis did affect even this group of countries (the prime risk group) initially. This provides further support for the view that, although confined to developing countries and Eastern Europe, the debt crisis affected confidence in the market as a whole.

The trends in spreads of the other groups of countries can be examined either on their own or in terms of the deviations from the prime risk group. Figure 6.11 shows the time-series profile for the OECD minor countries. Spreads for this group decreased steadily from 1977 until the end of 1982, from 1.5 per cent to just over 0.4 per cent. The rate of decrease slowed at the same time as the 1979 oil price rise. The debt crisis of late 1982 again appears to have had an effect, causing spreads to increase to 0.7 per cent in the first two quarters of 1983, before resuming their downward trend in 1984.

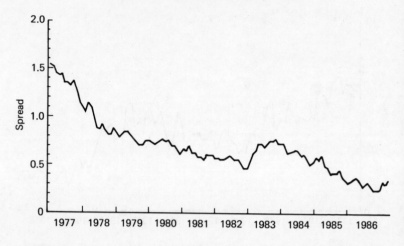

Figure 6.11   OECD Minor – 3-monthly Moving Average Spread, 1977–86

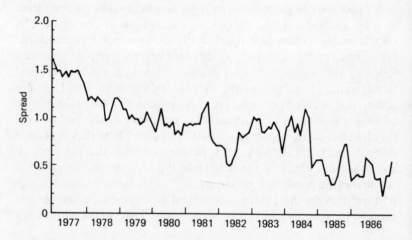

Figure 6.12   Oil Exporting Developing Countries – 3-monthly Moving
Average Spread, 1977–86

Figure 6.12 shows the movements in spreads for the oil exporting developing countries. Spreads declined until the second half of 1981. The 1979 oil price rise, not surprisingly, had no impact on the downward trend. Towards the end of 1982 spreads increased, but re-narrowed sharply in 1984 and remained at a low level throughout 1985 and 1986. Here too, the debt crisis of 1982 appears to have had

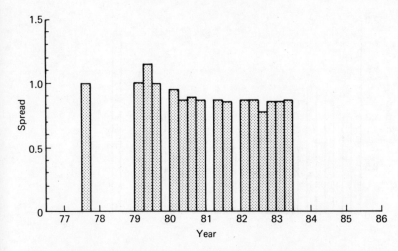

Figure 6.13   Nigeria – Quarterly Average Spread, 1977–86

an impact on spreads. However, one might have expected it to have had a greater impact in this group than it appears to have done, since several of the countries have had debt servicing difficulties (Mexico, Nigeria, Ecuador etc). Moreover, these countries have continued to have problems throughout 1985 and 1986, when spreads had again narrowed. Perhaps the re-narrowing of spreads indicates that countries without debt servicing problems continued to have access to the markets on favourable terms, whereas those with problems had no access (see section 6.3.5).

It is interesting to look at movements in spreads of the more prominent borrowers in this group – Nigeria, Venezuela and Mexico – who also happen to be among the top developing country debtors and have experienced repayment problems. Figures 6.13, 6.14 and 6.15 show the movements in spreads. Spreads for the whole of this group (see figure 6.12) appear not to have anticipated the debt crisis. As risk was increasing in the years previous to the crisis, because the debt servicing *level* relative to the debt servicing *capacity* of these countries increased, spreads should have increased. The fact that they did not appears to imply that either the banks did not assess risk properly, or, if they did, were unable to reflect their increasing perception of risk in spreads. This line of reasoning is also supported by the data for the individual countries which averages the spreads over each month. Mexico entered the New York bond market for the first time in four years with a successful bond issue, only six months

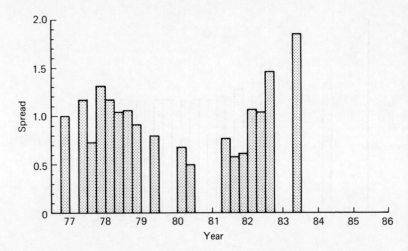

Figure 6.14 Venezuela – Quarterly Average Spread, 1977–86

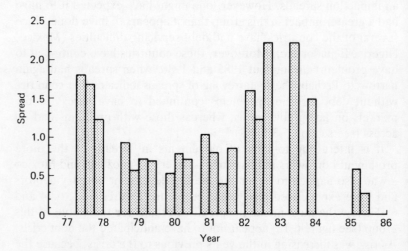

Figure 6.15 Mexico – Quarterly Average Spread, 1977–86

before the crisis broke. This suggests that there was little indication of the coming difficulties. Spreads on Mexican bank loans had moved up somewhat at the beginning of 1982; but they rose significantly above the level they had been at since 1979 only in the third quarter of 1982; Mexico announced that it could no longer meet its interest payments on 20 August 1982. Spreads for Venezuela seemed to be

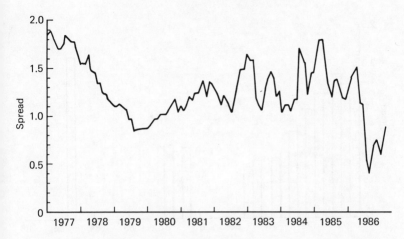

Figure 6.16   Oil Importing Developing Countries – 3-monthly Moving
Average Spread, 1977–86

included in the general rise that took place in late 1982 even although
Venezuelan debt was not initially implicated. On the other hand,
Nigeria did not seem to be included in the general reassessment of
spreads; it continued to borrow at just under 0.84 per cent.

For the oil importing developing countries, figure 6.16 shows the
pattern of movement in average spreads. From 1977 until the end of
1980, spreads decreased from around 1.75 per cent to 0.8 per cent.
After rising somewhat to 1.25 per cent in 1980–81, they fell back to
just over 1.0 per cent in the summer of 1982. The most notable
feature from the third quarter of 1982 until the end of 1985 is the
volatility of spreads: the three-monthly moving average spread has
varied between 1.0 per cent and 1.75 per cent. Variations tend to be
positively related to Brazil's presence in the market, widening when
Brazil is seeking funds (usually with spreads of 2 per cent) and falling
back subsequently. This is the result of a small sample of borrowers
in each month such that when Brazil does borrow, it dominates the
average. Since 1985, spreads for those countries which have been
able to borrow (mainly in Thailand, India and South Korea) have
been at low levels.

Figures 6.17 to 6.20 show the monthly average spreads for several
large debtors in this category – Argentina, Chile, The Philippines and
Brazil. The observations for Argentina are limited but clearly indicate the effect of the debt crisis and increasing worries about the
ability of Argentina to meet its debt service payments;[32] spreads

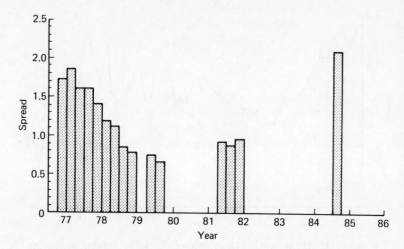

Figure 6.17   Argentina – Quarterly Average Spread, 1977–86

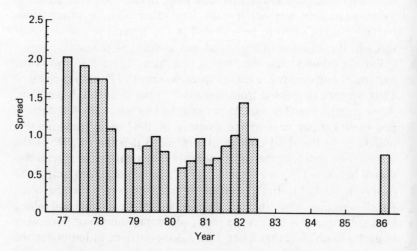

Figure 6.18   Chile – Quarterly Average Spread, 1977–86

increased to 2.25 per cent on new money and to 2.125 per cent on
rescheduled money, negotiated in 1985. Spreads, however, did not
appear to anticipate problems in repayment and increased only after
the Mexican crisis of 1982. The same is true of Chile. Spreads are
now as high as they were at the beginning of 1977 although a marked
increase took place only after the Mexican crisis. In the case of the

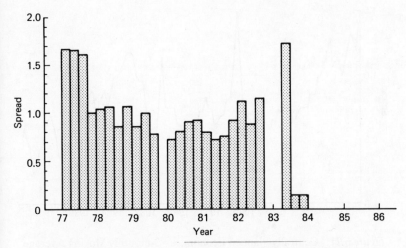

Figure 6.19   Philippines – Quarterly Average Spread, 1977–86

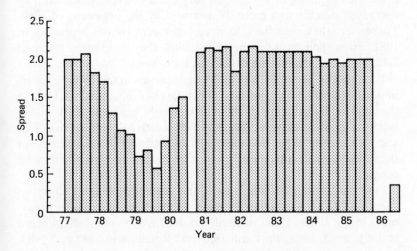

Figure 6.20   Brazil – Quarterly Average Spread, 1977–86

Philippines, spreads remained fairly stable around 0.9 per cent from the beginning of 1979 until the end of 1982. They increased dramatically in the last quarter of 1983, only after the government declared a moratorium on the repayment of principle. The rescheduling terms of 1984, however, were at spreads below 0.2 per cent.

Only in the case of Brazil did spreads increase rapidly before 1982.

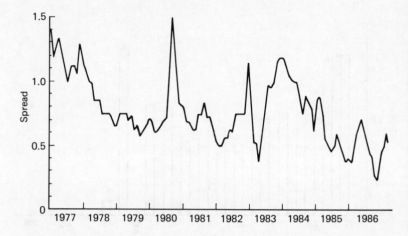

Figure 6.21   Centrally Planned Economies – 3-monthly Moving Average
Spread, 1977–86

From the beginning of 1977, when they stood at over 2 per cent, they decreased steadily to a mere 0.5 per cent by the beginning of 1980. Thereafter, they rose back to over 2 per cent by the beginning of 1981. From then until the middle of 1984, they were fairly stable at 2.125 per cent, decreasing slightly to 2 per cent.

It is thus not generally true to say that spreads in this category of oil importing developing countries reflect the risks inherent in it. Only in the case of Brazil were problems seemingly anticipated by movements in spreads, as we would expect if spreads fully reflect risk. This seems to suggest either that the banks do not properly analyse risk, or that they cannot implement the consequences of their findings on spreads.

Our final group of countries is the centrally planned countries (figure 6.21). These countries have also had problems with repayment in the 1980s. Cuba rescheduled debt in 1983 and 1984; Poland in 1981, 1982, 1983, 1984 and 1985 and Romania in 1982 and 1983. The time-series plot of the three-month moving average shows, in contrast to the other groups of countries, very few observations in each month, usually only one or two. Thus single observations tend to dominate. The Polish crisis affected only Poland; spreads for the other Eastern European countries, if they were able to come to the market (see section 6.3.5), tended to remain the same. Hence the first peak on the graph is due entirely to Poland. It is notable however that before the Polish problems, spreads were decreasing. Only after the crisis did spreads for Poland increase. The debt crisis of 1982 together with continuing difficulties of some centrally planned economies appears to have affected spreads in the second half of 1983 if only for a short period; by the middle of 1984, spreads were falling again. Indeed, to some extent, some Eastern European countries probably became more attractive given the unattractiveness of the LDCs.

From our description and analysis of movements in spreads it would appear that the debt crisis of 1982 did have a significant impact on spreads. However, the fact that in most cases, spreads did not anticipate the crisis suggests that the banks were either unable to forecast the crisis or to implement their forecasts. The 1982 crisis seemed to affect the whole market and there appeared to be a realisation that spreads had been generally too low for the risks incurred. However, this mood did not prevail for long. In the case of all country groups except the oil importing developing countries, spreads returned to their downward path by the beginning of 1984. In the case of the oil importing developing countries, spreads have tended to be marked by great volatility since 1982 and it is not clear what the new trend is.

Figures 6.22 and 6.22a show the deviations of each of the country groups from the prime risk grouping (OECD majors). These graphs

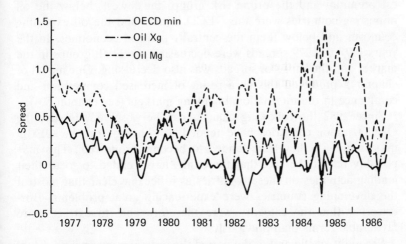

Where: OECDmin   =   OECD minor countries
          OilXg   =   Oil exporting LDCs
          OilMg   =   Oil importing LDCs
    Figure 6.22   Deviations from Prime Risk Group, 1977–86

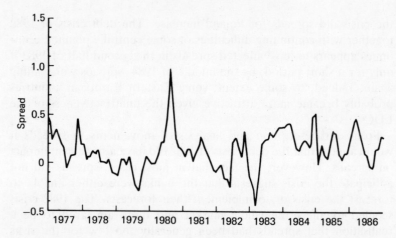

Figure 6.22a   Deviations from Prime Risk Group – Centrally Planned
Economies, 1977–86

are interesting in that they show that deviations from prime risk have
tended to follow a cyclical pattern: we may presumably conclude
from this that absolute risk differentials do not operate in the market.
At the beginning of the period there was a clear ranking of risk
premia across country groups; oil importing countries paid the greatest premium and the prime risk group, the lowest; below the oil
importing countries were the OECD minors and the oil exporting
countries and below them the centrally planned economies. In the
years 1977 to 1979 spreads were decreasing across all groups in the
market and the range of spreads was also decreasing. Our model of
chapter 5 predicted this as a result of increased competition and
confidence in the international banking markets (see chapter 5.4).

Since 1982 the following changes can be observed. Firstly, the
OECD minor countries have tended to converge on the OECD
majors that is, they have tended to become prime risk. This may
possibly reflect the fact that the banks have tended to focus their
lending activities on these countries as it became clear that most of
the developing countries were experiencing great problems. Borrowers within the category were therefore able to extract more
favourable terms than previously.

Secondly, at the end of the period the premium over prime risk of
the oil exporting developing countries was still lower than at the
beginning of the period, despite the fact that many of those countries
have experienced debt service problems.

Thirdly, in the case of the centrally planned economies, deviations from prime risk have tended to increase since 1982, probably following the difficulties with debt servicing which these countries have had. However, this increase followed upon a decrease that had placed centrally planned economies at prime risk status until 1980 and the Polish crisis. The great degree of volatility associated with this group is partly due to the limited data set.

The oil importing developing countries have had the greatest deviation from prime risk throughout the period. From 1977–79, spreads decreased for this group, converging on prime risk in the last quarter of 1979. Between 1982 and 1985, deviations increased significantly, moving away from the general trend experienced by other groups. This suggests that in absolute terms the risk of the oil importing developing countries was considered to be much higher than all the other groups which tend to show convergence just above prime risk. During 1986, however, the risk premia associated with this group have moved back into line with others.

In conclusion then it appears that banks have been able to distinguish between different groups of countries, although not to the extent that one might have expected. It is worrying that a large crisis is required before the banks will significantly reassess their perception of risk. In the years 1977 to 1982 spreads were generally decreasing. This seems to be indicative of the effect of competition and the increasing confidence in the depth of the Eurocurrency markets. The result was that spreads were reduced to very low levels and the range of spreads between the different groups reduced to the point where differences between prime risks and non-prime risks became almost insignificant. As a result, when the Mexican crisis occurred in August 1982, the market almost collapsed. Banks began to realise that the extent of their involvement in these countries implied that default by just one country could possibly lead to the collapse of some major banks. Spreads for all groups of countries increased and remained high until about 1984. Spreads for oil importing developing countries increased although perhaps not by as much as one would have expected given the proportions of the crisis. One may suggest two reasons for this. Firstly, the Baker initiative (1986) attempted to get the banks to lend new money at reasonable spreads, in the belief that any other reaction would intensify the crisis and perhaps make it worthwhile for a country to default outright. Secondly, perhaps spreads do not adequately reflect risks in this market and credit rationing is more common. This is the only explanation that would account for the new downward trend in spreads that appeared in 1985 – that is, those that have access to the market are getting even better terms as competition amongst suppliers is concentrated on fewer borrowers.

6.3.5   Credit Rationing

The last section alluded to credit rationing on several occasions. I now consider the effectiveness of credit rationing as a means of controlling risk exposure. Our theoretical analysis of chapter 5 suggested that banks might well practice credit rationing in a situation where they were unable to reflect risk adequately in a risk premium.

Ideally, a study of the effectiveness of credit rationing as a method of controlling risk exposure would examine the country exposure limits set by individual banks. As Appendix III points out, however, whilst all banks have exposure limits (that is, they practise credit rationing), they are not willing to divulge what the limits are and whether they have altered in the past 15 years. What we want to ascertain here is the extent to which country exposure limits were effective in controlling risk. The last section showed that spreads did not anticipate the 1982 crisis. Banks, however, may have reacted to their anticipation of impending crisis by cutting the volume of lending to high risk countries. This presumably is what an effective system of credit rationing would have led them to do.

The only data available are *ex post* figures on the extent of lending to individual countries by all banks. If banks as a group anticipated the crisis then we would expect these figures to show that decreasing amounts of new funds were lent to countries who have encountered debt servicing problems. If we find no evidence of a decrease in lending prior to the crisis then we can conclude that country exposure limits were ineffective in preventing the crisis.

We need to distinguish here post-1982 credit rationing (the above analysis applies only to the pre-1982 period). Analysis of the movements in spreads post-1982 showed that although spreads (especially in oil importing developing countries) reacted to the international debt crisis of 1982 by increasing sharply, this phenomenon did not continue and after some months, the long term downward trend resumed despite continuing difficulties with international debt servicing. This suggests that there may have been a 'split market' after 1982. One group of countries (to whom banks were still willing to lend) were able to borrow on better terms. Other countries may have been unable to borrow at any price. In the post-1982 period, if country risk assessment by banks was effective, then we would expect some discrimination by banks between countries – lending would have fallen only in those countries who subsequently had problems.

Table 6.3[33] shows the volume of new lending for various groups of countries[34] as well as for some individual countries selected because they are either rescheduling their debt or have a high debt volume outstanding. Table 6.4 shows the volume of debt rescheduled and the volume of new money raised within these rescheduling agreements by countries experiencing debt repayment difficulties.[35] The combination of the two tables allows us to distinguish between new money raised via rescheduling agreements and that which has been raised via normal market channels. This is achieved by comparing the totals of new money for any country in table 6.3 (which includes new money associated both with rescheduling agreements and with normal market channels) with that in table 6.4 (which includes only new money associated with rescheduling agreements).

It is apparent from table 6.3 that the effect of the 1982 international debt crisis was felt throughout the market. The volume of new lending in 1983 was less than that in 1982 for all groups of countries and not just for those that were experiencing debt servicing difficulties. This may suggest that the banks tend to react to a crisis in the first instance by cutting back on lending to all sectors of the affected market rather than by discriminating between borrower countries.

Looking at the group of socialist countries and especially at the effect of the Polish crisis which became apparent at the end of 1980, we see that total lending fell sharply after 1981 to $3353 million in 1982 and $1046 million in 1983.[36] Moreover, this decrease in new money not associated with rescheduling occurred for all members of the group and was not confined to countries experiencing debt repayment difficulties. Only the USSR continued to borrow to any great extent in 1982, and its lending was severely curtailed in 1983 after the general crisis became apparent.

This supports our tentative conclusion above that a crisis tends to result in a general imposition of rationing on all countries, in this case all socialist countries. Such an attitude, it can be argued, actually caused the spread of the crisis to other countries in the group.[37] Hungary, for example was forced to seek help from some western countries, after being unable to raise loans on the international market. After 1984 banks became more discriminating and only those countries who were actually in rescheduling negotiations or

Table 6.3   Annual Loan Volume ($ millions) – Selected Countries –
1979–1986

		1979	1980	1981	1982	1983	1984	1985	1986
OECD		34212	42789	111634	79497	61302	94076	177331	153485
SOCIALIST		8300	5006	4324	3353	1048	4849	4665	4758
Poland	*	901	1089	106	0	0	0	0	0
Romania	*	1100	458	337	0	0	0	150	0
USSR		1386	0	1147	2381	93	1048	1737	2071
Hungary		1047	550	573	458	647	1136	1234	1037
GDR		782	481	628	62	248	74	1100	1170
Yugoslavia	*	2291	1942	1522	439	2	82.7	48	32
OPEC		13726	11228	14494	16448	8003	6652	4389	3350
Algeria		2164	300	500	507	1910	298	1271	1237
Ecuador	*	1054	1009	541	495	25	0	0	220
Indonesia		778	1152	1137	1686	2041	2467	457	1045
Nigeria	*	1972	768	3209	1495	978	0	0	0
Venezuela	*	6164	6903	6771	7852	146	0	352	110
LDC		43873	28439	49347	42718	21100	17266	15167	10207
Argentina	*	2694	2307	3654	1398	250	0	0	85
Bolivia	*	47	0	424	7	0	0	0	0
Brazil	*	6883	5676	7060	6888	2010	3101	2689	228
Chile	*	666	885	2393	1258	107	0	0	37
Colombia		981	670	1181	629	519	480	1208	201
Costa Rica	*	272	168	0	0	0	0	0	0
Cuba	*	178	0	69	32	0	0	0	0
Dom. Rep.	*	195	220	76	0	0	0	0	0
Honduras	*	83	0	24	0	0	0	0	0
Hong Kong		1264	1736	3729	1674	1227	1195	1926	671
Ivory Coast	*	266	265	605	666	85	0	40	15
Jamaica	*	130	0	182	20	84	0	0	0
Korea		3246	2065	3979	4984	3848	3200	4243	1833
Liberia	*	105	0	27	30	44	14	16	0
Malawi	*	50	12	0	0	0	0	0	2
Malaysia		118	1050	1621	2261	1667	1416	45	1104
Mexico	*	10927	5332	13376	9905	4269	3975	634	0
Morocco	*	552	455	923	471	112	242	107	50
Panama	*	185	225	629	442	39	105	0	0
Peru	*	612	392	815	945	0	0	0	0
Philippines	*	1972	1321	1535	1398	905	188	40	0
Senegal	*	0	0	8	41	0	0	0	0
Sudan	*	0	0	30	62	0	0	0	0
Uruguay	*	67	116	216	220	0	0	0	0
Zambia	*	28	60	212	245	140	175	0	0
TOTAL (all countries)		101651	88427	181088	148499	94214	122843	201552	171800

Sources: Euromoney, International Loan Annual, 1984
Euromoney AMEX Syndication Guide

Definitions: Socialist – includes Yugoslavia; excludes Cuba and China
* = rescheduling

who had undergone rescheduling continued to be affected by the freeze on new lending (that is, Yugoslavia, Romania and Poland).

The move towards greater discrimination also reflects the breakdown in the umbrella theory[38] that was prevalent in the market in the pre-1981 period. This theory, which applied to the socialist countries of Eastern Europe, argued that the USSR would never allow one of its 'satellites' to default; in the event of any debt servicing difficulties, it would provide assistance. While the USSR did initially provide some assistance for Poland, once the magnitude of the problem became apparent, it did not do so on an indefinite basis. Although the banks appear to have practised credit rationing, in the sense that new lending through the normal market channels was severely restricted after a crisis had become apparent, it is noteworthy that Poland received $4600 million in new money in 1982, and Yugoslavia $2000 million in 1983 as part of their rescheduling packages (see table 6.4). This is a feature to which we return below.

The picture for the oil exporting OPEC countries is similar to that for the socialist countries. Lending decreased from 1982 to 1983 by 50 per cent and continued to fall up to 1986. However, in this case the decrease was generally confined to those countries with debt repayment difficulties. Other OPEC countries – Algeria and Indonesia are the examples in table 6.3 – do not appear to have been affected by the general slowdown in new lending that took place after 1982. For countries involved in rescheduling negotiations new lending has halted almost completely, and new money associated with rescheduling agreements has not been as forthcoming as in the cases of Poland and Yugoslavia.

With regard to the developing countries who include both oil importing developing countries and non-OPEC oil exporting countries, lending fell by 50 per cent from 1982 to 1983 and by another 50 per cent from 1983 to 1986. Moreover, very few countries increased their new borrowings in 1983 (the exception being a handful of countries, mainly African, whose borrowings in the market were few in number and small in amount). *Relative* decreases in the amount of new money forthcoming from the banks were greatest in relation to countries experiencing financial difficulties, especially in Latin America. Moreover, any new money that was available was granted only as part of a rescheduling package and IMF austerity programme.

A pattern appears to be emerging from our overview of developments in the post-1982 period. The effects of the crisis in Poland in late 1980 were confined to the socialist countries, although discrimination

Table 6.4 New Money: Rescheduling Volume ($ millions) – 1982–1986

	1982–84							1985–86						
	Short Term a. Resch.	New	Medium Term Resch.	New	IMF	BIS	IBRD	Short Term a. Resch.	New	Medium Term Resch.	New	IMF	BIS	IBRD
Poland			4625						700					
Romania			2550											
Yugoslavia	1200		3000	600	600	500				3500		300		
Ecuador	700		2100	431	170							d. 105		
Nigeria	2000			603			41		@6500			@2900		
Venezuela			*18400	1500										
Argentina		1100	7720							@45000	@1200			
Bolivia			* 450											
Brazil	8800	16100	4000	10900	6000	1450	350			7250	@ 150			
Chile	1300		2100	1300	866	350				150	* 75			
Costa Rica	225		1170				d. 54			100				
Cuba	200		170											
Dom. Rep.			b. 560											
Honduras			121				d. 66							
Ivory Coast			* 900		250		250			285				

Jamaica	n.a.					
Malawi	585					
Mexico	21700		48000	*2000		120
Morocco	*1880	8800				
Nicaragua	*140					
Panama	c. 278					
Peru	2930					d.350
Philippines	@ 3000	450	5800	925		d.615
Senegal	80					
Uruguay	629	240	2000			
Zaire	44	655				45
Zambia	46	350				d.211
	500	315				d. 212

KEY
* – under negotiation
@ – proposed
a. – mainly trade related debt which is usually refinanced
b. – includes short term debt
c. – includes new money
d. – SDR – millions

Source: Korner et al (1984), Euromoney International Loan Annual (1984), various issues of The Banker
Definitions Rescheduling includes refinancing

between these countries was initially limited. The effects of the 1982 crisis were far more widespread, although it has to be said that the crisis itself was more widespread in the first instance. Countries rescheduling in the post-1982 period are shown in table 6.4. New money granted to rescheduling countries after the crisis was limited to amounts negotiated as part of the rescheduling agreements and was conditional on the country signing and adhering to an IMF agreement. Nonetheless, large sums of new money were made available in this way (table 6.4) by the banks which in many cases were heavily involved in the countries already. Thus their exposure to these countries increased further. The secondary market subsequently provided a way of reducing that exposure by selling off subparticipations, but the question of who would bear the risk if further reschedulings were required remained unresolved (see above, chapter 1.4). In many respects this new lending can be considered to be involuntary lending: the banks would rather not have lent at all. However, they had little choice if they wished to recover what had already been lent – and crisis management by the authorities did not leave the banks the option of cutting their losses and getting out.

It would appear that whilst credit rationing in some form was a clear feature of the markets after the 1982 crisis, country limits may not have been important in the period leading up to the crisis. Lending to the countries which are now experiencing difficulties grew vigorously up until 1982 as table 6.3 shows. This implies that either country limits were being continually revised upwards or had not been reached. In either case, the banks were mistaken in their (implied) assessment of the exposure, which would be appropriate for these countries.

It would appear, in short, that banks were eager to continue to lend to the bad risk countries right up until the crisis became apparent. Prior to the crisis, therefore, credit rationing did not limit risk exposure. Only after the crisis broke did country exposure limits appear to take on any significance in affecting bank behaviour. By then, it was necessary to limit banks' freedom of action in order to forestall financial collapse.

6.4 CONCLUSION

This chapter has sought to examine the main contentions of chapter 5 for the case of the international credit markets. With respect to maturity transformation, data for London-based banks dealing in foreign currency showed that overall the degree of mismatching was significant. The largest increase in mismatching had occurred at the beginning of the period, 1973–1986. This was thought to have been the consequence of recycling the OPEC balance of payments surpluses. Between 1977 and 1982, there was no change in the level of mismatch despite increasing interest rate volatility and increasing exposure to developing countries. Together with an interbank market that cuts off funding whenever problems arise, this resulted in an increasingly risky environment. Since 1982 maturity mismatching has increased slightly, possibly due to rescheduling agreements which have in most cases carried greater maturities than the original debt. It is consistent with the notions (see chapter 5.4) that once the crisis becomes inevitable, banks tend to become locked into their unsustainable positions with little room for manoeuvre.

Sections 2 and 3 of the chapter examined the relationship between risk and return as measured relatively by the interest rate spread. Section 2 looked at the methods of country risk analysis employed by the banks over the past 15–20 years. This was found to have been generally inadequate and to have encouraged heavy reliance on the herd instinct. A risk assessment scheme should ideally allow a bank to determine, firstly, whether the market return is acceptable for the given level of risk, and thus whether the bank should lend or not; and, secondly, in combination with portfolio diversification considerations, how much the bank should lend at that price (that is, the exposure limit). However, the extent of the crisis since 1982 is at least circumstantial evidence that banks had not been able to make such decisions effectively. Our examination of movements in spreads over the period 1977 to 1986 (section 3) concluded that banks were able to distinguish to some extent between different crude risk categories, but had shown no signs of having anticipated the 1982 crisis. Only after the crisis was the downward trend in spreads halted. Moreover prior to the crisis, the range of spreads had been narrowing.

Once the crisis became evident, the whole market was affected. There was little discrimination between countries by the banks. Spreads initially became volatile, but by the end of 1984 had returned to their downward path. The question arose, therefore, to what extent credit rationing was effective in controlling risk exposure? Was the return to lower spreads the result of a shake-out of countries with debt repayment difficulties? Analysis in section 6.3.5 of the volume of lending to selected countries in the pre-1982 period showed that lending remained buoyant up until 1982, except in the case of the socialist countries, which were affected by the Polish crisis of late 1980. Reactions after the Polish crisis were repeated in a more general way after the 1982 crisis. The volume of lending at first decreased sharply for all groups of countries. Only after some time did the banks begin to discriminate between countries, and even then, 'involuntary lending' was prevalent. Banks would have preferred to cease lending to rescheduling countries as was obvious from interviews with bankers (Appendix III, p. 236), but could not do so if they wished to recover some, if not all, of the money that had initially been lent. Indeed we saw the effect of a general freeze on lending to socialist countries after 1981; countries which had not been in trouble had to seek assistance because they were unable to refinance their debt (for example, Hungary).

All in all, it appears that our abstract analysis of chapter 5.4 describes quite well the situation that developed in the international credit markets. Since 1983 there has been a split market; one category of borrowers (the non-rescheduling countries) continues to borrow at favourable rates in the 'free market': the other category (the rescheduling countries) is operating in a highly managed market where the banks, governments and international agencies (IMF and World Bank) are continuing to guide the international credit system through a phase of crisis adjustment, without the collapse of the system or threats to the viability of major banks.

7 Policy Implications of the Internationalisation of Capital

7.1 INTRODUCTION

This chapter draws together some conclusions from the previous chapters and examines proposals for domestic financial policy and for the international monetary system.

The general point that has emerged from this study is that domestic financial policies have taken on an increasingly international character.

Section 2 of the chapter summarises the conclusions of chapters 2 to 4 in which we discussed the mechanisms involved in the increasing internationalisation of capital, which began with its move 'offshore' to avoid domestic regulations and continued with the liberalisation of capital controls in Europe and the US.

Section 3 examines the implications of an internationalised banking industry for banking supervision and regulation. We discuss the future role for banks in international lending to developing countries in the light of our analysis in chapters 5 and 6.

Section 4 considers various proposals for the international monetary system, which attempt *inter alia* to facilitate solutions to the international debt crisis. Two issues are distinguished. Firstly and of immediate concern, is the question of the debt burden of developing countries. The aim here is to ensure the continued operation of the international banking system, without undermining the development objectives of developing countries. Secondly, we have to examine how the financing of balance of payments imbalances and of development should be conducted in the future, as well as how restrictions on independence resulting from the greater internationalisation of credit markets should be viewed. The first problem is a short run one of crisis management; the second takes a longer run view and entails an examination of the characteristics which the international monetary system should possess and what kind of reform, if any, is required to ensure that these characteristics become a reality.

The analysis of the previous chapters suggests that the following characteristics are desirable:

i) Greater control over destabilising capital flows which may undermine policy designed to influence the level and structure of real economic activity.

ii) An adequate level and distribution of balance of payments financing; this implies that there is an appropriate mechanism to allow smooth and equitable adjustment for all deficit and surplus countries.

iii) A coherent view of the role of the international banks in the above mechanisms, together with an improved system of regulation and supervision.

These matters underlie the discussion in the next sections.

7.2 INCREASED FINANCIAL INTEGRATION

In chapter 2 we asked why it might be desirable for a government to have monetary independence. It was argued that monetary policy is useful in influencing the level of aggregate demand in the economy and in helping to attain the 'correct' exchange rate. Monetary independence is a function of the degree of financial integration which was shown to depend crucially on the arbitrage mechanism. We sought to show, therefore, in chapters 3 and 4 the impact of the internationalisation of credit markets on the mechanisms which promote financial integration.

The 'chain arbitrage' model of chapter 3 shows that the Eurocurrency markets increased the number of arbitrage and speculative channels through which integration can be effected. The model highlighted the institutional nature of the determination of non-dollar Eurocurrency interest rates, which are derived by the subtraction of the forward discount from the Eurodollar rate. The implication is that interest rate parity should be expected to hold continuously between different Eurocurrency markets. This relation, in combination with the arbitrage relation between the Eurocurrency markets and their corresponding domestic markets led to the likelihood of increased interdependence. An examination in chapter 4 of the relationship between the sterling and dollar markets supported our hypothesis that interdependence had increased.

A major feature influencing this increased financial integration has been the financial policy of the developed countries. The Eurocurrency markets and the increasing internationalisation of capital can be seen as direct consequences of the regulatory mechanisms imposed on banking at a national level. In chapter 3 we showed that the existence of reserve requirements in particular imposed a cost on domestic banking. By moving 'offshore', banks could avoid this cost and thus narrow the differential between lending and borrowing rates: borrowing in the Euromarkets was cheaper and lending offered a greater return.

During the 1970s, many countries sought to protect their independence through extensive capital controls. A case study of the UK's experience in this respect was reported in chapter 4. Capital controls helped to forestall integration, by allowing a large (covered) differential to be maintained against sterling. The existence of exchange controls before 1979 was crucial to the preservation of some independence in the face of the internationalisation of capital. Prior to the abolition of controls, there were times when interest rates in the UK did not have to adjust (or had to adjust only partially) to a change in US interest rates. A covered interest differential against domestic sterling assets was sustainable. After the removal of controls, changes in US interest rates more frequently caused an expectation of a similar change in UK rates. However, when foreign exchange markets were stable, the forward premium could adjust, allowing some independence of policy. At other times, foreign exchange markets experienced bouts of (downward) speculative pressure on the pound and the resultant rigidity of the forward premium forced interest rate adjustment.

The other major factor which was found to have an impact on interdependence was exchange rate policy. In chapter 3, we restated the well-known Mundell–Fleming result that flexible exchange rates should allow greater insulation from exogenous monetary shocks, for a given degree of capital mobility. Prior to 1977 the UK authorities at times intervened heavily in the foreign exchange markets. Even after 1977, there were occasions when the authorities managed the exchange rate. This interventionist policy, as we saw in chapter 4, had a clear effect on interest rate policy and interdependence. The impossibility of running independent exchange rate and interest rate policy simultaneously manifested itself on several occasions, especially after 1979. The existence of capital controls prior to 1979 to some extent allowed separate interest rate and exchange rate policies to be pursued, because a covered interest differential against sterling domestic assets relative to Eurosterling and Eurodollar assets could be sustained.

In sum, the study of the removal of UK capital controls highlighted the increasingly interdependent environment in which UK monetary policy operated. Changes in US interest rates frequently generated expectations of a change in UK interest rates. Such expectations were less prominent before 1979, because a far greater range of policy options was open to the government.

7.3 BANK SUPERVISION AND REGULATION

The internationalisation of capital has, not surprisingly, been accompanied by the growing importance of the banks in the international monetary system.This section assesses their contribution to the financing of payments imbalances and discusses whether they should continue to play such an important role, in the light of the debt crisis and our previous analysis of it in chapters 5 and 6.

In chapter 6 we showed that during the 1970s the banks built up an increasingly risky international portfolio. Maturity mismatching increased in the early 1970s, and as a result funding risk. Risk premia were decreasing from 1977 up to the crisis of 1982, as was the spread of risk premia for different classes of risk. The quantity of lending to developing countries continued to expand right up to the crisis. After Mexico temporarily suspended payments on its external debt in August 1982, the volume of lending decreased sharply and spreads became very volatile. Since then, international bank lending has been characterised by a split market. Countries which the banks still consider to be creditworthy, have continued to receive funds on very good terms; countries which are involved in rescheduling receive funds only on an involuntary basis usually via negotiations with the IMF. International banking is thus at present in an unsettled position.

Some authors (such as Brunner and Friedman)[1] argued in favour of a free market solution to the debt crisis. Furthermore, they see no reason why normal commercial lending cannot meet the three criteria that the international monetary system should possess (see section 7.1). They argued that market forces should be left to resolve the crisis. Banks could ascertain the extent to which they would be required to make provision for these debts by placing the debt in the market, and in the event of failure to repay, the debt would be written off. As regards future lending to these countries, market forces would force the countries to remain creditworthy; if they did not, their debt would be seen to be trading at a discount, forcing up the cost of any future borrowing.

Such a proposal was flawed both as a solution to the debt crisis and as a suggestion for the continued participation of banks in future international lending. With respect to the debt crisis, there were two problems. Firstly, if the authorities had promoted such a proposal, the crisis to which it was supposed to be a solution, would probably have been intensified.[2] Bankers' confidence in the markets would have been undermined resulting in a withdrawal of funds from the interbank market, therefore causing a liquidity crisis. It is not certain that this could have been accomplished either without the failure of some banks or without the intervention of the central banks.

Secondly, it is not certain that the banks could have afforded to write off the losses which would have resulted from this free market policy: they did not have the reserves or capital base to allow this policy to be implemented smoothly, even without a decline in confidence exacerbating the problem. For all US banks, exposure to Eastern Europe and non-oil developing countries increased from 131.6 per cent of their combined capital base in 1977 to 155.0 per cent in 1982. The nine largest US banks had an even greater exposure, 235.2 per cent in 1982. If we include the five OPEC countries not in capital surplus (Venezuela, Ecuador, Algeria, Nigeria and Indonesia) then the figure for the top nine US banks increases to 282.3 per cent (Cline (1984)). This analysis leads Cline to conclude that even widespread moratoria would have had a severe impact on banks in western Europe. Although solvency might not have been threatened, the resulting erosion of the banks' capital base would have caused a sharp reduction in loans (as banks sought to maintain their capital requirements) with severe deflationary consequences. Again this would have required intervention by the authorities either to relax capital requirements (which does not seem to be a good long term suggestion) or to offset the deflationary impact.

Intervention by the authorities was thus inevitable after the 1982 crisis if the stability of the banking system was to be maintained (see section 7.4 for a critique of the actual method of intervention adopted and other proposals).

We argued in chapter 5.3.1 that bank failure has severe consequences for the economy as a whole because banks play an important role in the payments mechanism and are responsible for channelling savings to investment opportunities. The stability of the banking system is a public good, since it benefits both those who contribute to it and those who do not (Solow (1982) p. 241). As a result, the free rider problem arises, because it may profit someone to undermine the stability. Everyone therefore becomes a potential free rider and hence the stability of the system has to be ensured by government provision. Recognition of this fact leads us to reject the free market solution to the international debt crisis, because it could cause instability in the banking system.

This in turn, however, leads to the problem of moral hazard. We have effectively argued above that banks in danger of failing must be rescued. This, however, may lead banks to take on more risks than they would otherwise do, thereby increasing the chances of failure. What retribution will bankers face for bad banking, if the normal market mechanism of failure cannot be allowed to operate because of the externalities involved? This dilemma provides a case for increased monitoring of portfolios by some official body, such as the central bank.[3] Bankers themselves may complain about the level of regulation and supervision in favourable times, but '[o]nce equilibrium is threatened . . . only the adequacy of the state structure supporting the system can save it from collapse . . . and the whole capitalist class will expect them to provide both the resources and guarantees necessary to solve the problems which they have created' (Brett (1983) p. 226). If bankers expect intervention in times of trouble, then they should accept monitoring at all other times.

Having established the need to engage in supervision of banks at all times (that is, not just at times of crisis), we have to consider what form this might take. In this, we are no longer seeking a solution to the present crisis. Supervision helps to prevent a crisis and not to cure one. Rather we are seeking to determine whether it would be possible for commercial bank lending to meet longer term needs of balance of payments financing and the provision of development funds, as many authors claim.[4] There are two issues to address here. Firstly, what elements are required for successful supervision of banking. Secondly, because of the international nature of the problem, we have to determine whether such supervision can be implemented at an international level.

In chapter 5 we outlined the effects of an increasingly competitive environment in the banking industry, with empirical support following in chapter 6. For the banking system to contribute effectively to balance of payments financing and the development of developing countries, supervision must be adequate to forestall the problems which were highlighted in chapters 5 and 6. Moreover, it could happen that the level and type of supervision required is not compatible with the type of financing required by developing countries. We look first therefore at the kind of supervision that is implied by the characteristics of international banking which have helped to promote the debt crisis. After that we will determine whether our suggestions are compatible with developing country needs.

Banking supervision has two interconnected aims: to maintain confidence in the system and to ensure the solvency of financial institutions. The informal model of chapter 5.4 stressed the role played by confidence in the cycle of bank business. A build-up of confidence encourages banks to move into a new area when abnormal profits are initially being earned. Sudden withdrawal of confidence in an area can enhance the problems which have caused loss of confidence. Confidence is ultimately maintained by the presence of some form of insurance: 'I need to believe, at least to sleep well at night, that in the event of big trouble the central banks will be prepared to rescue at least the sound links of the financial community under their responsibility'.[5] This guarantee for the system and for depositors who entrust funds to the banks can be provided either by some form of deposit insurance or by a lender of last resort. Deposit insurance, however, cannot cope with a large domestic crisis, far less an international one where deposits are huge. The wholesale nature of the Euromarkets implies that rumours spread more quickly than they would if the deposits were held by private individuals. Confidence is unlikely to be maintainable therefore by an international deposit insurance scheme. As Solow (1982) argues, the lender of last resort is most likely to be a public body. This allows the access to large resources which would be required in the event of the collapse of several international banks.

Solow also argues that private insurance provided by the banking industry itself is not desirable, because default risk should not be shared among all financial institutions but rather should be borne by the stockholders of the bank concerned. However, Solow does not address the fact that in practice, there are difficulties either for a public body or for a private insurance scheme to apportion blame correctly. In the event of a crisis it is difficult to distinguish between banks which are insolvent, and those which are merely illiquid, for example as a result of the insolvency of one bank. In theory, the Bank of England, for example, only acts as a lender of last resort to those banks which are considered to be fundamentally sound. In practice during the Secondary Banking Crisis in 1973–4, the Bank found itself supporting banks which, as it became clear later, had solvency problems.[6] Notwithstanding that, it was clear that crisis management required a public body with the backing to prevent an erosion of confidence from spreading the crisis further. A public body is a necessary condition for crisis management. However, it is by no means guaranteed that the intervention by a public body is a sufficient condition for the prevention of collapse because the authority itself may pursue incorrect policies.

Whilst a lender of last resort helps to maintain confidence in the system, it is in the central bank's interests to ensure the continuing solvency of individual banks within that system by monitoring the risks undertaken. In chapter 6, we argued that the risks inherent in international banking had been increasing since 1974.

Maturity transformation became more extensive throughout the 1970s and 1980s, which led to both increased funding risk and increased interest rate risk (see chapter 6.1). This made it important for the supervisory authority to control the degree of mismatching. Although variable rate lending passed the interest rate risk onto the final borrower the risk was still present in the system and (see chapter 4 indirectly showed) borrower's repayments became increasingly dependent on US monetary policy.

The banks believed that by passing the interest rate risk on to the borrowers, they reduced their own risk. However, this essentially ignored the impact of interest rate changes on the ability of the borrower to repay. Variable interest rates increased the risk of default. The average interest rate on outstanding long term debt of developing countries rose from 4.5 percent in 1973–7 to 8.5 per cent in 1981–2, which in real terms (deducting the US inflation rate) implied an increase from –6 per cent to +3 per cent.[7] Cline (1984) calculates that the rise in interest rates in 1981 and 1982 above the 1961–80 average cost developing countries $41 billion. Thus whilst the banks removed the interest rate risk from their portfolios, the resulting decrease in interest rate risk was matched by an increase in the risk of the borrower experiencing debt servicing problems. So long as maturity mismatching occurs, interest rate risk will have an important role and both the borrower and the lender will be affected.

The level of mismatching of maturities has also led to increased funding risk. When mismatching is combined with a large interbank market, this risk can produce crisis, because of the speed with which rumours spread and action is taken. Deposits can be very volatile.

After Mexico's suspension of payments on its external debt in 1982, banks most closely linked with Latin America suffered a heavy loss of deposits within a short space of time.[8] The Bank of England for a time had to persuade other banks to maintain their deposits with these banks.

Maturity mismatching can therefore severely hamper the liquidity of banks and, where interest rates move against a bank or borrower, can cause losses which could threaten the banks' solvency. The supervisory authorities should therefore ensure that banks keep mismatching within prudent bounds. They should encourage banks to seek funds of a larger duration so as to limit their dependence on short term interbank deposits to finance medium term loans to developing countries.

The second area of concern examined in chapter 6 was that of sovereign exposure and country risk. In the early 1970s, when the banks were starting to build up their portfolios of sovereign loans, country risk analysis was very underdeveloped. The belief that sovereign risk was very low because countries could not go bankrupt was widespread until the early 1980s.[9] As a result of the banks' inability to assess risk adequately, interest rate spreads (which act as risk premia in the market) were influenced by factors other than risk such as the high degree of competition.[10] Spreads decreased throughout the period 1977–81 with the consequence that returns no longer reflected the risks involved.

Chapter 5 suggested that banks would practise credit rationing to control risk exposure because of the difficulty of discriminating between borrowers on the basis of price. In chapter 6.3.5 we suggested that exposure limits had not been effective in controlling risk. Only after August 1982 did banks attempt to limit lending to countries with repayment problems.

The findings of chapter 5 and 6 suggest that supervision requires to be tightened in several areas. Firstly, credit risk assessment systems should be improved to try to reduce the extent to which the herd instinct and headline banking determine banks' investment in sovereign borrowers. Standardised country risk should be introduced along with monitoring by the supervisory authorities of loans granted. This should help to reduce the detrimental side-effects of competition.

Secondly, exposure limits should be established and monitored by the central bank. Because of competitive forces and market failures described in chapter 5, the risk premium is unlikely ever fully to reflect the risk of a loan. Credit rationing is therefore the preferred method of risk control. The Bank of England in a consultative paper (Bank of England (1985)) recommended certain limits on exposures, indicating that there would in future be more control over banks' balance sheets. It was suggested that each bank should report all exposures above 10 per cent of capital to the Bank and no exposure to a single borrower or group of closely related borrowers taken together should exceed 25 per cent of capital.[11] When dealing with international banks, which operate in many different countries, it is more difficult to enforce such rules effectively, because they should apply to the consolidated balance sheet of the bank and its subsidiaries and affiliates. Greater co-ordination between central banks is required.

Another problem in the case of sovereign lending is to define what is meant by a borrower or a group of closely related borrowers. The Bank of England's consultative document is vague in this respect, saying merely that it expects a bank to set limits in accordance with its country risk analysis and that these limits will be monitored. Whilst it is difficult to lay down standard percentages for country limits and indeed not necessarily desirable, the absence of such guidelines implies that if the Bank of England is to monitor country exposure effectively, it has to examine each bank's portfolio in detail. This requires a much greater degree of interference in banks' commercial decisions than the Bank of England has ever been willing to undertake hitherto. In its consultative document, the Bank argues that the proposals seek to exert some control over lending, rather than involve itself in individual lending decisions (see Paragraph 4). However, such an approach is operationally possible only if the borrower or group of borrowers is clearly defined as is the case with a company or group of companies under one board of directors. When the group of borrowers is ill-defined and the setting of exposure limits is not obvious, then a supervisor must surely be involved to a greater extent in individual lending decisions. For example, should exposure to a developing country include only government guaranteed loans, or should private loans also be included? Should loans to multinational subsidiaries in the country also be included, because of the possibility that the assets could be nationalised? The answers to such questions require a more detailed examination of the structure of a bank's portfolio than is envisaged in the Bank of England consultative document.

Finally, there is the question of the type of lending that banks should undertake. Much of the lending in the 1970s was for balance of payments financing. As we argued in chapter 6.2, this is one of the more risky forms of lending, because it is not associated with any specific returns unlike, for example, a project. In the case of balance of payments financing, the returns are indirect in the sense that the finance allows the country to import components which are vital to its development. However, there is the danger that the funds could be misused, for example, for luxury consumption, in which case the foreign exchange required to repay the loan might not be readily forthcoming. Such problems arise in part because of the lack of conditionality and effective monitoring of commercial loans.

There are two difficulties with this apparent need for more rigorous supervision. Firstly, there is the question of the implementation at an international level. We saw in chapter 3 the importance of regulations in the US for the promotion of the Euromarkets in the early 1970s. More recently, the growth in importance of the offshore banking centres provides further evidence of international banks' desire to avoid the regulatory framework laid down in many developed countries. Indeed the Bank of England has always been reluctant to impose a heavy regulatory structure on international banks in London because such a move would put these banks at a disadvantage relative to their competitors in more favourable locations, thus undermining London's position as *the* international banking centre. Recent moves in the US further confirm this. As noted in chapter 1.4, the setting up of International Banking Facilities (IBFs) in New York in 1981 represents, firstly, an admission by the US authorities of the difficulty of competing in the international credit markets if regulations are imposed and, secondly, an attempt to induce the repatriation of disintermediated funds.

These factors have been recognised by central bankers since the mid-1970s: the setting up of the Committee on Banking Regulations and Supervisory Practices (the Basle or Cooke Committee) in early 1975 was evidence of this. They seek to ensure that no foreign banking establishment escapes supervision.[12] Whilst this committee has been a useful point of contact between the central bankers of the developed world, it was widely noted[13] that the failure of Banco Ambrosiano Holdings in Luxembourg in July 1982, where no central bank was willing to take the responsibility, showed up loopholes in the 1975 concordat. However, not only does there seem to be a need for the committee to be more precise on who is responsible, but there also needs to be agreement about the type of supervision which is required for international banks – exposure limits, maturity mismatching etc. A necessary condition for the adequate supervision of the international banking system is greater co-operation between the supervisory authorities to ensure that the system is adequate and not just that all banks are covered by one national authority. The prospects for an adequate international system of supervision do not look bright: indeed, competition among supervisors is becoming an increasingly likely outcome as manifested by the setting up of IBFs in New York, which represent an attempt to compete with London.

The second issue is whether a well-supervised banking system will ensure that the developing countries have access to the right kind of finance. In terms of the criteria put forward in the first section of this chapter, there appears to be some conflict with the closely supervised banking system described above. Firstly, a lower degree of maturity mismatching will entail a shortening of the maturities offered to borrowers, unless banks can attract long term funds. The present maturities offered to borrowers are arguably too short for many development projects. Yet these maturities already threaten to undermine the banking system because of the mismatching to which they give rise. Secondly, in the 1970s the distribution of lending was heavily skewed towards the high-/middle-income countries with a corresponding neglect of the poorer developing countries of sub-Saharan Africa and Asia.[14] Stewart and Sengupta (1982) calculate that at March 1980, low-income developing countries had net assets with the Euromarkets of $3.5 billion, whereas middle-income developing countries had net liabilities of $17.1 billion and upper-income developing countries had net liabilities of $59.2 billion. Low-income developing countries' share of the total external finance received by all non-oil developing countries fell from 16.9 per cent in 1973 to 14.3 per cent in 1980. This was the result of their inability to get access to private international credit at a time when that was becoming increasingly important in total flows to non-oil developing countries.[15] The oil price rise of 1973–4 affected their terms of trade adversely: 'the terms of trade . . . deteriorated by 16 per cent *vis-à-vis* industrialised countries, while those of middle-income countries improved by two per cent' (Stewart and Sengupta, 1982, p. 95). As a result their real export purchasing power fell between 1970 and 1980 and import growth was curtailed. Growth in per capita income fell from

1.3 per cent to 0.9 per cent from 1973–80. Whilst the needs of low-income developing countries were at least as great as those of middle- and high-income developing countries, commercial finance failed to meet these needs. Whilst the tightening of country limits by the supervisory authorities might possibly be accompanied by a greater degree of diversification of bank lending, it is unlikely that the poorer developing countries would benefit from a more closely supervised banking system.

Thirdly, in spite of spreads which are inadequate from the point of view of the banks, the borrowers have had to pay a high and variable cost for their funds[16], which many developing countries have found difficult to recoup from the return on their investment. This need not be due to misinvestment. Often projects in developing countries have a high social rate of return because they are designed to improve the infrastructure of the economy. The proceeds of these projects are usually not easily recovered, either through the market or through taxation, in a form which allows commercial repayment (Stewart and Sengupta (1982) and Llewellyn (1982)).

Fourthly, it is not clear that private commercial lending can guarantee that the funds provided have been used in an appropriate manner. Körner *et al* (1984) highlight several cases of 'cleptocracy' (*sic*), where those in power and in charge of distributing the borrowed funds have either squandered the finance on luxury consumption and military expenditure or re-exported it to foreign bank accounts for their own use. The problem of private domestic capital flight is more general. Figures quoted by Körner *et al* (1984) show that between 1980 and 1982 capital flight from developing countries was approximately $102 billion. For Mexico, Argentina and Nigeria estimated outflows were over 50 per cent of new debt.[17] Many loans were never invested but re-exported. Since 1984, much private debt has been socialised. Yet assets held abroad remain strictly private. Diaz-Alejandro (1984) notes that banks in OECD countries and offshore banking centres refuse to give details of the interest earned by Latin American residents on their foreign bank accounts to Latin American governments. This helps to promote capital flight.

Thus whilst it seems clear that closer supervision of international capital is desirable in the interests of the stability of the international banking system, it is not clear that such supervision would be compatible with the three criteria set forth in section 7.1. A solution to the debt crisis must therefore be sought elsewhere.

7.4 PROPOSED SOLUTIONS

The causes of the debt crisis of 1982 have been extensively researched[18] and include among other things the world recession in 1980–81, the rise in the dollar in the early 1980s, declining terms of trade of developing countries and high interest rates. These exogenous shocks combined with the attributes of the banking system (analysed in chapter 5 and 6) to produce the debt crisis which broke in 1982.

We ruled out in the previous section the completely market-orientated approach to the debt crisis, although such a solution would have been less costly for the borrowers than the solution that is presently being imposed (Brett (1985) p. 239). However, because of the probability that total reliance on the free market proposal would have caused a banking crisis, its wider implications would have been too disruptive for the international monetary system.

In the short run therefore some form of crisis management had to be undertaken by governments and international institutions in conjunction with the banks. Crisis management took the form of a 'case-by-case' approach.[19] This consisted of the International Monetary Fund (IMF) organising a 'rescue package' for each individual country experiencing debt repayment difficulties. Rescheduling of maturing debts, new finance from the banks and access to IMF finance were all made available on the condition that the debtor adhered to an agreed IMF policy package. The banks were keen to have IMF involvement in the reschedulings to impose conditions on debtors. This allowed the IMF to 'persuade' the banks to increase their lending to countries in difficulty by making Fund finance conditional on new bank finance.

This approach to crisis management allowed the banks time to accumulate reserves and strengthen their capital base. When the crisis broke in 1982, banks were not in a position to absorb the losses which would have resulted even from widespread moratoria far less widespread default.[20] Since 1982 banks have been accumulating reserves culminating in May and June (1987) in large sums being put aside as provisions against loans to developing countries. Citibank were the leaders, with a $3 billion write down in mid-May. Other banks followed – Chase Manhattan ($1.6 billion), National Westminster ($466 million) and Midland ($916 million) for example.

These provisions undoubtedly restored some of the financial community's confidence in banks (reflected in share price rises after the

Table 7.1   Negative transfers ($ billion)

Year	Developing countries	Highly indebted countries[1]
1982	17.80	3.85
1983	7.10	−7.50
1984	−7.30	−17.50
1985	−20.80	−26.10
1986	−30.70	−24.90
1987	−29.00	−20.00

[1] Argentina, Bolivia, Brazil, Chile, Colombia, Costa Rica, Cote d'Ivoire, Ecuador, Jamaica, Mexico, Morocco, Nigeria, Peru, Philippines, Uruguay, Venezuela and Yugoslavia.
Source: World Bank, *World Debt Tables*, vol. 1, Tables 1 and 2, 1987–88.

announcements), although it is not certain that the provisions made so far will be adequate to meet any non-repayment of debt (Huhne (1987)). It might be argued that these developments vindicate the authorities' approach to the debt crisis. Once the situation has improved as a result of this crisis management, normal commercial lending can resume. However, whilst the provisions have strengthened the position of the banks, it is not certain that the 'case-by-case' approach and the expected return to commercial lending represent a solution to the debt crisis. The approach can be criticised as a form of crisis management and as a long-run solution to the problems of balance of payments financing and the finance of development.

As a form of crisis management it has had a strongly negative impact on the debtor countries. The first problem with the 'case-by-case' approach is that since 1983 it has entailed a large outward flow of capital from indebted developing countries. This outflow has retarded development and is at variance with the principle that capital should flow to areas of highest social return. Table 7.1 shows the extent of these transfers from 1982 to 1987.

This raises the question of whether developing countries will be willing to continue to give priority to debt service. Lever and Huhne (1985) stress this point, arguing that the incentive not to default becomes weaker[21] the longer the negative transfers continue, because access to the capital markets is restricted in the future. Cline (1984) recognises the issue of negative resource transfer but argues that these transfers are a necessary component of the 'case-by-case' approach required to ensure that the developing countries become creditworthy on the international capital markets again. He does not tackle the question of the effect this may have on default incentive.

It can be argued that the provisions set aside by banks may exacerbate the negative transfer problem. Faber (1987) and Huhne (1987) point out that as banks build up their provisions they will become less willing to lend new money to debtor countries. This is probable because new money since 1982 has been provided by the banks involuntarily. The incentive for debtor countries to continue to co-operate in the rescue packages is further reduced if new money is less forthcoming.

Diaz-Alejandro (1984) and Griffith-Jones and Sunkel (1986) point out a second problem with the 'case-by-case' approach which may also result in a withdrawal of the support of the developing countries. As argued in section 7.3 curtailment of the crisis has the character of a public good because of the externalities associated with instability in the banking system. Diaz-Alejandro argues that the resulting intervention of the IMF, Federal Reserve and BIS in co-operation with the international banks has the characteristics of an international credit cartel, with the possibility of monopoly profits being captured by the banks. There is some support for this in terms of the large fees which banks have received in the recycling process. Griffith-Jones and Sunkel (1986, p. 134) suggest that there is a need for more co-ordination between borrowers to increase their bargaining strength to extract concessions from their creditors.

The third problem with the 'case-by-case' approach is that it has offered no debt relief to developing countries. The Baker proposals (1986) only sought to improve the terms of the rescheduling through a reduction in spreads and an increase in maturities. The authorities have shown little interest in proposals which concentrate on some form of combined interest and principal relief for debtor countries. Solutions such as those put forward by Kenen, Bradley, Rohatyn and others[22] envisage the conversion of the debt to either long term, lower interest loans or bonds. These would be held either by an existing international agency or by a new agency which would pay banks in long term bonds issued on itself. The international agency would purchase the debt at a discount, its size varying from country to country. The debt could then be rescheduled on a low interest long term basis providing some relief to the debtors.

As forms of crisis management these proposals attempt to deal with the 'debt overhang'. They recognise the need for maturing debts to be converted into longer term subsidised finance for developing countries which would help to ensure continued developing country co-operation. However, they do not consider the question of a long run solution to the problems of payments imbalances and the provision of development finance.

This leads us to the second level on which we can criticise the 'case-by-case' approach – its long run implications. This approach views the problems of developing countries as temporary and assumes that once they are back in a creditworthy situation, commercial bank lending can resume.[23] This view implies that there is no inherent difficulty with commercial bank lending as a means of financing balance of payments deficits or development. Section 7.3 argued that banks' involvement in the debt crisis (analysed in chapters 5 and 6) pointed to the need for closer supervision of banks to promote stability in the international financial system. However, we also argued that the kind of finance which such a supervised banking system could provide is incompatible with the kind of finance required by developing countries.

An alternative set of approaches recognise defects inherent in commercial lending to developing countries and call for some kind of guarantee to be given to commercial banks undertaking development lending. One variant of this suggested by Wallich (1984) envisages an insurance fund to insure either specific loans or banks' loan portfolios. The difficulty with this approach is that it is not clear whether such an organisation would have access to the funds required to protect the banking system against major banking failures.

Different variants on this approach have been suggested by Zombanakis (1983) and Lever and Huhne (1985) who argue that international agencies should give a 'green light' for projects in developing countries of which they approve. This would indicate to the commercial banks that such projects are 'safe' and offer a good investment. Under the Lever and Huhne plan, the banks would, in return, write down debt regarded as bad or doubtful and provide new funds under guarantee. The borrower would ensure that sound domestic policies were undertaken, in return for an end to the negative transfers characteristic of international capital flows since 1983.

There seem to be three possible objections to such guarantees. Firstly, if debts which the IMF had guaranteed go bad, would the IMF have the resources to honour their guarantees? Lending may well be restricted by a lack of funds backing the IMF guarantees. Secondly, it does not seem right that the commercial banks should profit from lending when someone else is assuming the risk. Lever and Huhne appear to accept this as the cost of ensuring a resumption of lending to developing countries in order to prevent default. Finally, there is the more important question of what kind of conditions should be imposed on borrowers, that is, what form should IMF conditionality take? Lever and Huhne (1985, p. 141) only see a need to prevent negative transfer and not to alter the terms of conditionality.

The arguments presented above lead us away from advocating a continuing role for the banking system in channelling funds to developing countries and towards a greater role for international institutions. This view raises a wide range of issues connected not only with international finance but also with economic development, North–South relations etc, which are beyond the subject matter of this book.

In conclusion, I propose to touch on three of the issues which have to be addressed regarding the structure and operation of such an agency:[24] the power structure, the question of adjustment and the economic policies which it would advocate. There has been much literature recently[25] on the role of the IMF within the international system and a discussion of the issues raised in that literature will be helpful here.

The power structure of the IMF is basically determined by the quotas that is, the contributions which each member makes to the Fund's resources. This structure reflects the political balance of power of the 1940s, with the US having just under 20 per cent of the total vote (Körner *et al* (1984)). Any change in quotas thus requires the approval of the US since 85 per cent must be in favour of such a change. This structure operates to maintain the *status quo* at the time of the Bretton Woods conference. The result of this domination by the US and the other OECD countries has been increasing hostility towards the IMF from the developing countries who argue that they have no effective voice in policy decisions. This has been reflected in the unwillingness of developing countries to use the IMF (Stewart and Sengupta (1982, p. 119)). An increase in the representation of developing countries is needed. Stability can only be achieved when those involved feel that they have a say in the decision making processes that affect them.

The second branch of reform is in the area of adjustment of balance of payments disequilibrium. At present, all the burden of adjustment falls on deficit countries. The scarce currency clause of the IMF articles was meant to ensure that surplus countries also had to adjust, but it was never invoked, partly because it was not in the interests of surplus countries who have the power within the IMF. They wished to maintain their strong position because it represented market domination by their domestic export orientated industries (Brett (1985) pp. 261–2).

The third area which is a candidate for reform is that of IMF conditionality. This has come to the fore because of the importance that the IMF has assumed in rescheduling agreements. Countries with debt repayment problems now gain access to new money only if they sign and adhere to an IMF stabilisation programme. The controversy is not about conditionality *per se*, but rather about its form. As Brett (1985) argues, those who are providing the finance must be satisfied that it is being used in a positive fashion. This is important in view of the misuse of funds that occurred during the 1970s as we noted above. The fact that the funds have ultimately to be repaid is the main justification for conditionality (Spraos (1984)).

Conditionality implies limitation of sovereignty. To some degree this is a necessary result of greater interdependence in the world economy. The IMF argues that it is *a*) politically neutral and *b*) concerned only with questions of money and finance and not with development. However, its stabilisation programmes are based on a strongly held ideological view which embraces the principles of the market economy and has profound implications for the development of developing countries. The practical result is an insistence on fairly standard stabilisation programmes which emphasise deflation through a reduction of the public sector deficit in order to improve the balance of payments and control inflation, an opening up of developing country economies to free trade and capital movements and a reduction in the role of the state.[26] Spraos (1984) argues that there is a fundamental flaw in all Fund adjustment programmes – the Fund is guilty of using *instruments* as *targets*. The *target* is a viable balance of payments (not necessarily a zero current account). Yet the IMF has concentrated mainly on targeting three of the many instruments which could be employed to meet the true target. Spraos argues that setting targets for these instruments – credit ceilings, budget deficits and devaluation – is inefficient for three reasons. First, an instrument should not be fixed but rather able to adapt to exogenous shocks. Secondly, the true target – the balance of payments – may improve even if the targeted instruments fail to meet their performance criteria. Thirdly, it is a divisive approach. If the balance of payments were targeted this would leave the IMF's clients to determine which instruments they wished to use to meet that target.

Balance of payments deficits of developing countries are often the result of structural deficits (Stewart and Sengupta (1982, pp. 119–20)). If deflationary policies are used to correct such deficits, then its degree has to be particularly severe. This results from the inelasticity of import demand. Moreover, such a reduction in imports is likely to impinge on development programmes. Spraos' approach has the advantage that both structural deficits and demand determined deficits can be dealt with using different policies (instruments).

The fact that the success of IMF stabilisation programmes has been mixed is further evidence that the present emphasis of these programmes is misplaced. This has been noted by many authors including ones (such as Dornbusch (1984) and Diaz-Alejandro (1984) p. 365) who are inclined to be less critical of the IMF's fundamental philosophy than those mentioned above. Indeed, Körner *et al* argue that the very fact that reschedulings have for many countries been a frequent recurrence is partly a result of the inadequacy of the IMF programmes. In general, they argue, 'the Fund pays far more attention to creditors' interest in rapid and profitable repayment than to the development options of the debtor country' (Körner *et al* (1984) p. 71). As a result, some countries have been negotiating consecutive IMF stabilisation programmes, because the fundamental structural problems have not been tackled. What has to be recognised is that it is not true to say that the IMF's policies are the result of undisputed economic theory.[27]

In conclusion, therefore, what is required, at this time, but which is unlikely to be forthcoming, is a forum which would enable these issues to, at least, become part of an international political agenda from which at present they are excluded.

7.5 CONCLUSIONS

This book has examined some implications of the internationalisation of credit markets. We considered the growth of the Eurocurrency markets and the liberalisation of controls on capital as mechanisms promoting internationalisation. Two main implications were identified for domestic financial policy. Firstly, monetary and exchange rate policy is now conducted within a highly interdependent international monetary system; the most powerful economies exert a large influence upon the smaller, open ones notwithstanding floating exchange rates. Secondly, supervision of the banking industry can no longer be confined to the domestic sphere. Moreover, a banking system less prone to crises may prove difficult to reconcile with a continuing role for banks in the international monetary system along the lines followed prior to the international debt crisis of 1982. The market failures inherent in the banking industry provide a case for more official intervention. At the same time, substantial reforms may be necessary before official monetary institutions can play a deeper and less controversial role in balance of payments financing.

Appendices

APPENDIX I: MOVEMENTS IN THE COVERED INTEREST DIFFERENTIAL AND THE FORWARD DISCOUNT, 1975–79

The hypothesis that the covered interest rate differential against sterling assets varied with the forward discount and the interest rate policy of the authorities is confirmed by a month-by-month examination of events over the period 1974–79 as a whole.

In 1975, the covered differential against sterling was much narrower than it had been during 1974, because the forward discount on sterling was narrower. The Eurosterling rate was very similar to the LA rate especially during the second half of the year, with the difference rarely rising above 2 per cent. Both Eurodollar rates and Eurosterling rates fell. The forward discount was steady during 1975 because of greater confidence in sterling for several reasons:

i) Tighter supervision by banks of their foreign exchange departments following a Bank of England memorandum (20 December 1974) suggesting improvements in supervision. This was the result of concern about such supervision because of losses incurred from operations in the foreign exchange markets by banks in several countries during 1974 (see BEQB March 1975, p. 21).

ii) The state of the UK economy; at the beginning of 1975, it was recognised that pay restraint would offer a more acceptable solution to the inflation problem than deflation, because of the latter's adverse effect on unemployment. In July, the Chancellor of the Exchequer negotiated a pay deal limiting pay rises to £6 per week from 1 August 1975.

In the first six months of 1976, there was a widening of the differential between the LA and Eurosterling rates. Whilst the Eurodollar rate was steady because of the stability of US domestic interest rates, the forward discount widened following political uncertainty after the Prime Minister's resignation in March, and because of industrial relations problems in the car industry. As a result, the Eurosterling rate increased to maintain interest rate parity between the Eurosterling and Eurodollar markets. The existence of exchange controls again allowed the LA rate to remain below the Eurosterling rate widening the differential as the latter rate rose.

Towards the end of August and the beginning of September 1976, the pound came under increasing downward pressure. The main reason for this was the disturbing monetary developments which took place over the period. Publicly announced monetary targets were first adopted in 1976, although the Treasury had been using unpublished targets since 1973. This change to publicly announced targets was the result of the Treasury's belief that the financial community held essentially monetarist views and such targets were therefore necessary to inspire confidence (Gowland (1978) p. 123). How-

226

ever, growth in M3 had risen to 9 per cent in the first half of 1976–77, a rate well in excess of the authorities' target of 12 per cent for the whole financial year. Interest rates rose but this did not halt the slide of the pound, and the forward discount sharply widened, aggravated also by other factors such as the continuing deficit on current account and industrial relations problems in the car industry. The result of this was a large differential against domestic sterling assets relative to Eurosterling assets, as the Eurosterling rate increased sharply to over 21 per cent in October, whilst the LA rate rose only slowly in response to the general rise of UK interest rates.

For much of 1977, financial markets were fairly confident about the UK economy. The IMF Letter of Intent arrived and improved economic indicators such as that of monetary growth which showed it to be under control. At the beginning of the year, the authorities were able to accept some fall in interest rates, whilst indicating that monetary policy was still aimed at reducing inflation. With the Eurodollar rate also stable, the covered differential against domestic sterling almost disappeared. In May there was a brief bout of speculative pressure against sterling as reports circulated that the IMF believed a realistic exchange rate for the pound to be about $1.50. Although the forward discount widened sharply, the LA rate rose only slowly, causing an increase in the covered interest differential against UK domestic assets which was sustainable only because of the presence of exchange controls.

In the first half of 1978, the UK current balance of payments weakened and the future course of inflation became more uncertain both because of faster growth of monetary aggregates; £M3 rose by 16 per cent in the year to mid-April, well outside the target of 9–13 per cent: and because the average increase in earnings of 14.5 per cent in the eleven months to June 1978 was outside the 10 per cent guidelines. These factors led to expectations of exchange rate depreciation. At the same time interest rates in the UK were constant, whilst those in the US began to rise, as credit expansion fuelled the upswing in economic activity. With a widening forward discount on sterling, this caused the covered differential against domestic sterling to rise also.

APPENDIX II:MATURITY TRANSFORMATION
STATISTICS: PERCENTAGE CLAIMS AND
LIABILITIES IN EACH MATURITY CLASS

Table 1   All Banks
Table 2   British Banks
Table 3   American Banks
Table 4   Japanese Banks
Table 5   Other Foreign Banks
Table 6   Consortium Banks
Source: Bank of England Quarterly Bulletin, Statistical Appendix
Note: 'aver' = average   'mons' = months
        'liabs' = liabilities   'yr' = year
        'mon' = month   'yrs' = years

Table 1 All Banks

date	<8 days as %liabs	<8 days as %claims	8 days—<1mon as %liabs	8 days—<1mon as %claims	1mon—<3mons as %liabs	1mon—<3mons as %claims	3mons—<6mons as %liabs	3mons—6mons as %claims	6mons—<1yr as %liabs	6mons—<1yr as %claims	1yr—<3yrs as %liabs	1yr—<3yrs as %claims	>/=3yrs as %liabs	>/=3yrs as %claims
aver 73	19.09	14.86	19.45	18.77	26.18	24.76	20.86	20.84	8.84	8.21	2.49	4.81	3.09	7.75
aver 74	21.59	17.57	20.31	17.63	27.40	24.02	18.23	16.60	6.54	6.94	2.21	5.35	3.73	11.88
aver 75	20.81	15.58	17.48	14.87	28.63	23.82	18.88	15.51	7.15	6.64	3.15	6.94	3.90	16.63
aver 76	20.66	16.25	17.97	13.97	28.48	23.46	18.65	15.40	7.50	7.04	4.24	8.62	2.49	15.26
aver 77	21.94	16.77	17.46	13.60	27.44	22.37	18.74	16.11	7.89	7.51	4.70	9.73	1.82	13.91
aver 78	21.29	15.54	17.30	13.72	27.83	23.06	19.29	16.26	8.38	8.06	4.07	9.19	1.84	14.17
aver 79	21.48	16.27	17.51	13.93	27.67	23.28	20.23	17.31	7.67	7.42	3.61	7.44	1.83	14.34
aver 80	21.06	16.31	18.94	15.34	27.87	23.10	19.67	16.72	7.53	7.35	3.15	6.61	1.73	14.57
aver 81	20.52	16.28	19.71	16.16	29.27	23.95	19.55	16.90	6.48	6.68	2.68	6.36	1.78	13.69
aver 82	20.44	15.73	19.66	16.41	29.21	24.64	20.16	17.32	5.95	6.28	2.69	6.25	1.89	13.37
aver 83	21.94	15.68	20.51	16.53	28.75	23.55	18.21	14.67	5.72	6.15	2.66	7.02	2.20	16.40
aver 84	21.92	16.30	20.94	16.48	27.62	22.63	17.47	14.32	6.59	6.51	2.62	7.11	2.84	16.64
aver 85	22.39	16.39	20.99	16.41	27.19	22.14	16.87	14.36	6.23	6.47	2.59	6.83	3.75	17.40

Table 2 British Banks

date	<8 days as %liabs	<8 days as %claims	8 days—<1mon as %liabs	8 days—<1mon as %claims	1mon—<3mons as %liabs	1mon—<3mons as %claims	3mons—<6mons as %liabs	3mons—<6mons as %claims
aver 73	16.50	14.36	18.02	18.02	24.74	22.54	22.40	21.36
aver 74	19.44	17.89	17.65	14.42	27.38	21.56	19.17	15.15
aver 75	19.00	14.60	16.16	11.89	26.59	18.16	19.40	12.91
aver 76	18.86	13.90	17.32	11.98	26.43	17.77	19.50	12.37
aver 77	20.33	14.95	16.60	11.96	25.18	17.06	20.22	12.97
aver 78	19.75	15.45	17.03	11.99	27.28	18.36	20.58	13.03
aver 79	21.33	17.71	17.01	11.41	27.62	17.94	21.92	13.95
aver 80	23.18	19.87	18.22	12.47	27.12	17.44	20.59	13.62
aver 81	25.45	20.24	19.36	13.96	27.50	18.39	18.88	13.26
aver 82	23.83	19.86	19.86	13.28	27.31	18.65	19.62	13.34
aver 83	24.82	18.45	19.11	12.36	27.46	17.31	18.63	11.13
aver 84	23.45	17.42	19.98	12.91	26.86	16.63	18.08	11.65
aver 85	23.74	16.64	20.76	12.87	26.38	17.04	16.76	11.38

6mons—<1yr as %liabs	6mons—<1yr as %claims	1yr—<3yrs as %liabs	1yr—<3yrs as %claims	>/=3yrs as %liabs	>/=3yrs as %claims
10.36	9.19	3.25	6.99	4.72	7.54
8.39	8.34	3.60	8.75	4.40	13.89
9.64	8.15	5.12	11.55	4.07	22.75
9.66	7.74	5.66	13.67	2.53	22.56
10.66	8.25	4.24	12.59	2.77	22.21
9.59	8.24	2.88	11.40	2.88	21.56
7.71	7.70	2.34	9.69	2.06	21.60
7.47	7.62	1.57	7.72	1.55	21.31
5.50	6.71	1.56	7.60	1.74	19.84
6.04	6.26	1.78	7.83	2.11	20.78
6.17	5.72	1.87	9.52	1.95	25.53
7.62	6.68	1.80	9.84	2.21	24.86
6.33	6.50	2.30	9.60	3.73	25.98

Table 3 American Banks

date	<8 days as %liabs	<8 days as %claims	8 days-<1mon as %liabs	8 days-<1mon as %claims	1mon-<3mons as %liabs	1mon-<3mons as %claims	3mons-<6mons as %liabs	3mons-<6mons as %claims
aver 73	22.52	15.09	20.13	20.18	25.67	25.77	18.96	21.18
aver 74	28.58	19.64	19.81	17.75	25.25	25.97	16.13	18.07
aver 75	27.23	18.52	16.85	15.37	26.99	25.54	17.35	17.04
aver 76	26.09	20.34	18.67	14.59	26.93	24.50	16.99	16.87
aver 77	27.32	20.30	17.71	13.56	26.82	23.79	16.57	17.79
aver 78	26.73	18.20	17.57	14.02	27.10	24.31	17.17	17.69
aver 79	26.35	18.48	17.86	14.14	26.84	25.45	18.13	18.77
aver 80	27.25	19.52	19.57	16.03	26.35	24.47	17.68	18.68
aver 81	25.22	18.27	20.12	16.32	28.68	25.88	17.23	17.70
aver 82	25.47	17.81	20.47	16.68	29.10	27.32	17.40	18.15
aver 83	29.27	18.79	19.64	16.84	27.66	26.02	15.18	14.63
aver 84	31.15	23.20	20.05	15.68	24.99	23.95	14.49	13.43
aver 85	31.71	22.35	19.43	15.21	24.28	22.04	13.72	13.98

6mons-<1yr as %liabs	6mons-<1yr as %claims	1yr-<3yrs as %liabs	1yr-<3yrs as %claims	>/=3yrs as %liabs	>/=3yrs as %claims
8.47	8.91	2.39	3.37	1.88	5.50
5.58	6.57	1.93	4.13	2.62	7.87
6.20	6.48	2.61	5.21	2.75	11.84
6.37	6.70	3.72	6.56	1.24	10.44
6.61	7.20	4.09	7.70	0.91	9.65
7.57	7.66	2.79	7.02	1.08	11.11
7.48	7.47	2.04	5.55	1.30	10.14
6.03	6.51	1.83	5.13	1.27	9.64
5.74	5.39	1.91	5.87	1.09	10.59
4.14	5.02	2.44	6.00	0.99	9.07
5.10	5.75	1.87	6.06	1.28	11.91
5.80	5.06	1.71	5.92	1.82	12.75
6.20	6.09	2.40	6.27	2.25	14.06

Table 4 Japanese Banks

date	<8 days as %liabs	<8 days as %claims	8 days–<1mon as %liabs	8 days–<1mon as %claims	1mon–<3mons as %liabs	1mon–<3mons as %claims	3mons–<6mons as %liabs	3mons–<6mons as %claims
aver 73	19.88	19.89	21.40	17.87	29.38	25.81	17.07	13.40
aver 74	13.30	18.64	23.70	18.83	31.95	23.59	18.94	13.50
aver 75	9.63	14.37	18.89	15.71	35.19	27.73	20.22	15.16
aver 76	11.89	15.59	17.20	14.39	34.19	28.50	18.48	14.70
aver 77	14.36	15.41	18.01	15.12	30.87	25.91	17.60	15.23
aver 78	13.44	11.55	16.41	13.95	27.82	25.76	17.56	15.96
aver 79	14.51	11.39	16.47	14.35	26.84	24.92	19.54	18.43
aver 80	12.14	10.33	16.99	14.62	28.27	25.39	21.28	19.86
aver 81	13.21	10.83	18.06	16.43	30.14	27.26	22.30	21.44
aver 82	13.64	9.96	17.77	17.06	29.69	27.48	24.55	21.74
aver 83	15.76	10.92	20.11	17.53	29.78	26.61	21.17	18.07
aver 84	16.21	11.76	20.04	17.03	28.70	25.01	19.79	17.18
aver 85	18.30	12.52	19.80	16.85	27.97	24.52	19.48	16.97

6mons–<1yr as %liabs	6mons–<1yr as %claims	1yr–<3yrs as %liabs	1yr–<3yrs as %claims	>/=3yrs as %liabs	>/=3yrs as %claims
3.76	2.07	2.45	2.83	6.05	18.13
2.61	2.23	1.45	2.21	8.27	21.00
4.51	2.96	2.45	3.57	9.11	20.53
5.22	4.20	5.55	6.12	6.66	16.36
6.17	5.64	10.08	9.71	2.93	12.98
9.26	7.07	12.19	9.31	3.30	16.40
9.02	6.67	10.36	6.79	3.49	17.45
9.42	7.45	8.75	6.54	3.14	15.78
8.36	7.51	5.33	4.58	2.61	11.95
7.58	7.29	4.41	4.58	2.37	11.89
5.83	6.84	4.36	5.11	2.98	14.91
6.96	7.76	4.07	5.45	4.24	15.81
6.69	6.96	2.91	5.04	4.85	17.14

Table 5 Other Foreign Banks

date	<8 days as %liabs	<8 days as %claims	8 days-<1mon as %liabs	8 days-<1mon as %claims	1mon-<3mons as %liabs	1mon-<3mons as %claims	3mons-<6mons as %liabs	3mons-<6mons as %claims
aver 73	16.53	14.58	19.46	18.52	26.71	27.64	23.56	25.10
aver 74	17.50	14.05	21.99	21.74	29.30	26.23	18.54	17.19
aver 75	19.46	13.31	18.14	17.59	28.64	25.92	19.54	17.18
aver 76	19.71	13.32	17.19	15.25	28.29	25.17	19.66	16.89
aver 77	20.27	14.90	16.94	14.88	27.75	23.83	20.38	17.76
aver 78	20.23	15.25	17.62	15.62	28.53	25.12	20.49	17.88
aver 79	21.40	16.47	17.69	15.99	28.35	25.42	20.61	18.42
aver 80	19.94	15.49	19.76	18.80	28.73	25.02	20.12	16.93
aver 81	18.81	16.54	20.75	18.46	30.22	25.51	19.18	16.20
aver 82	19.80	16.52	20.83	18.92	30.18	26.03	18.45	16.65
aver 83	20.36	16.02	22.44	19.60	29.34	25.08	16.97	14.99
aver 84	20.17	16.05	22.74	19.62	28.56	25.05	16.55	14.67
aver 85	20.51	17.20	23.20	19.62	28.18	23.98	15.77	14.34

6mons-<1yr as %liabs	6mons-<1yr as %claims	1yr-<3yrs as %liabs	1yr-<3yrs as %claims	>/=3yrs as %liabs	>/=3yrs as %claims
9.91	8.46	1.74	2.67	2.09	3.02
7.45	7.42	1.83	3.37	3.42	9.99
8.29	7.84	2.84	5.58	3.09	12.59
9.15	8.88	3.69	7.21	2.34	13.29
8.68	8.37	3.81	8.28	2.17	11.98
8.31	8.72	3.19	7.84	1.63	9.79
7.53	7.55	2.83	6.19	1.59	9.97
7.47	7.31	2.27	5.53	1.71	10.91
6.68	7.23	2.37	5.76	1.99	10.43
6.21	6.26	2.29	5.27	2.08	10.33
5.88	6.01	2.44	6.19	2.55	12.12
6.71	6.32	2.51	6.09	2.76	12.20
5.92	6.13	2.66	6.05	3.76	12.66

Table 6 Consortium Banks

date	<8 days as %liabs	<8 days as %claims	8 days-<1mon as %liabs	8 days-<1mon as %claims	1mon-<3mons as %liabs	1mon-<3mons as %claims	3mons-<6mons as %liabs	3mons-<6mons as %claims
aver 73	15.40	10.82	18.33	15.85	28.22	19.22	23.61	15.48
aver 74	16.84	11.90	22.85	13.09	29.70	17.09	20.16	11.67
aver 75	15.99	11.15	20.42	11.38	32.49	17.43	21.51	10.79
aver 76	16.81	11.01	19.44	10.70	31.52	16.60	22.70	11.57
aver 77	16.90	11.45	19.75	10.78	30.35	17.43	23.04	11.19
aver 78	16.33	10.52	17.46	10.21	31.05	17.08	25.14	12.33
aver 79	15.60	11.72	19.45	10.77	31.28	15.95	25.63	13.09
aver 80	15.41	10.54	19.64	11.19	32.30	16.85	25.28	12.73
aver 81	15.96	10.92	21.31	11.45	31.60	15.21	24.49	12.25
aver 82	18.87	11.05	20.57	10.85	30.56	14.53	23.92	11.57
aver 83	19.02	13.06	21.78	8.74	30.51	12.26	21.97	8.95
aver 84	21.95	12.31	21.19	9.15	29.98	11.70	20.98	8.77
aver 85	20.49	12.48	22.64	10.33	31.40	12.70	19.67	8.80

6mons-<1yr as %liabs	6mons-<1yr as %claims	1yr-<3yrs as %claims	1yr-<3yrs as %liabs	>/=3yrs as %claims	>/=3yrs as %liabs
8.59	7.34	2.30	11.95	3.56	19.34
5.25	6.39	1.92	12.40	3.28	27.46
6.25	6.42	2.01	13.51	1.30	29.30
6.66	6.31	2.28	16.81	0.59	26.79
7.10	7.26	2.23	18.74	0.62	23.14
7.28	8.50	2.04	19.24	0.62	22.12
5.52	7.57	1.97	17.31	0.56	23.59
5.40	7.62	1.46	15.74	0.53	25.33
5.01	7.19	1.14	15.04	0.49	27.94
4.37	7.74	1.04	16.11	0.65	28.15
4.81	7.12	1.19	18.01	0.72	31.86
3.67	6.53	1.43	19.23	0.81	32.29
3.76	6.78	1.28	18.36	0.76	30.54

APPENDIX III: SUMMARY OF INTERVIEWS

1.   Introduction

75 letters were sent out to a variety of banks in London, which according to Hambros Euromarket Directory were involved in the Eurocurrency markets in London. 25 replies were received, of which nine refused to grant me an interview with someone involved in the markets, whilst 16 did. One other bank arranged for me to meet someone from a London subsidiary of a European bank. Altogether these 17 banks included a wide range of the different institutions involved in the Eurocurrency markets;

5 British merchant banks
2 British banks
3 Japanese banks
1 Scandinavian bank
1 European bank
2 American banks
2 consortium banks
1 Latin American bank

The following is a summary of the replies to questions put to each of these bankers, in the period August–October 1986.

2.   General Questions

Questions of a general nature sought to establish the extent to which each bank was involved in international banking and in the medium term syndicated loan market in particular. All the banks interviewed had participated, at one time, in the syndicated credit Eurodollar markets, although the extent to which they had participated and the extent to which they still participated differed significantly. The merchant banks were the least involved of any of the banks at present. Their involvement in the 1970s was fairly limited due to capital constraints and their generally more conservative attitude. This allowed them to run down operations in medium term lending and to concentrate on the Eurobond market, which had always been their priority. Where they had participated in the Eurocurrency market, they tended to concentrate on the developed industrial nations (for example, EEC nations, Scandinavia, Japan, Australia and Canada), although all had had some exposure to problem debtor countries in Latin America and elsewhere.

At the other end of the scale of participation in syndicated credit markets are the two consortium banks, and the Latin American Bank branch. They have relied almost entirely on medium term syndicated loans and trade finance. These banks were set up with that exclusive role in mind, and because of their great involvement have been unable to move out of the market when problems became evident.

The other banks have been and still are involved in medium term credit syndication, although on a lesser scale in relation to their portfolio than the consortium banks. These banks tend to be either large banks involved in retail as well as wholesale banking or subsidiaries of the same.

3.   Concentration and Type of Assets (Loans)

This question was posed with a view to ascertaining the degree to which banks target certain geographical areas, to benefit possibly from economies of scale in information gathering. Overall, it was found that involvement in syndicated lending had been concentrated within specific geographical areas, which differed among the banks interviewed.

The consortium banks and the Latin American bank branch in London were set up to deal not only with syndicated Eurodollar loans, but also to specialise in such loans to Latin America. The reasons given were the advantages of having either institutionalised or personal links with one or more countries within Latin America, in terms of acquiring information. Such links are subject to economies of scale, which result in some concentration of the portfolio on several targeted countries. Relative to these banks, all the other banks in the survey were more diversified, although to differing degrees. The merchant banks concentrated mainly on Europe, Australia and Canada, but all banks surveyed had had some involvement in Eurocurrency syndicated loans which were being rescheduled, or had been rescheduled.

With regard to the type of institution for which the loan was provided, all preferred sovereign or sovereign guaranteed state companies' loans. These were seen as the least risky. Where loans were concentrated in developing countries, the desire for government guarantees was even more pronounced and loans to private companies were extremely rare. The reason, according to one banker, is that in countries with very high rates of inflation, which is true of many developing countries involved in the syndicated lending markets, private companies are a very high risk, because management has to be very astute to avoid the easily arising cash-flow problems associated with such economic conditions. There was some emphasis on company lending among merchant banks or the larger retail banks which (especially in the case of the former) have traditionally had closer links with company finance and moved into the Eurocurrency markets partly with a view to offering their customers such facilities.

4. Country Risk Analysis

The aim of the questions in this section was to determine what kind of assessment was used in trying to establish the risk involved in lending to a particular country and whether any changes had occurred as a result of the international debt crisis. Generally the *quantitative/qualitative* method (chapter 6.2) was prevalent.

Most bankers interviewed expressed some concern about their banks' methods of country risk analysis, but very few seem to have instigated changes in the actual method used in the light of the current problems. Most use a method of assessing short run economic factors, such as balance of payments situation, foreign exchange reserves, inflation, growth and debt levels. This analysis is then overlaid with some subjective assessment of political stability. Both the economic and political factors may be reviewed in the light of personal contacts or visits to the country. None of this analysis is very detailed; the number of experts in economic or political analysis is very small, even within the large banks.

Very few have attempted any changes in the light of current difficulties. One banker suggested that no change meant that the previous system had been effective; in view of the results of much of the country lending, this opinion appears to be optimistic. Of the banks that have changed their method of assessment, one has attempted to move into more project-orientated finance which is likely to generate foreign exchange reserves; the need for economic and political assessment of the country is then arguably less important. Another has felt a need to take a longer term view of a country in which it is thinking of investing and monitor trends in the key economic variables rather than relying too much on their levels.

In conclusion, it appeared that few banks had a detailed system of analysis. While there is a problem of information, most of which is gathered from international official institutions such as the OECD, IMF and World Bank, there seemed to be little objective use of such information as is available. Decisions as to the viability of a country tend to be subjective.

5. Rescheduling

The extent to which the banks surveyed are involved in rescheduling, varied enormously. A couple of banks have almost 100 per cent of their portfolios involved. All those interviewed had been or still were involved to some extent. Among the banks that are heavily involved, there is often little room to manoeuvre, in terms of altering portfolios, although there is the secondary market in Latin American debt, for example, which allows some changes to be made to existing portfolios. These banks are essentially waiting for some of the countries in which they specialise to be accepted back in to the market. Those with much smaller involvement, mainly the merchant banks, are getting out by selling some of their participations in the secondary markets at heavy discount. Indeed, the majority of merchant banks preferred to write off these loans rather than put up new money, which they felt they were under political pressure to do. Those who are heavily involved do not like to put up new money either and would like to get out completely, but where they have billions of dollars invested in a rescheduling country, they have little choice, if they wish to recover some of the existing loans.

The possible withdrawal of some of the banks involved to only a small extent in the negotiations, raises the questions of a possible breakdown in the united front which bankers are officially taking with respect to forgiving some of the debt. However, banks who want and are able to get out (potential 'free-riders') have tended to try to keep that view very quiet in the market and to offload the affected part of their portfolios slowly in the secondary market. Many of those interviewed, even where their banks were heavily involved in rescheduling, although stressing that it was not their bank's official policy, expressed their personal opinion that some of the debt of these countries would have to be cancelled in the future, and that banks were using rescheduling to gain time to build up sufficient reserves to deal with such a possibility. IMF agreements are considered, without exception, to be a necessary condition before rescheduling will be considered. As one banker put it, the IMF acts as the 'honest policeman'; although banks do not receive detailed information from the IMF, they essentially trust the institution such that if it recommends rescheduling, then the banks will go along with this.

There was general agreement among those banks interviewed that rescheduling was something they would have to go along with, if they could not offload their participations in the affected loans. While this position was in many cases adopted under protest, they also felt that in the long run it would enable them to recover more of the debt than if they called the loans into default now.

6. Spreads and Fees

The first question related to spreads and fees in the syndicated medium-term market concerned the determination of spreads and whether there is/was a relationship between risk and return in the market. To analyse this we need to determine the extent to which spreads reflect returns.

The vast majority of bankers thought that there had been a deterioration in the risk-return relationship. The merchant banks were very strong on this – returns were, in their opinions, totally inadequate for them to consider getting involved in the markets. Several reasons were given for the deterioration. Firstly, the most popular reason was that competition in the markets had increased. In the opinion of several bankers, this led to returns not even covering costs, far less risks. The degree of competition had increased *a)* because Japanese banks, and to some extent American and German banks, were engaging in aggressive pricing; *b)* because of the 'sheep' or 'herd' mentality in financial markets, which made many banks want to become involved in every new area – the result of this was overbanking: that is, too many producers chasing too few consumers and; *c)* because once a new, good name is found, all banks move in and spreads fall below that required for them to reflect a risk premium. For example, at the time of interviewing (September 1986) Portugal was one country to which banks were keen to lend.

Secondly, many banks were interested, and still are, in establishing a position in the market and building up their balance sheets and are willing to subsidise their operations in the syndicated credit markets through other parts of their operations.

Thirdly, several respondents indicated that demand for credit had been decreasing. This had helped to produce a borrowers' market, with lengthening maturities and declining spreads. In conclusion, most bankers were dissatisfied with the risk-return relationship. This included two out of the three Japanese banks in the market; if they are pricing aggressively, then they are certainly aware of it and willing to take the consequences.

The second area of interest was the extent of any trade-off between spreads and maturities; that is, where a borrower sought a loan of greater maturity, he would be required to pay a greater spread to compensate the banker for the likely increased maturity transformation incurred. The general feeling was that a trade-off of this kind existed, but that it was not very systematic. Since 1985–6, with rescheduling and the pressure to keep spreads down and increase maturities at the same time (the Baker initiative), whatever relationship did exist has become even weaker.

Thirdly, in view of the trend away from using LIBOR as the benchmark interest rate, to which the spread would be added, the question posed was what influenced the choice of base interest rate. The general response was that it was a purely cosmetic exercise; US prime, or whatever interest rate is chosen, is usually higher than LIBOR, thus allowing spreads over US prime to be lower than those quoted over LIBOR for a given return. This is the reason why only spreads over LIBOR were included in the quantitative analysis of chapter 6.3. Some countries prefer pricing over US prime because they believe that the spread is a very important statistic in the market and anything to lower it was welcomed. This indicates a lack of rationality on the part of borrowers. A Japanese bank suggested that many of his bank's customers in 1986–7 preferred Japanese long term prime rate, because it was quite low, and if you believed that the Yen was strong, then such borrowers would gain so long as the Yen did not rise even further.

Regarding fees, most respondents argued that they were there mainly to cover administration costs, but some thought that they were of greater importance than this. One argued that fees moved positively with spreads, implying that when spreads are being squeezed, fees are too and therefore provide little cushion to cover administration costs.

7. Credit Rationing

All banks indicated that they practise credit rationing.They have exposure limits for countries and economic sectors, which are set each year by Head Office.There are also limits on interbank deposits based on a risk assessment of banks with whom they deposit. All respondents were unwilling to reveal these limits.

8. Funding of Loans

About half of those interviewed relied on the interbank market to fund 100 per cent of their dollar loans; and the rest, unless dollar-based banks with a customer base, used the market heavily. Where there was a natural deposit base, then this was used. For example, the British merchant banks obtained sterling from the deposits of non-bank customers: since the merchant banks were not so heavily involved in the Eurocurrency markets, they were able to dispense with large deposits from other banks.

With regard to whether a bank might pay a premium above LIBOR to attract deposits, only the Japanese (in 1974) and the South American banks (throughout the 1970s and 1980s) had had to and were willing. All the others refused a) because if they did it for one bank, they would have to for all and b) because it would amount to admitting to being a bad risk. Since 1974, Japanese banks have been able to get funds at zero premium, because they have been viewed a better risks.

There was no clear evidence that there had been a systematic reduction in the average cost of funds to all banks over time. At any point in time, there is a range of deposit rates at which interbank funds can be obtained. Banks have moved around within that range (the Japanese being a good example). Across all banks, however, there is no evidence that this range of prices has decreased implying that on average a decrease in the cost of funds has not compensated for the decline in spreads. This accounts for the generally held belief that returns have decreased over the last 10 years. It is also noteworthy that most Treasury departments price funds internally (that is, to other departments) at LIBOR, so the syndication department should take this as a benchmark when determining spreads.

Although there was some rationing by price in the market, there was also quantity rationing. The two consortium banks had found it difficult to keep the deposits they had in 1982. At this time, one banker told me, the Bank of England was keeping a close watch on small banks to determine whether they were having difficulties. They were in touch with the banks every week asking which banks had refused to redeposit with them, and then exerted pressure on the latter to redeposit. Nonetheless, it did not prevent one bank losing two-thirds of its deposits within six months of the onset of the crisis in 1982.

The banks are usually involved in both depositing and borrowing in the interbank market. Quantity rationing was found to be universal. As one banker put it, grading banks with which you deposit on the basis of price is very difficult because the market is so competitive. In order to protect yourselves, there is a need to impose limits on each bank with which you deal in the markets.

9. Maturity Transformation

Given that on average some 90 per cent of loans made are funded in the interbank market, that interbank deposits are for six months (at most) and that the maturity of the loans made is usually not less than five years, positive maturity transformation is very evident in the market. Moreover, my study of the banks in London revealed that it had increased greatly over the period 1973–5 and less so over the past four years. I therefore asked bankers why this might have occured. Those who had an opinion thought that the increase over the period 1973–5 was due to competition in the market forcing longer loans; indeed this is believed to be important in the trend towards greater transformation since 1982. More important with respect to the increase between 1982–6 are the rescheduling agreements which have increased the maturity of loans as part of Baker's attempt to improve the international debt situation.

Maturity transformation involves two kinds of risk – interest rate risk and funding risk. Some of the banks interviewed matched the roll-over period of their loans with that of their deposits, thus eliminating interest rate risk. However, a significant number, especially the larger banks, admitted to deliberately mismatching in order to take a view on interest rate movements in the hope of profits. With respect to the second risk – funding risk – all banks recognised the danger involved, but generally felt that there was little they could do; longer term money was more difficult to get and more costly and with spreads as low as they have been, this increased cost would cut profits further or increase losses. The best method of dealing with the funding problem was thought to be maintaining a good relationship with other banks, thus minimising the risk of deposits being withdrawn in a crisis. One of the banks had attempted to lengthen its funding structure by issuing Floating Rate Notes, Preference Shares etc, thereby decreasing their dependence on short term funding.

Notes and References

Introduction

1. The Euromarkets comprise those banks and their customers that deal in Eurocurrencies. The latter are currencies transacted in banks outside the currencies' countries of issue.

1. The Eurocurrency Markets: History and Structure

1. BIS (1964) p. 127.
2. BIS (1964) p. 129.
3. The BIS (1964, p. 127) identify two grey areas that exist, given their above definition; firstly, not all the dollar liabilities nor assets can be regarded as Eurodollars. With respect to liabilities, banks may arrange for credit through their US associates, independent of their Eurodollar business. With respect to assets, banks may place assets in the US money market, again for reasons totally unconnected with their Eurodollar business. We cannot distinguish such cases from the statistics, because they are the result of different motives. Secondly, the dollar deposits may have been acquired indirectly through the conversion of deposits which had been made in another currency. This affects our figures for each individual Eurocurrency market and not the figures for total liabilities and assets.
4. See sections 1.2 and 1.3.
5. See BIS (1964) p. 130.
6. Where 1 billion – 1 thousand million. This will be the case hereafter.
7. The BIS report several statistics. They do not provide a 'global' figure which includes all financial centres in the world. In 1963, the statistics initially covered nine European countries (Belgium, France, Germany, Italy, Luxembourg, Netherlands, Sweden, Switzerland and the United Kingdom) with Canada and Japan included later that year. In 1977, the European segment was extended to include Austria, Denmark and Ireland.

    Data from US banks (foreign branches) together with data from US branches in offshore centres, namely the Bahamas, Cayman Islands and Panama have been included since 1973. Hong Kong and Singapore were added in 1975 and the Lebanon in December 1977 and from September 1979 to September 1981. (Dennis (1984)).

    Increasingly, greater emphasis has been put on the growth of international banking in general rather than the narrower Eurocurrency concept. Although a strictly 'world-wide' measure is not presented, the countries covered include a very large proportion of the volume of international banking (Dennis (1984) p. 23).

    Johnston (1983) categorises these various statistics. The 'broadly defined gross measure' (BDGM) can be defined as;

$$BDGM = IBL - ELdom + Lfor$$

where:

IBL = international bank lending

$ELdom$ = external lending by banks in domestic currencies

$Lfor$ = lending by banks in foreign currencies to residents.

It is a gross measure, because it includes all interbank deposits/liabilities between countries, and it is a broad measure because it extends over the widest geographical area (that is, it includes all the countries mentioned above).

If we restrict the geographical coverage to reporting banks in the European Area alone, excluding lending by the 'offshore' branches of US banks and Canada and Japan, we derive the narrowly defined gross measure. It is this measure that is included in the first two columns of table 1.1a, up until 1981. After 1981, we include external lending by banks in their domestic currencies: in other words, we move closer to a measure of total international bank lending.

I quote these figures because they give the most comprehensive time series published by the BIS. Nevertheless, it can be noted that whichever measure was shown, the overall picture would be the same.

8. See Johnston (1983) p. 11.
9. See Section 1.3 for a fuller discussion of non-dollar Eurocurrencies.
10. See BIS (1964) p. 129.
11. Johnston (1983) p. 40.
12. Johnston (1983) p. 42.
13. These examples are taken from Johnston (1983). See also Dennis (1984) for an outline of the principles involved.
14. Not all switched positions are included since some represent double counting. Johnston (1983) cites the following example: the London bank which has received the switched dollar funds from the German bank may switch into sterling and on-lend the sterling to another London bank. This second London bank, in turn, may switch the sterling back into dollars to fund a loan to a non-bank. In this case, the credit flow would be double-counted if all switches were included.
15. Maturity transformation occurs in a bank if the volume of its claims is different from that of its liabilities within a given maturity range (for example, one to three months). See chapter 6.1 for an analysis of maturity transformation in the Eurocurrency markets.
16. See Johnston (1983) p. 57.
17. See McKenzie (1976) p. 88.
18. The liquidity balance method of calculating the US balance of payments was the most widely used measure by the authorities (see Clendenning (1970)). We essentially want to divide the balance of payments into two sections: *i*) net autonomous transactions; *ii*) net balance of compensatory financial transactions.

    i) represented the deficit/surplus. The main problem was determining whether short term capital movements belonged to category *i*) or *ii*). In the US, this was resolved by distinguishing between short term capital flows initiated by residents and non-residents. If the latter altered the short term assets that the non-resident held in the US then it would fall into category *ii*): if a resident made the same change, it would fall into category *i*), and be an autonomous transaction.

19. Johnston (1983) p. 10.
20. See Bell (1973) p. 84.
21. See BIS (1964) p. 140.
22. Johnston (1983) p. 14.
23. This regulation had its impact prior to 16 May 1973 when three-month maximum interest rate ceilings were abolished for time deposits over $100 000. This implied that US domestic assets that were substitutes for Eurodollar deposits were no longer subject to Regulation Q.
24. See BIS (1965).
25. A Certificate of Deposit (hereafter CD) is a time deposit which matures after a specific period. It is negotiable and can be sold in the secondary market before maturity. They were initially introduced in 1961 by New York banks.
26. The effective cost of borrowing extra funds in the Eurodollar market is derived by dividing the actual Eurodollar rate by the proportion of funds that can be loaned out.
27. See section 1.3 and chapter 4 for a more detailed analysis of the case of Germany and the UK.
28. See Bell (1973) p. 91.
29. In 1974, the Eurocurrency market accounted for about 25 per cent of total financing requirement of deficit countries: other channels included direct investment, concessionary loans and other capital market finance (see Johnston (1983) p. 148 and Stanyer and Whitley (1981)). By 1979, Euromarkets accounted for 50 per cent of financing.
30. See Ellis (1981) p. 353.
31. Ellis (1981) p. 360.
32. Goodman (1980) p. 37.
33. Goodman points to one specific risk particularly associated with international banking, that of political risk associated with sovereign lenders that is, the lender may choose to default and the legal protection in this case is much less than in the case of a private lender's default. See also chapter 6.2.
34. See Marston (1976) in particular.
35. See, for example, McMahon (1985), Kettell and Magnus (1986) and Johnston (1983).
36. See, for example, W. Shepherd, *Market Power and Economic Welfare*, New York, 1970 and Kamien and Schwartz (1975).
37. See, for example, Kamien and Schwartz (1975) for a review of the empirical literature.
38. Table 1.5; The basis for determining inclusion in this table is the origin of the institution's ownership. Each institution, even if it has several different forms of representation, is included only once. Thus the table shows the number of foreign banks represented in London and not the number of representations of foreign banks.

Whilst the rule regarding origin of ownership is clear in theory, a number of problems arise in practice. Branches of foreign banks and UK registered subsidiaries of foreign banks are obviously not included. Some subsidiaries of British banks are included such as Crocker National

Bank (controlled at that time by Midland Bank) because they have a distinct non-British representation in London. Some old British companies now in foreign hands are included, as are others which are not controlled by a single foreign bank and which may have a British partner (for example, consortium banks). See Blanden (1983), (1984a, b), (1985) and (1986) for more details and examples.

39. See Brimmer and Dahl (1975); Buttrill-White (1982); and chapter 1 above.

40. Lees (1976) p. 126. A consortium bank is owned by a group of (around five) other banks, usually large banks, which are well-established in their own domestic markets.

41. *The Banker*, May 1983, p. 10.

42. See Brimmer and Dahl (1975), Goldberg and Saunders (1980) and Buttrill-White (1982).

43. Under Competition and Credit Control (CCC) a reserve ratio of 12.5 per cent applied to both foreign and domestic banks. After 1973, and the apparent failure of CCC to control monetary growth, there was a return to quantitative ceilings on sterling bank lending which now applied to all banks. These were removed in 1979 and reserve requirements were abolished in 1980.

44. Table 1.6; the total number of direct representations shown in this table is greater than those in table 1.5. This is the result of some duplications, for example, those banks with more than one representation, which were omitted from table 1.5.

45. Norinchukin Bank from Japan was the only one not in London in 1984. It set up an office in London in 1985. Blanden (1984b) p. 93.

46. Lees (1976) p. 11.

47. Butrill-White (1982) p. 49.

48. See Euromoney (1984) for a wide-ranging description of these new international banking centres.

49. Because there are no official figures on the size of the market and because the banks are not forthcoming about the extent to which they participate, it is difficult to know how large this market has grown.

50. See *The Banker*, November 1983, p. 63 and Grant (1983, p. 132), who both argue that the desire to receive front-end fees for new loans is one reason why banks like to sell off existing loans.

51. It would appear that the legal situation has not been clarified with regard to subparticipation documents as there have been no test cases.

2 Interdependence and Monetary Policy

1. Llewellyn (1980) recognises these issues, calling them 'constitutional' and 'effective' sovereignty respectively.

2. See particularly Llewellyn (1980) who invokes several definitions of integration.

3. Kenen (1976) p. 16.

4. See Kenen (1976) p. 15.

5. Tests involving this definition include Frenkel and Levich (1975) and Minot (1974).

6. Divergences can be measured by the standard deviation and the coef-

ficient of variation of compatible interest rates in different countries. See Cooper (1971).

7. Llewellyn (1980) p. 170.
8. Sterilisation mechanisms operate to the same end as insulation mechanisms, but are policy induced (see Llewellyn (1980)).
9. Two assets are substitutes for one another when they have similar characteristics that is, similar risk, length to maturity and so forth.
10. Llewellyn (1980) p. 173.
11. The direct controls such as the Supplementary Special Deposits scheme were an effort to control the level of bank lending to the private sector, which proved to be the most difficult part of £M3 to control. The controls consisted of ceilings on interest bearing eligible liabilities of commercial banks.
12. Keynes (1936) Chapter 12 (VII).
13. See for example, Mundell (1963), Fleming (1962) and Mckinnon and Oates (1966).
14. A definition of the correct exchange rate would allow for capital flows that occur as a result of countries being at different stages of development. For example, those at a low state of development would be expected to import capital for development purposes. *Cf.* Krueger's (1983) discussion of Kouri and see Krueger (1983) pp. 63–7 for a discussion of purchasing power parity.
15. See, for example, Meade (1951) for the elasticities approach and Alexander (1952) for the absorption approach.
16. This approach stems from the work of Mundell and Johnson on the monetary approach to the balance of payments (see Frenkel (1976) for a survey of this approach). The monetary approach (a revival of the classical theory) was followed by the portfolio balance approach (for a survey of the literature see Allen and Kenen (1980)). The essential difference between the two (see Krueger (1983) p. 81) is that whereas the monetary approach concentrates on domestic residents' demand for holding domestic money, whilst assuming perfect substitutability between domestic and foreign bonds, the proponents of the portfolio approach emphasise differences in the degree of substitutability between various domestic and foreign assets.
17. Niehans (1977) anticipated this approach: see also an analysis of the approach in Dornbusch (1980).
18. See Williamson (1983) for a discussion of the costs associated with exchange rate misalignment.
19. Many would argue that this occurred in the UK in the early 1980s. See, for example, Allsopp (1985). Layard (1986, p. 72) estimates that half of the deficiency in aggregate demand in the early 1980s was due to low competitiveness because of the appreciation of the pound.
20. Sterilisation could also be achieved through transactions in the domestic securities market alone, see Llewellyn (1980) chapter 12.

3   The Effect of the Eurocurrency Markets on the Arbitrage Process

1. Mundell (1963) and Fleming (1962) separately developed models exam-

ining the impact of monetary and fiscal policies under different exchange rate regimes. Since their initial articles, many additions and modifications have been added to the models. The model here is not a precise representation of their work, but it is in that spirit.

2. Where domestic prices are the prices of non-tradeable goods and imports.

3. Within the literature on international capital movement, we can identify two types of model.

   i) A flow model, which postulates a relationship between interest rate differentials and capital flows that are continuous. As long as an interest rate differential is maintained, a constant capital flow will accompany it. As Krueger (1983, p. 80) points out, there are difficulties associated with treating the 'flow of asset accumulation as a function of the interest rate or interest rate differential. Presumably, the desired level of asset holdings is a stock and one would have to explain why stock adjustment to the desired level was not instantaneous'.

   ii) The portfolio stock adjustment model, which remedies the fault of the flow model, posits that the demand for assets is a stock demand and that equilibrium will be established when wealth holders are satisfied with their portfolios given the level of interest rates and risk. Movements of capital within this framework occur when there are changes in the interest rate differential, causing a once-for-all stock adjustment of investors' portfolios, assuming there is no growth in portfolios. With portfolio growth, the long run outcome is that a greater proportion of the portfolio will be invested in the foreign assets.

4. Assuming that the authorities can control the money supply.

5. This is the case only if we assume constant terms of trade. If we relax this assumption, then some interdependence will result.

6. See for example, Branson and Hill (1971), Herring and Marston (1977) and Argy and Kouri (1974).

7. We are assuming that there is no credit rationing, because we are in a general equilibrium world. We relax this assumption in chapter 5. At present, however, its inclusion would complicate the analysis and detract from the main issue under investigation.

8. For example, if the central bank wanted to reduce domestic liquidity it would buy domestic currency spot and sell it forward (that is, engage in a swap). Banks would thus switch from holding domestic currency with the central bank to holding foreign currency reducing the volume of domestic high powered money (see Llewellyn (1980) p. 139).

9. This is not necessary to achieve flow equilibrium. The diagram below shows a flow equilibrium at E'.

   In this case, speculators believe that the expected future spot rate is such as to give a forward discount of OB on dollars. (The expected future spot rate is depreciated against the actual spot rate by an amount OB). The interest parity level of the forward exchange rate is such that the forward rate is depreciated against the spot rate only by an amount OC. Flow equilibrium occurs at E' where speculators are willing to sell OA of forward dollars, which arbitrageurs are willing to buy. The representation in figure 3.2 (p. 58) is both a flow and a stock equilibrium.

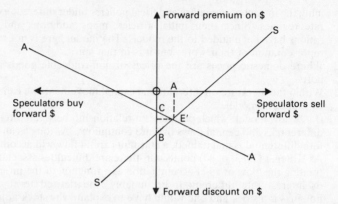

Figure 3.3   Flow Equilibrium in the Forward Exchange Market

10. See, however, chapter 7.3 for a critique of this view. For the present, it is enough that banks believed that the risks were smaller.
11. Ellis (1981) p. 351.
12. All that is theoretically required is that Eurobanks hold less than domestic banks: this assumption made here simplifies the analysis.
13. Many reasons have been put forward for this – see Officer and Willet (1970).

4   Some Empirical Analysis of the US and the UK

1. Following earlier relaxation UK exchange controls were finally abolished on 23 October 1979 (see section 4.5.2).
2. This is not strictly a transaction cost, but does increase the size of the band within which arbitrage is unprofitable.
3. They examine the case of arbitrage between US and UK Treasury bills.
4. He examines the case of arbitrage between US Treasury bills and both Canadian and UK Treasury bills.
5. This is important because it would lead to bias in the estimated coefficients.
6. For an explanation of the instrumental variables technique see, for instance, Koutsoyiannis (1977).
7. The interest rate ceiling became effective when deposit rates rose to their ceiling level and would have risen higher had it not been for the existence of Regulation Q.
8. That is, January 1961 – June 1966, February 1967 – April 1968 and July 1970 – March 1971.
9. See also Kreicher (1982) who uses this same method of an arbitrage tunnel to examine the period 1970–81.
10. This is taken to be the secondary CD rate adjusted for reserve requirements and federal deposit insurance. His justification for using the secondary CD rate is that: 'It appears to be the practice among large US banks to use the secondary market three-month CD rate as a reference

when lending funds' (Johnston (1983) p. 134). See section 4.3 for a discussion of this point.

11. This is measured as the primary CD rate adjusted for reserve requirements.

12. Subsequent to the completion of this research, Giavazzi (1987) has noted that the impact of exchange control abolition removed the differential between Euromarket interest rates and UK domestic interest rates (Giavazzi (1987) pp. 108–9).

13. The Eurodollar and Eurosterling interest rates are middle market rates for the last working day of the month. The interest rates and forward premium are taken from the *Bank of England Quarterly Bulletin*, Statistical Appendix.

14. Other calculations for periods of different lengths showed similar results.

15. Regulation Q, three-month maximum interest rate ceilings were abolished on 16 May 1973 for time deposits over $100 000. This means that US domestic assets that are substitutes for Eurodollar deposits were no longer subject to Regulation Q. We do not expect to find, therefore, any influence from Regulation Q. In contrast, other US monetary policies may have affected the Eurodollar market.

16. Johnston (1983) and Kreicher (1982) claim that during 1979, US banks faced an inward arbitrage incentive, implying that they became net takers from the Eurodollar market. Kreicher argues that this was the result of a fall in Eurodollar rates as new deposits increased substantially in the wake of the second oil price shock (see Kreicher (1982) p. 17). The official BIS figures quoted here, whilst showing a decline in net supplies of funds to the Eurodollar market during 1979, do not support the contention that US banks were overall net demanders of funds. Kreicher (1982) looks only at US' banks positions *vis-à-vis* their foreign branches rather than their total external position which is given by the BIS figures.

17. The US domestic CD rate has been adjusted for reserve requirements and FDIC as implied by the formula. The latter cost is 0.036 per cent (see Kreicher (1982, p. 13) and Johnson (1983, p. 141, n. 9)). Reserve requirements (RR) have varied over the period 1979–84 (see the *Federal Reserve Bulletin*). From January 1979–July 1980, the RR was 6 per cent basic plus a 2 per cent supplementary RR (that is, 8 per cent in total). In July, the supplementary RR was abolished. In November 1980, the basic RR was reduced to 3 per cent. There were also marginal reserve requirements in place between October 1979 and July 1980. However, these do not represent a cost on all domestic borrowing because they apply only to increases in banks' CD liabilities over a certain base. Hence it is difficult to include them in an adjusted CD rate of the type presented here, because their impact on the cost of borrowing will vary from bank to bank.

18. These graphs are based on figures from the *Federal Reserve Bulletin* (Statistical Appendix). The rates are average monthly rates on three-month Eurodollar deposits and three-month secondary CDs.

19. The declared reason was that it was thought that the 'relationship between the monetary base and aggregate nominal demand . . . [was] likely to be more stable and predictable than the corresponding relation-

ship invoking the various money supply measures' (*FRBNY Quarterly Review*, Winter, 1979–80, p. 1).

20. *FRBNY Quarterly Review*, 1979–80, pp. 54–5.
21. Bank of England (1984) p. 133, para. 29.
22. *FRBNY Quarterly Review*, Summer 1980, pp. 9–10.
23. A shift of funds from savings deposits (not part of M1–B) to automatic transfer accounts (part of M1–B) was also responsible for this money supply figure.
24. The Federal Reserve refused to adjust the broad range for the Federal Funds rate (at that time 15–20 per cent) despite the fact that the rate had fallen below the bottom end of the range.
25. *FRBNY Quarterly Review*, Spring 1983, p. 39.
26. See *FRBNY Quarterly Review*, Spring 1983, pp. 46–54 for a detailed account of these institutional developments.
27. *FRBNY Quarterly Review*, Spring 1984, p. 39.
28. *FRBNY Quarterly Review*, Spring 1984, p. 39.
29. See BIS *Annual Report*, 1979/80, pp. 106–110.
30. The interest rates are taken from the *Bank of England Quarterly Bulletin* (Statistical Appendix). They are middle market rates quoted on the last working day of the month. The LA temporary loan rate is a parallel money market rate. A high proportion of interbank deposits are deposited in the LA market, suggesting that it is a good substitute for Eurodollar or Eurosterling markets (see Einzig (1974)).
31. *BEQB*, March 1974, pp. 25–27.
32. *BEQB*, March 1974, p. 11.
33. *BEQB*, June 1974, p. 125, p. 142.
34. See *BEQB* March 1975, p. 20.
35. See also the *Bank of England Quarterly Bulletin* for detailed monthly accounts of interest rate and exchange rate movements.
36. See Appendix I, p. 226, for a summary of events in 1975–79.
37. See *BEQB* (June 1979) p. 130 and *BEQB* (1979, September) p. 271. The UK was becoming more self-sufficient in oil production: self-sufficiency was expected to be reached in 1980 (BEQB March 1979, p. 34). The net import bill for oil was therefore being reduced, helping to strengthen the pound. This was an important factor in the abolition of exchange controls: the exchange rate had been arguably too high to allow the UK to compete in world markets because of North Sea oil (see *The Banker*, May 1979, p. 19, and *The Economist*, 27 October 1979).
38. See Cairncross (1973) p. 56.
39. With the exception of loans to governments in default and governments that had not funded their war debts.
40. Enacted during the financial crisis of 1931, the Act took the UK off the Gold Standard.
41. Yeager (1966) p. 343.
42. *The Economist*, 26 September 1931, p. 555.
43. Persons living outside the UK could now sell sterling at the $4.03 parity for dollars or other currencies.
44. *BEQB* December 1980.
45. There was concern over the level of reserves owing to the need under the

Bretton Woods system to intervene to maintain the fixed exchange rate in accordance with the IMF Articles of Agreement. When a currency is weak, under a fixed exchange rate regime, there is a cost in terms of fluctuations in exchange reserves involved in maintaining the declared par exchange rate and the need for foreign currency reserves is great. The floating of the pound in 1972 did not radically reduce the need for reserves, since the government was fairly active in managing the exchange rate until the end of October 1977 (see BEQB December 1977). Since then intervention has taken place to maintain orderliness in the foreign exchange markets, and indeed on occasion to try to stabilise the exchange rate. We discuss exchange rate policy more fully in section 4.6 of this chapter.

46. The authorities did permit some enlargements by allowing foreign borrowing to finance an investment in foreign securities, for example.

47. The price of foreign exchange in this market commanded a variable premium, which fluctuated according to the demand and supply in the market. When selling the proceeds of sales of foreign assets only 75 per cent could be sold on the investment currency market. The other 25 per cent had to be sold in the official foreign market. Thus only 75 per cent of the premium was potentially recoverable. For a fuller discussion, see *BEQB* September 1976, p. 314.

48. Permission was required to open and operate a foreign currency account. This was usually given only to firms with trading interests abroad or persons with sources of income from abroad and regular commitments (see Bank of England (1977), p. 12).

49. See Einzig and Quinn (1977), p. 94.

50. Article 67 of the Treaty of Rome stated that:
    'Member states shall, in the course of the transitional period and to the extent necessary for the proper functioning of the Common market, progressively abolish as between themselves restrictions on the movements of capital belonging to persons resident in member states and also any discriminatory treatment based on the place in which capital is invested'.
    Prior to December 1962, there were four categories according to the degree of liberalisation which was obligatory. In a directive (December 1962), categories 1 and 2 were essentially combined. Category 1 covers direct investments and their liquidation, dealings in quoted securities across countries, personal capital flows, and short/medium term credit connected with transactions in goods and services. These must be fully liberalised, apart from temporary recourse allowed in exceptional circumstances. Category 2 refers to new issues by enterprises, medium/long term credits of a purely financial nature and transactions in unquoted securities. The directive (December 1962) called for these to be liberalised conditionally, that is, restrictions can be reimposed if economic conditions warrant it and if the Commission allows it.
    Category 3 refers to short term capital movements, the opening of and payments into bank accounts. There are no recommendations concerning these. McMahon (1964).

51. See Parker (1978), Appendix on changes in February 1979.

52. *BEQB* June 1979, p. 111.
53. *BEQB* June 1979, p. 111.
54. *BEQB* March 1980.
55. Laidler (1985) p. 36. See also note 11, chapter 2.
56. Allsopp (1985) p. 3–4.
57. Allsopp (1985) p. 5. This was especially marked in terms of normalised unit labour costs: competitiveness according to this measure fell 20 per cent in 1979 alone.
58. See note 11, chapter 2.
59. For all full classification of all the possibilities, see Llewellyn (1979).
60. See Llewellyn (1979), p. 47.
61. *BEQB*, December, 1980, pp. 228–9 and March 1981, pp. 38–9.
62. See *BEQB* December 1976, p. 411.
63. Other instances of UK interest rates changing in response to changes in interest rates abroad occurred in October 1979, August–October 1981, and the first half of 1984.

5 Competition, Stability and Efficiency in International Banking

1. Friedman and Schwartz (1982).
2. See Fisher (1932), Keynes (1936), Kalecki (1971), Minsky (1982a, b) and Kindleberger (1978).
3. Overindebtedness can be defined as a state where firms, banks or individuals in the economy have insufficient liquidity to meet liabilities currently falling due. This leads to distress selling (that is, selling of assets to acquire liquidity) which may become widespread.
4. McClam (1982), p. 286.
5. The question of supervision and regulation is discussed in chapter 7 where we examine the validity of the neoclassical view, given the analysis which is to follow in this chapter and the empirical work of chapter 6.
6. That is, will always choose to finance the investment with the lowest risk for any given level of expected return.
7. This is the *raison d'être* of financial intermediaries. Since they can hold a diversified portfolio of loans, they can offer loans at risk premia which take into account only the systematic risk of the loan and hence offer loans at lower interest rates than the average saver, who would be unable to have such a diversified portfolio.
8. This argument is an interpretation of Keynesian notions of regional multipliers.
9. The weights are derived from regressing bank revenue from interest earning assets against a composition of earning assets.
10. Moreover, these non-lending activities contribute 10 per cent to bank income. (Greenbaum (1967a)).
11. He recognises that capital inadequacy would mean bankruptcy. However, he makes the simpler assumption that capital inadequacy implies costly rearrangement of the bank's portfolio, because the costs of bankruptcy are more difficult to assess. Clearly, this assumption is a weakness, but the reserve case still applies.

12. An example is the deposits of dollars in Europe, which were placed by the Soviet Union for political reasons. This, as we saw in chapter 1, was one of the early factors behind the establishment of the Eurodollar market.

13. Jaffee and Modigliani note that Freimer and Gordon do not have to include a demand for loans curve for their concept of strict credit rationing, even though it is similar to equilibrium rationing. This is because Freimer and Gordon argue that the bank sets a 'conventional' interest rate. The banker then grants loans to customers up to the amount indicated by the bank's supply curve for each customer, given the 'conventional' interest rate.

14. Where acceptable is defined as safe or non-crisis producing.

15. That is, without causing the adverse selection or incentive effects to operate.

16. See Artis and Lewis (1981), chapter 5.

17. See Hewson (1975), Niehans and Hewson (1976) and Weston (1980).

18. Liquidity can be defined both in terms of assets and liabilities. The more basic definition is that in terms of liabilities: liquidity relates to the ability to meet current/future, expected/unexpected obligations (debts). Defining liquidity on the asset side of the balance sheet produces the following: liquidity relates to the ability to transform assets into means of payments that enable us to meet these obligations. Liquidity is produced by banks if the maturity of loans is greater than the maturity of the deposit which financed the loan.

19. See, for example, Kindleberger (1978), Revell (1978), Barclay (1978) and Minsky (1982a, b).

20. It should be noted that a recent body of literature on rational speculative bubbles has sought to explain financial crisis within a neoclassical rational expectations framework (see Blanchard and Watson (1982) and Capie and Woods (1986)). See Oppenheimer and Gibson (forthcoming) for a discussion of the applicability of these models to the international debt crisis.

21. Demand may also increase but since we have assumed that the banks are quite eager to take part in new opportunities, supply is still likely to outstrip demand.

22. Indeed, the exogenous shock may help to promote such a trend. See also chapter 1.4.

23. This may result in a conflict with the need for diversification to spread risk and may account for increasing concentration of loans to some LDCs (see chapter 6).

24. Llewellyn (1982) points to the cases of the American banks in 1974 and Japanese in 1977 whose entrance into the market, after regulations preventing entry were removed caused once-for-all stock increases in international lending which put pressure on profits.

25. See Revell (1980), Pitman (1985), Group of Thirty (1982b) and Bance (1979) to name but a few.

26. We can note here that there may be some potential borrowers who are not experiencing such easy conditions: that is, those whom the banks do not see as creditworthy for example, poorer developing countries.

27. See Brett (1983), p. 227 and Edwards (1981).

28. For example, as banks did with the OPEC borrowers; they never took into account what would happen if the cartel broke down.
29. *Cf.* the secondary banking crisis in the UK in 1973–4, when new entrants engaged in imprudent activities which were profitable because of the general boom in property prices, but which proved to be crisis producing when economic euphoria declined as a result of problems appearing. In this case, many of those involved were new entrants, but even the more established banks, with their greater experience, became involved (see Reid (1982)).
30. See Pecchioli (1982), p. 48 and Brimmer and Dahl (1975), p. 360.
31. See Bagehot (1878), p. 50, Fisher (1935) and Oppenheimer (1985). Cycles of optimism and pessimism may lead to procyclical lending, that is, where the banks are willing to lend more on the upswing of the cycle when borrowers are less in need of credit: on the downswing, when credit is necessary, banks are less willing to lend. The withdrawal of credit after 1982 caused many countries to experience repayment difficulties which they would otherwise not have done. Procyclical lending intensifies a crisis (see chapter 6).
32. See Group of Thirty (1982b), p. 30.
33. See Chari and Jagannathan, 'Banking Panics, Information and Rational Expectations Equilibrium', *BRC Working Paper*, no.112, Northwestern University, J L Kellogg School of Management, 1984 and Postlewaite and Vives, 'Bank Runs as an Equilibrium Phenomenon', unpublished, University of Pennsylvania, 1984. Both these papers are discussed in Diamond (1987) and it is to that discussion which I refer.
34. Diamond and Dybvig (1983).
35. Batchelor (1986).
36. For example, Diamond and Dybvig (1983), Batchelor (1986) and Diamond (1987).
37. The bank is insolvent because the contract specifies that the bank will pay a return (less than the return on a unit invested if left until period 2) even if the deposit is liquidated in period 1. The value of this return depends on the number of depositors expected to withdraw in period 1. However, the value of its assets in the event that all are liquidated in period 1 is equal only to the initial value of the deposit.
38. Sunspots have been characterised as extrinsic / extraneous uncertainty (for example, 'animal spirits', crowd psychology) which thus have nothing to do with 'economic fundamentals' (Diamond (1987) p. 93). Sunspots can generate self-fulfilling prophecies which result in fluctuations in economic activity even within rational expectations models with full price flexibility (see for example, Azariadis (1981), Cass and Shell (1983), Woodford (1987) and Diamond (1987)). As such they provide a rationale for government intervention to smooth the fluctuations.
39. Diamond and Dybvig (1983) recognise that the existence of such risk may lead to a moral hazard problem (see chapter 7.3). They argue, as we do, that the existence of moral hazard may provide a case for bank regulation or supervision.
40. Banks extend their *loans* on a fixed nominal value basis because this reduces information and monitoring costs associated with granting a loan

whose return depends on the project's outcome (Goodhart (1987) p. 86).
41. This is discussed further in chapter 7.

6 Maturity, Transformation, Risk-Return Analysis and Credit Rationing in the Euromarkets

1. The reporting area includes Belgium, Luxembourg, France, the Federal Republic of Germany, Italy, the Netherlands, Sweden, Switzerland, the UK, Canada, Japan and the US.
2. Ellis (1981) uses data from the Bank of England on the maturity distribution of assets and liabilities in foreign currencies of banks in London for the period 1975–1981.
3. See section 6.1.3 for an analysis of the methods he employs.
4. Liquidity is a property of the balance sheet as a whole. A position can be described as liquid even though the assets held are not due to mature for five years, as long as no liabilities need to be met prior to that. When we introduce uncertainty with respect to the timing of our obligations, an investor's liquidity preference is shifted towards the more liquid end of the spectrum of assets to allow greater flexibility, in the event that obligations fall due earlier than expected.
5. Nagy (1984) p. 1.
6. Nagy (1984) estimates that the annual cost at mid-1983 of evaluation of 100 countries and in-depth studies of 20 was $850 000.
7. Kettell and Magnus (1986) p. 63.
8. Nagy (1984) p. 10. See also Appendix III, p. 237.
9. Friedman in Ensor (1981).
10. Caldwell and Villamil in Ensor (1981).
11. Yassukovich (1976).
12. Nagy (1984) p. 14.
13. See, for example, Thompson (in Ensor (1981)), Caldwell and Villamil (in Ensor (1981)), Sofia (1979) and Nagy (1984, chapter 6).
14. See for example, Tunney (in Ensor (1981)) and Puz (1977).
15. Sofia in Ensor (1981) and Nagy (1984).
16. Sofia in Ensor (1981).
17. Although some countries, for example, Brazil, used the interbank market to secure additional loans which then proved to be non-withdrawable.
18. See also Heffernan (1986).
19. Group of Thirty (1982a) p. 10.
20. Many of the merchant banks, who had been involved only to a small extent, were able to sell off most of their participations and thus run down their involvement in the Eurocredit markets.
21. *Cf.* the portfolio approach employed by Fleming and Howson (1980), which is similar but emphasises the opportunity cost of lending in the Euromarkets as the main determinant of spreads.
22. See Goodman (1980) p. 49; he examines the period 1973–1979.
23. See Fleming and Howson (1980) p. 317; they also examine the period 1973–1980.
24. Goodman (1980) divides the period 1972–80 into four parts:

> *i*) 1970 to 1972 – lender's market;
> *ii*) late 1972 to mid-1974 – borrower's market;
> *iii*) mid-1974 to mid-1977 – lender's market;
> *iv*) mid-1977 to mid-1980 – borrower's market.

This emphasises the tendency for conditions to move cyclically. A lender's market is associated with shorter maturities and higher spreads. A borrower's market is associated with longer maturities and lower spreads.

25. See Saade (1978, 1981) and Bance (1983, 1984).
26. Fleming and Howson (1980) p. 314.
27. Fees are not generally publicised, whereas spreads are. Thus the sample of loans which include both spreads and fees is much smaller than that which includes spreads alone.
28. World Bank *Lending in International Capital Markets*.
29. I have included FRNs within these spread calculations firstly because they give some indication of the spreads borrowers are able to get, and secondly because banks themselves tend to keep the majority of the issue (see *The Banker*, February 1984, p. 55). Although such notes are more liquid than Eurocredits (even with a secondary market) this is true – as I argued in chapter 1.4 – only in normal market conditions. Their main influence is in 1985 and 1986.
30. See, for example, Goodman (1980) who looks at movements in spreads from 1972 to 1979.
31. Goodman (1980) p. 45.
32. Bance (1983).
33. Years 1979–83 were taken from the Euromoney *International Loan Annual*, 1984. Years 1984–1986 were calculated from the same data used by Euromoney. Loans of all currencies are included, with non-dollar loans being converted to dollars at the end-of-month exchange rates. This table is likely to underestimate the volume of lending as only published loans are included.
34. The groupings shown are slightly different from the ones in sections 6.3.2 and 6.3.4 because the source (Euromoney (1984)) used different groupings for the period 1979–1983 and these are followed in the calculations here. Nonetheless this is not important as the individual country volumes are more important.
35. If we compare the medium term new money loans of table 6.3 with that of new money under rescheduling agreements in table 6.4, we can see that there are discrepancies. For example, in the case of Brazil, table 6.3 shows that over the period 1982–4 Brazil raised $11 999 million in new money. Table 6.4, however, has a figure of $10 900 million. This difference arises because table 6.4 only includes new money that was granted as part of the rescheduling agreement. Table 6.3 includes new money not associated with rescheduling, usually borrowed by private companies without government guarantee.
36. These figures exclude Poland's and Yugoslavia's new money deals which accompanied their rescheduling agreements in 1982 and 1983 respectively.
37. Montagnon (1983) p. 43.
38. Montagnon (1983) p. 44 and Magnus and Kettell (1986) pp. 65–6.

7 Policy Implications of the Internationalisation of Capital

1. See Kettell and Magnus (1986) p. 164, Lever and Huhne (1986) p. 138 and Lomax (1982).
2. Lever and Huhne (1985) p. 138.
3. Lepetit (comment on Solow (1982)) and Flannery in Gardener (1981) both use this argument.
4. See, for example, Cline (1984) and Lever and Huhne (1985).
5. Lepetit, comment on Solow (1982), p. 251.
6. See, for example, Reid (1982) and Gardener (1986) p. 10.
7. See Cline (1984) p. 12.
8. See Appendix III on p. 239.
9. See chapter 6.2.
10. Chapter 6.3.
11. However, the Johnson Matthey Bankers collapse suggested that the Bank of England had not adequately supervised JMB's exposures under the criteria set out in this document. 40 per cent of JMB's portfolio was loaned out to one country (see Ollard and Routledge (1985)). Thus at the domestic level, it seems that the Bank of England was particularly slack. Ollard and Routledge indicate that the whole episode suggests a revision of the Bank of England's supervisory methods.
12. See Blunden (1977), Johnston (1983), Muller (1985) and Peake (1986) for a more detailed discussion of their aims and agreements.
13. See, for example, Grant (1982).
14. This point has a lot of support in the literature – see, for example, Stewart and Sengupta (1982), Brett (1985) and Killick (1981).
15. Commercial loans increased from 49 per cent of total flows to non-oil developing countries in 1973 to 60 per cent in 1980 (Stewart and Sengupta (1982) p. 94).
16. See Brett (1985) p. 233 which is confirmed by our findings in chapter 6.
17. See also Ros (1987) and di Tella (1987) who examine capital flight in Mexico and Argentina respectively.
18. See, for example, Cline (1984), Allsopp and Joshi (1986) and Diaz-Alejandro (1984).
19. Cline (1984) provides a comprehensive survey of this approach.
20. Cline (1984) pp. 26–7. See also section 7.3.
21. The costs of default no longer outweigh the benefits (if we analyse default in terms of Eaton and Gersovitch (1982)). The cost of default is the lack of access to the international capital markets in the forseeable future. Where access is denied in the present (which is the case given the negative transfers), then the costs of default are much less and the benefits could conceivably outweigh these costs.
22. See Cline (1984), Kettell and Magnus (1986), Lever and Huhne (1985) and Griffith-Jones and Sunkel (1986) for a more detailed discussion of their proposals. Here we look only at the broad principles of the approach rather than the exact detail.
23. The main proponent of this view is Cline (1984).
24. This agency need not be a new one. Indeed, reforms of existing international financial institutions would be preferable to avoid duplication

and the expense of setting up a new body. Reform, however, is important and we address this question now, with reference to the IMF in particular, but the conclusions apply to all public international financial institutions.

25. Some relevant literature includes Körner *et al* (1984), Stewart and Sengupta (1982), Spraos (1984), Brett (1985), Diaz-Alejandro (1984), Dornbusch (1984), Lever and Huhne (1985) and various articles from the IDS Bulletin (January, 1983).

26. I do not wish to look at these policies in great detail here. Stewart and Sengupta (1982) and Körner *et al* (1984), among others, provide a thorough critique of specific IMF programmes which show, in my view, the validity of the arguments being presented here.

27. Griffith-Jones (1983) p. 51.

Bibliography

Abbreviations

AER	*American Economic Review*
BEQB	*Bank of England Quarterly Bulletin*
BIS	Bank for International Settlements
CUP	Cambridge University Press
EER	*European Economic Review*
FRBNY	Federal Reserve Bank of New York
IEA	Institute of Economic Affairs
JF	*Journal of Finance*
JIE	*Journal of International Economics*
JMCB	*Journal of Money, Credit and Banking*
JME	*Journal of Monetary Economics*
JPE	*Journal of Political Economy*
OEP	*Oxford Economic Papers*
OUP	Oxford University Press
PEIF	Princeton Essays in International Finance
PSIF	Princeton Studies in International Finance
QJE	*Quarterly Journal of Economics*
Scan.JE	*Scandinavian Journal of Economics*

AKERLOFF, G., (1970) 'The market for lemons; Qualitative uncertainty and the market mechanism', *QJE*, 84, pp. 488–500

ALDI, A. F., (1977) 'Foreign Exchange and other Problems – Franklin National Bank' in Altman and Sametz (eds) *Financial Crises: Institutions and Markets in a Fragile Environment*, New York, Interscience

ALEXANDER, S., (1952) 'Effects of a Devaluation on a Trade Balance' *IMF Staff Papers*, 2, pp. 263–78

ALHADEFF, D., (1954) *Monopoly and Competition in Banking*, University of California Press

ALIBER, R. Z., (1974) *National Monetary Policy and International Financial Integration*, University of Chicago Press

— (1973) 'The Interest Rate Parity Theorem: A Reinterpretation' *JPE*, 81(6), pp. 1451–9

ALLEN, P. R., (1976) *Organisation and Administration of a Monetary Union* PSIF, No. 38

ALLEN, P. R., and KENEN, P., (1980) *Asset Markets, Exchange Rates and Economic Integration*, CUP

ALLSOPP, C. J., (1985) 'The Assessment: Monetary and Fiscal Policy in the 1980s', *Oxford Review of Economic Policy*, 1(1), pp. 1–20

ALLSOPP, C. J., and JOSHI, V. R., (1986) 'The Assessment: The International Debt Crisis', *Oxford Review of Economic Policy*, 2(1), pp. i–xxxiii

ANGELINI, A., Eng and F. Lees (Angelini *et al* (1979)) *International Lending, risk and the Euromarkets*, Macmillan, London

257

ARGY V., and HODJERA, Z., (1973) 'Financial Integration and Interest Rate Linkages in Industrial Countries' *IMF Staff Papers*, 20(1), pp. 1–77

ARGY, V., and KOURI, P., (1974) 'Sterilisation Policies and the Volatility of International Reserves' in R. Z. Aliber (ed) *National Monetary Policies and the International Financial System*, Chicago University Press

ARTIS, M. J., and LEWIS M. K., (1981) *Monetary Control in the United Kingdom*, Phillip Allen

AZARIADES, C., (1981) 'Self-fulfilling prophecies', *Journal of Economic Theory*, 25, pp. 380–96

BAGEHOT, W., (1878) *Lombard Street; a description of the money market*, London, 7th edition

BALTENSPERGER, E., (1972) 'Economies of Scale, Firm size and Concentration in Banking', *JMCB*, 4(3), pp. 467–488

BANCE, N., (1979) 'Trading the lead banks: who's competing hardest?' *Euromoney*, August 1979, pp. 14–30

— (1983) 'Swedish signing lifts market morale', *Euromoney*, May 1983, p. 21

— (1984) 'Back to the Borrower's Market', *Euromoney*, May 1984, p. 61

BANK FOR INTERNATIONAL SETTLEMENTS *Annual Reports*, 1963/4 to 1985/6, Basle

BANK FOR INTERNATIONAL SETTLEMENTS (1983) 'The international interbank market', *BIS Economic Papers*, no. 8, July, 1983

BANK OF ENGLAND (1977) *A guide to UK Exchange Controls*

— (1984) *Operation and Control of Monetary Policy*, London

— (1985) *Large Exposures Undertaken by Institutions Authorised under the Banking Act 1979*, Bank of England Consultative Paper, London

BARCLAY, C., (1978) 'Competition and Financial Crises – Past and Present', in Barclay, Gardener and Revell (eds), pp. 1–23

BARCLAY, C., GARDENER, E. P. M., and REVELL, J., (1978) *Competition and Regulation of Banks*, University of Wales Press, Cardiff

BATCHELOR, R. A., (1986) 'The avoidance of Catastrophe: Two nineteenth century banking crises', in Capie, F., and Woods, G. E., (eds) *Financial Crises and the World Banking System*, Macmillan, London

BELL, F. W., and MURPHY, N. B., (1968) *Cost in commercial banking: A quantitative analysis of bank behaviour, and its relation to bank regulation*, Research Report, No. 41, Federal Reserve Bank of Boston, Boston

BELL, G., (1973) *The Eurodollar Market and the International Financial System*, Macmillan, London

BEQB (1970) 'The Euro-currency Business of the Banks in London', *BEQB*, 10(1), pp. 31–40

— (1976) 'The Investment Currency Market' *BEQB*, 16(3), p. 314

— (1980) 'The Foreign Exchange Market in London', *BEQB*, 20(4), pp. 437–444

BENSTON, G., (1972) 'Economies of Scale in Financial Institutions', *JMCB*, 4 pp. 312–41

BERNOULLI, D., (1954) 'Exposition of a new theory on the measurement of risk', *Econometrica*, 22, pp. 23–36

BIRD, G., (1985) *World Finance and Adjustment: An Agenda for Reform*, Macmillan, London

BLANCHARD, O. J., and WATSON, M. W., (1982) 'Bubbles, rational, expectations and financial markets', in Wachtel (ed), pp. 295–315

BLANDEN, M., (1983) 'The foreign Banking Community Grows', *The Banker*, November 1983, pp. 111–120

—, M., (1984a) 'Foreign Banks: The impetus slackens', *The Banker*, February 1984, pp. 89–93

— (1984b) 'Newcomers to the City' *The Banker*, November 1984, pp. 93–105

— (1985) 'Foreign Banks Regroup' *The Banker*, November 1985, pp. 101–105

— (1986) 'Bigger Role for foreign banks in London' *The Banker*, November 1986, pp. 69–73

BLUME, M. E., (1971) 'On the Assessment of Risk', *JF*, 26(1), pp. 1–10

BLUNDEN, G., (1977) 'Control and Supervision of the Foreign Operations of Banks', in Wadsworth *et al* (eds), *Development of Financial Institutions in Europe*, Sijthoff-Leyden

BRANSON, W. H., (1969) 'Minimum Covered Interest Differential for Interest Arbitrage Activity' *JPE*, 77(6), pp. 1028–35

BRANSON, W. H. and HILL, R., (1971) *Capital Movements in the OECD Area: An Econometric Analysis* OECD Occasional Studies, Paris

BRETT, E. A., (1983) *International Money and Capitalist Crisis*, Heinemann, London

—, E. A., (1985) *The World Economy since the War: the Politics of Uneven Development*, Macmillan, London

BRIMMER, A. F. and DAHL, F. R., (1975) 'Growth of American international banking: implications for public policy' *JF*, 30(2), pp. 341–63

BRUCKER, E., (1970) 'A Microeconomic Approach to Banking Competition', *JF*, 25(5), pp. 1113–1141

BUTTRILL-WHITE, B., (1982) 'Foreign Banking in the United States: A Regulatory and Supervisory Perspective', *FRBNY Quarterly Review*, Summer 1982

CAIRNCROSS, A., (1973) *Control of Long-term International Capital Movements*, Brookings Institution

CALDWELL, J. A., and VILLAMIL, J. A., (1981) 'Factors Affecting Creditworthiness', in Ensor (ed) pp. 19–25

CAPIE, F., and WOODS, G. E., (1986) *Financial Crises and the World Banking System*, Macmillan, London

CASS, D., and SHELL, K., (1983) 'Do sunspots matter' *JPE*, 91(21), pp. 193–227

CHALMERS, E. B., (1969), ed. *Readings in the Eurodollar*

CHARI, V., and JAGANNATHAN, R., (1984) 'Banking Panics, Information and Rational Expectations Equilibrium', *BRC Working Paper*, No. 112, Northwestern University, J. L. Kellogg School of Management

CLENDENNING, W., (1970) *The Eurodollar Market*, Clarendon Press, Oxford

CLINE, W. R., (1984) *International Debt: Systemic Risk and Policy Response*, Institute for International Economics, Washington DC

COOPER, R. N., (1968) *The Economics of Interdependence*, McGraw-Hill, New York

— (1971) 'Towards an International Capital Market?' in C. Lindeberger and A. Schonfield (eds), *North American and Western European Economic Policy*, St. Martin's Press, New York

— (1972) 'Eurodollars, Reserve Dollars, and Asymmetries in the International Monetary System', *JIE*, 2(4), pp. 325–44

CORDON, W. H., (1972) *Monetary Integration* PEIF, No. 93

CROCKETT, A. D., (1976) 'The Euro-currency Market: An Attempt to Clarify Some Basic Issues' *IMF Staff Papers*, 23(2), pp. 375–86

CURTIN, D., (1981) 'The Mysterious Charm of Borrowing over Prime', *Euromoney*, June 1981, p. 46

DAVIES, S. I., (1976) *The Euro-bank: its origins, management and outlook*, Macmillan, London

— (1980) 'Why Strategic Planning is the Key to Eurobanking', *Euromoney*, August 1980, p. 86

DENNIS, G., (1984) *International Financial Flows*, London, Graham & Trotman

DIAMOND, D. W., and DYBVIG, P. H., (1983) 'Bank Runs, Deposit Insurance and Liquidity', *Journal of Political Economy*, 1983, pp. 401–19

DIAMOND, P., (1987) 'Multiple Equilibria in Models of Credit' *AER Papers and Proceedings*, 77(2), pp. 82–86

DIAZ-ALEJANDRO, C. F., (1984) 'Latin American Debt: I don't think we are in Kansas any more', *Brookings Papers on Economic Activity*, 2, pp. 335–389

DI TELLA, G., (1987) 'Argentina's most recent Inflationary Cycle, 1975–85' in Thorp and Whitehead (eds), *Latin American Debt and the Adjustment Crisis*, Macmillan, London

DORNBUSCH, R., (1980) *Openeconomy Macroeconomics*, Basic Books, New York

— (1984) 'On muddling through the Debt Crisis', *World Economy*, 7

DORNBUSCH, R., and FISCHER, S., (1980) 'Exchange Rates and the Current Account' *AER*, 69, pp. 639–49

DUE, J. F. and CLOWER, R. W., (1966) *Intermediate Economic Analysis*, 5th ed., Irwin, Illinois

DUFFEY, G., and GIDDY, I., (1978) *The International Money Market*, Prentice Hall

EATON, J., and GERSOVITZ, M., (1981) *Poor Country Borrowing in Private Financial Markets and the Repudiation Issue*, PSIE, no. 47

EDWARDS, F. R., (1981) 'Financial Institutions in the 21st Century: After the Crash?' in Verheirstraeten (ed) *Competition and Regulation in Financial Markets*, Macmillan, London

EINZIG, P., (1974) *Parallel Money Markets: Volume 1; The new money markets in London*, Macmillan, London

EINZIG, P., and QUINN, B., (1977) *The Euro-dollar System*, Macmillan, 6th ed.

ELLIS, J. C., (1981) 'Eurobanks and the Interbank Market', *BEQB*, 21(3), pp. 351–64

ENSOR, R., (1981) *Assessing Country Risk*, Euromoney Publications, London

EUROMONEY (1984) *International Banking Centres*, Euromoney Publications, London

EVITT, H. E., (1945) *Exchange and Trade Controls in Theory and Practice*, Pitman & Sons, London

FABER, M., (1987) 'Guardian Third World Review', *The Guardian*, Saturday 6 June

FEDER, G., and JUST, R. E., (1977) 'A Study of Debt Servicing Capacity Applying Logit Analysis', *Journal of Development Economics*, 4, pp. 25–38

FIELD, P., (1980) 'Meet the new Breed of Banker: the political risk expert', *Euromoney*, July 1980

FINANCIAL MARKET TRENDS (1982) 'The Medium-Term Euro-credit Market in 1978–81' *Financial Market Trends*, March 1982

FISHER, I., (1932), *Booms and Depressions*, New York

FLANNERY, M. J., (1986) 'Deposit Insurance Creates a Need for Bank Regulation', in Gardener (ed), pp. 257–269

FLEMING, A., and HOWSON, S., (1980) 'Conditions in the Syndicated Medium-term Eurocredit Market', *BEQB*, 20(3), pp. 311–18

FLEMING, M., (1962) 'Domestic Financial Policies Under Fixed and Under Floating Exchange Rates' *IMF Staff Papers*, 9, pp. 369–79

FLOOD, R. P., and GARBER, P. M., (1982) 'Bubbles, Runs and Gold Monetization', in Wachtel (ed), pp. 275–93

FRANK, C. R. and CLINE, W. R., (1971) 'Measurement of Debt Servicing Capacity: an Application of Discriminant Analysis', *JIE*, 1, pp. 327–344

FREEDMAN, C., (1977) 'A Model of the Euro-dollar Market' *JME* 3(3), pp. 467–78

FREIMER, M., and GORDON, M. J., (1965) 'Why Bankers Ration Credit' *QJE*, August 1965, pp. 397–416

FRENKEL, J. J., (1976) 'A Monetary Approach to the Exchange Rate: Doctrinal Aspects and Empirical Evidence' *ScandJE*, 2, pp. 200–24

FRENKEL, J. J., and LEVICH, R. M., (1975) 'Covered Interest Arbitrage: Unexploited Profits', *JPE*, 83

FRIEDMAN, I. S., (1981) 'The Evolution of Country Risk Assessment', in Ensor (ed) pp. 9–15

FRIEDMAN, M., (1953) 'The Case For Flexible Exchange Rates' in *Essays in Positive Economics*, Chicago, University of Chicago Press

— (1969) 'The Eurodollar Market: Some First Principles' *Morgan Guaranty Survey*, October 1969, pp. 4–14

FRIEDMAN, M., and SCHWARTZ, A. J., (1963) *A Monetary History of the United States, 1867–1960*, Princeton University Press

FRIEDRICH, K., (1970) 'The Eurodollar system and International Liquidity' *JMCB*, August 1970

FRYDL, E., (1979) 'The debate over regulating the Eurocurrency market', *FRBNY Quarterly Review* 4(4), pp. 11–20

GARDENER, E. P. M., (1981) *Capital Adequacy and Banking Supervision*, University of Wales Press, Cardiff

— (ed) (1986) *UK Banking Supervision Evolution, Practice and Issues*, Allen and Unwin, London

GIAVAZZI, F., (1987) 'The Impact of EEC Membership', in Dornbusch, R., and Layard R., *The Performance of the British Economy*, OUP

GOLDBERG, L., and SAUNDERS, A., (1980) 'The causes of US bank expansion overseas' *JMCB*, 12(4), pp. 630–643

GOODHART, C. A. E., (1975) *Money Information and Uncertainty*, Macmillan, London

— (1987) 'Why do banks need a central bank?', *OEP*, 39, pp. 75–89

GOODMAN, L. S., (1980) 'The Pricing of Syndicated Eurocurrency Credits', *FRBNY Quarterly Review*, 5(2), pp. 39–49

GOWLAND, D., (1978) *Monetary Policy and Credit Control: The UK Experience*, Croom Helm, London

GRANT, C., (1982) 'Can the Cooke Committee stand the heat?', *Euromoney*, October 1982, p. 39

— (1983) 'The Liquification of the Euromarkets', *Euromoney*, October 1983, p. 132

GREENBAUM, S. I., (1967a) 'A Study of Bank Costs', *National Banking Review*, 4, pp. 415–34

— (1967b) 'Competition and efficiency in the banking system: empirical research and its policy implications', *JPE*, August 1967, pp. 461–78

GRIFFITHS, B., (1970) *Competition in Banking*, Hobart Paper, no. 51, IEA

GRIFFITH-JONES, S., (1983) 'A Chilean Perspective', *IDS Bulletin*, 14(1), pp. 50–4

GRIFFITH-JONES, S., and SUNKEL, O., (1986) *Debt and Development Crisis in Latin America, The end of an illusion*, Clarendon Press, Oxford

GROSSMAN, S. J., and STIGLITE, J. E., (1976) 'Information and Competitive Price Systems', *AER*, 66, pp. 1246–53

GROUP OF THIRTY (1982a) *How Bankers see the World Financial Markets*, New York

— (1982b) *Risk in International Bank Lending*, New York

HAEGELE, M. J., (1980) 'The Market still knows best', *Euromoney*, May 1980, p. 121

HEFFERNAN, S. A., (1986) *Sovereign Risk Analysis*, Allen and Unwin, London

HENDERSHOTT, P., (1967) 'The Structure of International Interest Rates' *JF*, 22, pp. 455–65

HENDERSON, D., and WALDO, D., (1980) *Reserve Requirements on Euro-currency Deposits: Implications for Euro-deposit multipliers, Control of a Monetary Aggregate and Avoidance of Redenomination Incentives*, International Finance Discussion Paper, no. 164

HERRING, R., and MARSTON, R., (1976) 'Euro-currency and National Money Markets' in Stem, Makin and Logue (eds), *Euro-currencies and the International Monetary System*, American Institute for Public Policy Research, Washington

— (1977) *National Monetary Policies and International Financial Markets*, North-Holland

HESTER, D., and TOBIN, J., (eds) (1967) *Financial Markets and Economic Activity*, Yale University Press, New Haven

HEWSON, J., (1975) *Liquidity Creation and Distribution in the Eurocurrency Markets*, Lexington Books, Mass.

HEWSON, J., and SAKAKIBARA, E., (1975) *The Eurocurrency markets and their implications*
— (1976) 'A General Equilibrium Approach to the Euro-dollar Market' *JMCB*, 8(3), pp. 297–323
HIRSCH, F., (1974) 'Control of international liquidity and the Eurodollar market' in Johnson and Nobay (eds) *Issues in Monetary Theory*, OUP
— (1977) 'The Bagehot Problem' *The Manchester School of Economics and Social Studies*, 45, pp. 241–57
HODGMAN, D. R., (1960) 'Credit Risk and Credit Rationing' *QJE*, May 1960, pp. 258–78
HOWCROFT, B., and SOLOMON, C., (1985) *Syndicated Lending by Banks*, Bangor Occasional Papers in Economics, no. 22, University of Wales Press
HUHNE, C., (1987) 'Just a drop in an ocean of bad debt', *The Guardian*, Wednesday 24 June
IPSEN, E., (1983) 'After Mexico, the Regionals are in Retreat', *Euromoney*, January 1983, p. 58
JAFFEE, D. M., and MODIGLIANI, F., (1969) 'A theory and test of credit rationing', *AER*, vol LIX, pp. 850–72
JOHNSTON, R. B., (1983) *The Economics of the Eurocurrency Market*, Macmillan, London
KALECKI, M., (1971) *Selected Essays on the Dynamics of the Capitalist Economy*, CUP
KAMIEN, M. I., and SCHWARTZ, N. L., (1981) 'Market Structure and Innovation, A Survey', *JEL*, 13, pp. 5–37
KAPUR, I., (1977) 'An Analysis of the supply of Euro-currency finance to developing countries' *Oxford Bulletin of Economics and Statistics*, 39(3), pp. 171–81
KENEN, P., (1976) *Capital Mobility and Financial Integration*, PSIF, no. 38
KETTELL, B., and MAGNUS, G., (1986) *The International Debt Game*, Graham & Trotman, London
KEYNES, J. M., (1936) *The General Theory of Employment, Interest and Money*, Macmillan, London
KILLICK, T., (1981) 'Euromarket recycling of OPEC surpluses: Fact or Myth?', *The Banker*, January 1981, pp. 15–23
KINDLEBERGER, C. P., (1975) 'Quantity and price, especially in financial markets' in Kindleberger, C. P., *International Money*, ch. 18, Allen & Unwin, London
— (1978) *Manias, Panics and Crashes*, Macmillan, London
KINDLEBERGER, C. P., and LAFFARGUE, J. P., (1982) *Financial Crises: Theory, History and Policy*, CUP
KLOPSTOCK, F., (1968) *The Euro-dollar Market: Some Unresolved Issues*, PEIF no. 65
KNIGHT, M., (1977) 'Eurodollars, Capital Mobility and Forward Exchange Markets', *Economica*, 44(173), pp. 1–21
KÖRNER, P., *et al* (1986) *The IMF and the Debt Crisis*, English translation, London, 1986
KOUTSOYIANNIS, A., (1977) *Theory of Econometrics*, Macmillan, London, 2nd ed.

KREICHER, L. L., (1982) 'Eurodollar Arbitrage', *FRBNY Quarterly Review*, Summer 1982, pp. 10–21

KRUEGER, A., (1983) *Exchange Rate Determination*, CUP

KRUGMAN, P., (1984) 'Comment on Diaz-Alejandro', *Brookings Papers in Economic Activity*, 2, pp. 390–1

LAIDLER, D., (1985) 'Monetary Policy in Britain: Successes and Shortcomings', *Oxford Review of Economic Policy*, 1(1), pp. 35–43

LAYARD, R., (1986) *How to beat Unemployment*, OUP

LEES, F. A., (1976) *Foreign Banking and Investment in the US*, Macmillan, London

LEPETIT, J. F., (1982) 'Comment on Solow', in Kindleberger and Laffargue

LEVER, H., and HUHNE, C., (1985) *Debt and Danger: The World Financial Crisis*, Penguin

LEVIN, J., (1974) 'The Euro-dollar Market and the International Transmission of Interest Rates', *Canadian Journal of Economics*, 1974

LLEWELLYN, D. T., (1979) 'End of UK Monetary Control' *The Banker*, December 1979

— (1980) *International Financial Integration*, Macmillan, London

— (1982) 'Avoiding an International Banking Crisis', *National Westminster Quarterly Review*, August 1982, pp. 28–39

LOGUE, D. E., *et al* (1976) 'Financial Markets Survey, Synthesis and Results' in Stem, Makin and Logue (eds) *Euro-currencies and the International Monetary System*, American Enterprise Institute for Public Policy Research, Washington, 1976

LOMAX, D. F., (1982) 'The Recycling folly', *The Banker*, August 1982

MCCLAM, W. D., (1972) 'Credit Substitution and the Euro-currency Market' *Banca Nationale del Lavoro Quarterly Review*, 25(103), pp. 323–63

MCCLAM, W. D., (1982) 'Financial Fragility and instability monetary authorities as borrowers and lenders of last resort' in Kindleberger and Laffargue (1982)

MCKENZIE, G., (1976) *The Economics of the Eurocurrency System*, Macmillan, London

MCKINNON, R., (1979) *Money in International Exchange*, OUP

MCKINNON, R., and OATES, W., (1966) *The Implications of International Economic Integration for Monetary, Fiscal and Exchange Rate Policy*, PSIF, no. 16

MCMAHON, C., (1964) *Sterling in the Sixties*, OUP

— (1985) 'Change and Development in International Financial Markets', in The Institute of Bankers *Competition and Cooperation in International Banking*, London, 1985

MARSTON, R., (1976) 'Interest Arbitrage in the Euro-currency Markets', *EER*, 7, pp. 1–13

MEADE, J., (1951) *The Balance of Payments*, OUP

MELTZER, A. H., (1967) 'Major issues in the regulation of financial institutions', *JPE*, August 1967, pp. 482–501

METAIS, J., (1982) 'Less Developed Countries' rising indebtedness and the lender of last resort in international context' in Kindleberger and Laffargue (1982)

MINOT, W. G., (1974) 'Tests for Integration between Major Western European Capital Markets' *OEP*, November 1974, pp. 424–439

MINSKY, H. P., (1982a) 'The financial instability hypothesis: capitalist processes and the behaviour of the economy' in Kindleberger and Laffargue (1982)

— (1982b) *Inflation, Recession and Economic Policy*, Wheatsheaf Books Ltd

MONTAGNON, P., (1983) 'Eastern Europe: is it coming back to the market?', *The Banker*, October 1983, pp. 41–44

MONTI, A., (1974) 'The changing criteria of external creditworthiness for developing countries – a banker's view', in *International Economics and Banking*, Skandinaviska Enskilda Banken, Stockholm

MULLER, H., (1985) 'Supervisory Cooperation – A Condition for Fair Competition in International Banking', in Institute of Bankers *Competition and Cooperation in World Banking*

MUNDELL, R., (1963) 'Capital Mobility and Stabilisation Policy Under Fixed and Flexible Exchange Rates', *Canadian Journal of Economics*, 29(4), pp. 475–85

— (1968) *International Economics*, Macmillan, London

MUSGRAVE, R. A., and MUSGRAVE, P. B., (1982) *Public Finance in Theory and Practice*, 3 ed, McGraw-Hill

NAGY, P. J., (1981) 'The use of quantified country risk in decision making in banks' in Ensor (ed), pp. 103–110

— (1984) *Country Risk*, Euromoney Publications, London

NIEHANS, J., (1978) *The Theory of Money*, Johns Hopkins University Press, Baltimore

— (1977) 'Exchange Rate Dynamics with Stock/Flow Interaction', *JPE*, 85(6), pp. 1245–57

NIEHANS, J., and HEWSON, J., (1976) 'The Eurodollar market and Monetary Theory', *JMCB*, February 1976, pp. 1–28

OLLARD, W., and ROUTLEDGE, N., (1985) 'How the Bank of England failed the JMB test', *Euromoney*, February 1985, p. 49

OPPENHEIMER, P., (1985) 'Governments, Markets and the Role of International Agents', in The Institute of Bankers, *Competition and Cooperation in World Banking*, London

OPPENHEIMER, P., and GIBSON, H. D., 'Rational Speculative Bubbles and the International Debt crisis', forthcoming

OECD (1981) *Regulations affecting International Banking Operations* Paris, OECD

— (1982) *Controls on International Capital Movements* Paris, OECD

OFFICER, L., and WILLET, T., (1970) 'The Covered Interest Arbitrage Schedule: a Critical Survey of Recent Developments', *JMCB*, 2(2), pp. 247–52

PARKER, A., (1978) *Exchange Controls*, Jordans, London

PECCHIOLI, R. M., (1982) *The Internationalisation of Banking*, OECD, Paris

PEAKE, D. J., (1986) 'International Banking: Regulation and Support Issues', in Gardener (ed)

PITMAN, B., (1985) 'Organising for the Future' in Institute of Bankers, *Competition and Cooperation in World Banking*, London, 1985

POSTLEWAITE, A., and VIVES, X., (1984) 'Bank Runs as an Equilibrium Phenomenon', unpublished, University of Pennsylvania, June 1984

PUZ, R., (1977) 'How to find out when a sovereign borrower slips from A–1 to C–3', *Euromoney*, December 1977, p. 67

REID, M., (1983) *The Secondary Banking Crisis, 1973–75*, Macmillan, London

REVELL, J., (1973) *The British Financial System*, Macmillan, London

— (1975) *Solvency and Regulation of Banks*, Bangor Occasional Papers in Economics, no. 5, University of Wales Press

— (1978) 'Competition and Regulation of Banks', in Barclay, Gardener and Revell (eds), pp. 48–63

— (1980) *Costs and Margins in Banking: An International Survey*, OECD, Paris

RICH, G., (1972) 'A Theoretical and Empirical Analysis of the Euro-dollar Market', *JMCB*, 4(3), pp. 616–35

RICHARDSON, G. B., (1960) *Information and Investment: A study in the working of the competitive economy*, OUP

ROS, J., (1987) 'Mexico from the oil boom to the debt crisis: An analysis of policy responses to external shocks, 1978–85', in Thorp and Whitehead, *Latin American Debt and the Adjustment Crisis*, Macmillan, London

SAADE, N. A., (1978) 'Spreads may swing, but the long-term trend is down', *Euromoney*, December 1978, p. 73

— (1981) 'How Banks can live with Low Spreads', *Euromoney*, November 1981, p. 139

SARGEN, N. P., (1976) 'Commercial Bank Lending to Developing Countries', *Federal Reserve Bank of San Francisco*, Spring 1976, p. 29

SCHLOSSBERG, G., (1981) 'Today's Euromarket Tactic: Funding for Profit', *Euromoney*, October 1981, p. 328

SHAVELL, S., (1976) *On Moral Hazard and Insurance*, Harvard Discussion Paper, no. 494

SHILLER, R. J., (1979) 'The volatility of long-term interest rates and expectations models of the term structure', *JPE*, 87(6), pp. 1190–1212

— (1981) 'Do Stock prices move too much to be justified by subsequent changes in dividends?', *AER*, 71, pp. 421–36

— (1987) 'Ultimate Sources of Aggregate Variability', *AER Papers and Proceedings*, 77(2), pp. 87–92

SOFIA, A. Z., (1979) 'How to rationalise country risk ratios', *Euromoney*, September 1979, p. 76

— (1981) 'Rationalising Country Risk Ratio', in Ensor (ed), pp. 49–68

SOLOW, R. M., (1982) 'On the lender of last resort' in Kindleberger and Laffargue (1982)

SPRAOS, J., (1984) 'IMF Conditionality – A Better Way', *Banca Nationale del Lavoro Quarterly Review*, 151, pp. 411–21

STANYER, P., and WHITLEY, J., (1981) 'Financing World Payments Imbalances', *BEQB*, 21(2), pp. 187–99

STEWART, F., and SENGUPTA, A., (1982) *International Financial Cooperation: A Framework for Change*, Pinter, London

STIGLITZ, J. E., and WEISS, A., (1981) 'Credit Rationing in Markets with Imperfect Information', *AER*, 71(3), pp. 393–410

STILLSON, R., (1974) 'An Analysis of Information and Transaction Services in Financial Institutions', *JMCB*, 6, pp. 517–535

TINIC, S., and WEST, R., (1979) *Investing in Securities: an efficient markets approach*, Addison-Wesley, Mass.

THOMPSON, J. K., (1981) 'An index of economic risk' in Ensor (ed), pp. 69–74

TOBIN, J., (1967) 'Comment' [on Meltzer (1967)], *JPE*, 1967, pp. 508–9

TOBIN, J., and BRAINARD, W., (1963) 'Financial Intermediaries and the Effectiveness of Monetary Controls' *AER Papers and Proceedings* 53(2), pp. 383–400

TUNNEY, J. J., (1981) 'Bank perspectives on measuring risk', in Eusor (ed), pp. 83–85

VALENTINE, R., (1973) 'A profit orientated approach to liquidity management' *Euromoney*, July 1973, pp. 24–27

VAUBEL, R., (1979) *Choice in European Monetary Union*, IEA

VINER, J., (1964) *Problems of Monetary Control*, PEIF no. 45

WACHTEL, P., (1982) *Crises in the Economic and Financial Structure*, Lexington Books, Mass

WALLICH, H., (1984) *Insurance of Bank Lending to Developing Countries*, Group of Thirty, May 1984

WESTON, C. R., (1980) *Domestic and Multinational Banking*, Croom Helm, 1980

WILLET, T., (1976) 'The Euro-currency Market, Exchange Rate Systems and National Financial Policies' in Stem, Makin and Logue (eds) *Eurocurrencies and the International Monetary System*, American Enterprise Institute for Public Policy Research, Washington

WILLIAMSON, J., (1983) *The Exchange Rate System*, Institute for International Economics, Washington DC

WOODFORD, M., (1987) 'Three questions about sunspot equilibria as an explanation of economic fluctuations' *AER Papers and Proceedings*, 77(2), pp. 93–98

YASSUKOVICH, S. M., (1976) 'The growing political threat to international banking' *Euromoney*, April 1976, pp. 10–15

YEAGER, A., (1966) *International Monetary Relations; Theory, History and Policy*, Harper and Row, 2nd ed.

ZOMBANAKIS, M., (1983) 'The International Debt Threat: A way to avoid a crash', *The Economist*, 30 April, pp. 11–13

Index